FLANNERY O'CONNOR'

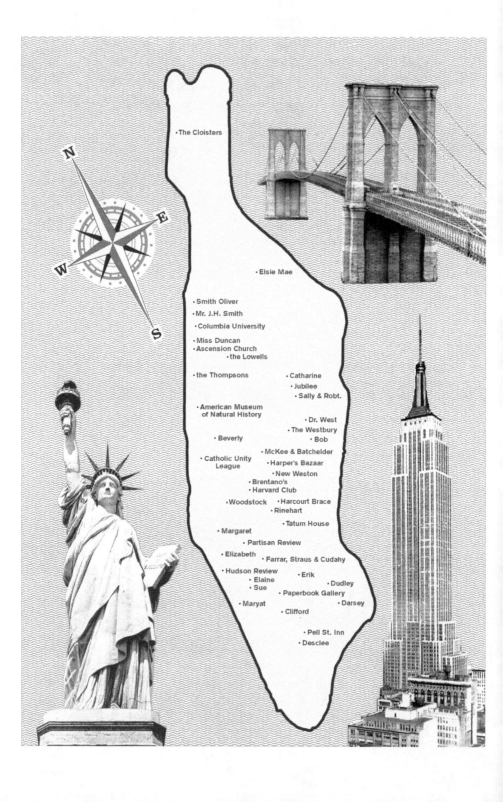

FLANNERY O'CONNOR'S MANHATTAN

KATHERYN KROTZER LABORDE

Fordham University Press

NEW YORK   2024

Fordham University Press has no responsibility for the persistence or accuracy of URLs for external or third-party Internet websites referred to in this publication and does not guarantee that any content on such websites is, or will remain, accurate or appropriate.

Fordham University Press also publishes its books in a variety of electronic formats. Some content that appears in print may not be available in electronic books.

Visit us online at www.fordhampress.com.

Library of Congress Cataloging-in-Publication Data available online at https://catalog.loc.gov.

Printed in the United States of America

26 25 24ˑ   5 4 3 2 1

First edition

for Tom Bonner, friend and mentor

Contents

Preface: In Search of Flannery's Manhattan

I

May was in full bloom when I found myself spending three days in the Stuart A. Rose Manuscript, Archives, and Rare Book Library at Emory University. It was 2016, and I was there to read letters that had been acquired from the Mary Flannery O'Connor Charitable Trust late in 2014 and had not been made available until the fall of 2015. The letters I wanted to peruse were written by Mary Flannery O'Connor, then a student in the Writers' Workshop at the University of Iowa, in the days when she was becoming Flannery O'Connor. They were addressed to her mother, Regina Cline O'Connor.

I was there to start working on what would lead to a book I had in mind. It was a book of essays. But the book I had in mind when I arrived at Emory was not the one I would end up writing.

These near-daily (and, in 2016, still unpublished[1]) letters are generally brief but give quick details of the life O'Connor lived from 1945 to 1947. Most of the letters are handwritten, the stationery has browned with age, and the affection and interest O'Connor expresses toward her mother is genuine (and, considering how she writes about mothers later in her fiction, somewhat surprising). O'Connor talks of skirts she wants her mother to hem. She speaks of going to dinner with one person or another. She mentions the food she purchases at the A&P and the homemade mayonnaise she begs her mother to send, adding that store-bought mayonnaise is not nearly as good as what Regina can whip up.[2]

Yes, she called her mother *Regina*. And until the end of 1947, O'Connor signed her letters *MF*.

As one does before visiting an archive, I had requested certain materials—items other than the letters—to be on the ready for my visit. There was Regina's travel diary from a trip she took with Flannery to Lourdes. There was a strand of purple pearls and a necklace of gold ones, too. There were religious cards, medical records, childhood writings, address books. There was even a gallstone (which I didn't particularly want to see, but I was amused to find it as part of the collection).

With only three days to spend in the archives, I decided to focus on the letters and asked for them, box by box. But at one point, unable to down one more morsel of writing about meals O'Connor had either devoured or disdained, I decided to look at something, *anything*, that didn't start with the words *Dear Regina*. I asked for Series 1, Box 3, File 7—the first listing of the first series in the archive.

Inside the file were her personal address books. Two black, a red, a brown, and a white, each sized to fit easily in a woman's hand and designed to reside in the shallow top drawer of a desk or the bottom of a cluttered purse. Each page of each book was filled with O'Connor's roundish writing. Growing excited, I scheduled a return trip to take photos of every scribbled page so I could peruse these books at my leisure.

If one is lucky, there are moments in a person's life that change their plans, perhaps even their path. In stopping to look at those five little books, I became that kind of lucky.

II

The personal address book, whether stately and leather-covered or flimsy and wire-bound, is filled, over the years, with information. People's names, street names, cities and states, countries, phone numbers, zip codes, and more. Such a chronicle is a progressive work created over time.

The first layer of entries might be neat and uniform, each stroke of a letter committed in the same shade of blue. But people move. Marry. Die. We remove some folk from our lives, and others pointedly remove themselves. And in their absence, we fill the gaps with new people, whether friends, relatives, or business associates. Eventually, the once orderly address book becomes a mess of scratch-outs and squish-ins, different inks and pencil leads, lines and cross-outs, X's and arrows. The book itself becomes a story told by disrupted alphabetizations, corrections, and the occasional odd note—such as this notation of an invitation I found in the brown address book:

4:00 PM June 19–1948

Christ Church—Park Ave
at 60th St.

5:00 PM—John Thompson's
214 Riverside Drive

This was an address book, not a calendar or planner, and so this notation stood out. This note seemed the sort one would make when on the phone with a friend, the address book already open to their listing. At least, that is how it seemed to me.

I turned to the Internet. Within minutes, I knew that Christ Church, located on the Upper East Side, was a nondenominational church with Methodist roots. Still scouring the Internet, I learned that June 19, 1948, had been a Saturday. After more digging, this time referring to her letters, I discovered that O'Connor had arrived at Yaddo Artists and Writers Colony in Saratoga Springs, New York, on the first of June that year. She was but a train ride away from the Christ Church event.

I didn't know who John Thompson was, and I wondered if she herself had known when she took down the information. And what sort of gathering was it? A funeral? A wedding? A christening?

All I could do was wonder and guess.

III

Besides, there was much to be made of the many, many names that filled not only that page but all the pages of each book. These five little books spanned almost twenty years. Considered together, they provided a telescope's view into O'Connor's universe, within which a galaxy of worlds existed. There was the ever-changing world of friends and the ever-growing world of acquaintances. There were the shadowing spheres of family and of friends of family.

There were nuns, priests, and monks. College professors. Physicians. Agents. Editors.

Writers.

IV

One's address books, of course, are maintained for the practical purpose of keeping track of contact information. As I write this simple and obvious sentence, I can't help but add, "or, at least, they once were."

Many people now keep track of addresses and phone numbers on their smartphones and computers rather than in paper books. We still update contacts, but the old information disappears unless we make an effort to keep the outdated listings. With this change of method, we indeed have lost those confusing messes of cross-outs, arrows, and lines, but, in truth, we have lost far more. We have lost access to possible portals to times past: our own and those of others, be they relatives, friends, or public figures.

Fortunately, O'Connor did not live in a time of digital recordkeeping. To take the what-if a little further, in our age of encouraging the decluttering of every shelf, drawer, and closet, I can't help but be grateful that these books were not tossed out as trash. Because they were not, the account of O'Connor's life is all the more complete for them. These simple, utilitarian, and messy books offer illumination in so many ways, but particularly as they toss light on previously unexplored avenues of her life, such as the Southern midcentury writer's time in, and connections to, New York City.

V

Such an exploration has to start somewhere. This one began with looking through the many pages for names of those O'Connor had known both famously and well, hoping to discern a New York connection to each.[3]

I looked for those most influential to her career: her editor, Robert Giroux; her agent, Elizabeth McKee; and her critic and mentor, Caroline Gordon. While it was obvious that Giroux and McKee would have New York listings, I wasn't sure about Gordon. As it turned out, there were no Manhattan addresses for her, but her various entries eventually proved valuable in dating the books.

I looked for Robert and Sally Fitzgerald, a couple O'Connor met in Manhattan and followed to Connecticut. In the brown book, I found the address of their York Avenue apartment, where the three were introduced in March 1949.

I looked for two women who were among O'Connor's closest friends during her last decade. Betty Hester, known as "A" in *The Habit of Being*, had no New York address. (This was not a surprise.) But Maryat Lee, the inspiration for O'Connor's liberal characters, lived on Sixth Avenue.

Finally, I sought the names of three men O'Connor was known to have been interested in at one point or another. There was Erik Langkjaer, the traveling textbook salesman who would drive 100 miles out of his way to visit O'Connor's home in Milledgeville, Georgia, a farm called Andalusia. In one of the books was the address of a New York apartment on University Place.

Long before she met Langkjaer, there was the poet Robert Lowell, whom O'Connor got to know at Yaddo. He was handsome, charismatic, intelligent, and, to her delight, in 1948, rediscovering Catholicism. In the brown book, his New York address was listed under "Mr. & Mrs. Robt. Lowell"; he shared the home on West 104th with poet Elizabeth Hardwick, whom he married in the summer of 1949.

And before O'Connor knew Lowell, there was Robie Macauley, a fiction writer she met through the Iowa Writers' Workshop. Macauley and O'Connor spent a great amount of time together, though he was engaged to another. Still, they went to parties together and went out to dinner regularly. They sat on the boarding house porch swing and talked for hours about writers and writing. In particular, they spoke of her writing. He recognized her incredible talent.

There was no New York address for Macauley in her book, though there was one for his fiancée, Anne Draper. Her Washington Place address was not listed under a dedicated entry for Draper, or even under one for Macauley, but as part of an entry for another friend, Faye Hancock Messick (listed formally as "Mrs. Hank Messick"), whom O'Connor knew from both Iowa and (as it was then known) Georgia State College for Women (GSCW).[4]

VI

Exploring the pages of address books line by line was not enough. Some fieldwork was needed to find Flannery O'Connor's Manhattan. So, in June 2016, I took a trip to New York City. I wanted to step inside the two buildings where O'Connor had resided in 1949: Tatham House in Murray Hill and the Manchester in Morningside Heights.

I stayed in a hotel around the corner from Tatham House, a midrise located at the corner of 38th and Lexington. Back in the day, the building's twelve stories offered rooms to young, unmarried professional women. Perhaps still upset about the abrupt and extraordinary circumstances that had landed her there in the first days of March (see Chapter 2), O'Connor didn't like her accommodations and complained, though comically, about how the building smelled like "an unopened Bible."[5]

I walked toward the building, its brown bricks checkered by windows. I was charmed by the arched green awning that shielded the door from the elements. As I crossed the threshold, my eyes immediately fell on the beautiful wooden staircase and the twin red elevators, which led to the current eighty apartments that were, I imagined, far nicer than the original 250 dorm rooms. Having spoken briefly by phone with the super earlier that morning—though not for long, as the connection had been poor—I took a seat on the padded wooden bench by the window and waited for him.

With morning light grazing my shoulders, I took it all in: the high ceiling, cream-colored archways, touches of wrought metal, marble tile floor. Narrowing my focus to what was right before me, I regarded the skinny metal mailboxes lined up along the lobby wall and imagined O'Connor retrieving a letter from Regina.

Glancing to my left, I considered the twin elevators, each painted a deep red, framed by a black sill, and accessorized by a round window. I imagined O'Connor entering an elevator upon returning from a meeting with her agent or exiting one to grab a bite to eat at a nearby deli. I wondered if there would have been an elevator operator back in the day. For that matter, I was curious whether there had been a doorman to greet the young, respectably-heeled residents. I had initially planned to ask the super this question, but I changed my mind when, after our in-person hello, he suggested that the bad phone connection was undoubtedly my fault because I likely used some Southern carrier.

I did not argue with him. I asked some simple questions about the building. I got some simple answers back. I knew better than to ask to be shown around.

Afterward, I felt slightly relieved to step back onto the street. Picturing a twenty-three-year-old Flannery standing there as I was at the corner of Lexington and East 38th, I imagined her facing a similar puzzle of buildings, people, taxis, and noise.

I imagined her experiencing her share of regional slights, especially since she had such a thick Georgian accent. It was an aspect of her Manhattan that I had not considered until that moment.

And in that moment, I took her along with me. Together, we crossed Lexington and headed toward a Starbucks.

VII

When I was young, I attended a Catholic elementary school where we were all made to use cartridge pens, even though ballpoint pens were readily available (and far less messy). For this reason, I take note when I see the thicker, fuller penmanship produced by fountain pens.

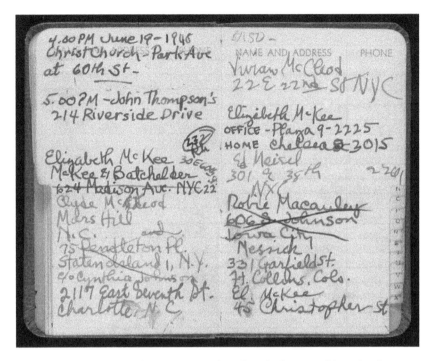

FIGURE 1: A notation of an invitation found in the brown address book. (Used with permission from Flannery O'Connor Papers, Stuart A. Rose Manuscript, Archives, and Rare Book Library, Emory University.)

The June 19 notation in the brown address book had been written in heavy black ink (see Figure 1).

And because I've always been fascinated by how we write differently in different moments, I tend to notice such variances in the jottings of others (and, to be honest, my own). So, it is clear to me that, although two lines are skipped between the June 19 notation and what follows, both were written at the same relative time.

And what follows the notation is the name and address of O'Connor's agent.

> Elizabeth McKee
> McKee & Batchelder
> 624 Madison Ave. NYC 22

The address was (later) scratched out, and a cramped and curving replacement squeezed in. Following the trail of ink density rather than what was written directly below McKee's information (in a different ink),

I skipped over to the facing page where her office and home phone numbers were listed. Later, I would realize that what we had here was O'Connor's first recording of McKee's contact information. Knowing how McKee was instrumental in the writer's success, this discovery was an exciting one.

I doubted there was a connection between the June 19 event and McKee. Still, it seemed logical that a person would add a note (such as this) to a page (such as that) if the book were already open to that page. Who had O'Connor been talking to when she wrote down the information? I examined the two pages before me.

There was an entry for Clyde McLeod, O'Connor's colleague at Iowa, that included both the family home in Mars Hill, North Carolina, and a Staten Island address in care of a friend. (For a time, McLeod worked for Simplicity Patterns on Madison Avenue, writing directives such as "fold along perforated lines and stitch" on the patterns.[6]) The New York address is lightly X'd out in favor of the Charlotte address that follows.

On the facing page, listed above McKee's phone numbers, is a misspelled entry for Vivienne [Koch] MacLeod, a writer O'Connor met at Yaddo. Following McKee's phone numbers are entries for writer Ed Maisel (also misspelled), another Yaddo chum. Next comes the (crossed out) Iowa address of Robie Macauley. Following that is the post-Iowa address of workshop colleague Hank Messick and, finally, McKee's home address in Greenwich Village.

In all, six people were spread over eight listings, one stacked on top of the next with hardly a space skipped, and recorded in ink or pencil—six people who had been part of O'Connor's writing life in the late '40s. I knew the June 19 invitation was connected somehow to one of them, but O'Connor had not made it obvious who.

VIII

In June 2017, I readied myself for my second visit to her Manhattan and planned to stay in Morningside Heights near the Manchester. I booked a room in a two-star hotel where I was lucky to have my own bathroom.

Back in 2016, I had brought my (then) boyfriend along. We stayed near Tatham House in Murray Hill. In addition to going where everyone goes—the Statue of Liberty, Museum of Modern Art, Rockefeller Center, and Times Square—we took a cab across town to the Manchester and discovered a delightful Hungarian pastry shop nearby. After coffee, we hopped across the street to see the Poets' Corner at St. John the Divine. Later, we had cocktails at Campbell's Apartment and sandwiches at Bloom's Delicatessen. With my mission in mind, we made time to walk around the Church of St. Agnes, near Murray Hill, with the thought that perhaps O'Connor had kneeled in a pew there.

But in 2017, I wanted to be on my own as O'Connor herself had been in the summer of '49. Aside from making a trip to Washington Heights to see the Cloisters (a spectacular museum that O'Connor had visited twice), my goal was to stay put in the Upper West Side.

I wanted to walk at least once to Columbia University because O'Connor had walked there daily, taking many a meal in the student dining hall. I wanted to attend Mass at Ascension Roman Catholic Church because O'Connor had, and to meet New York friends for dinner because O'Connor did. In particular, I wanted to spend afternoons walking to Upper West Side addresses listed in her address book, using the corner of 108th and Broadway—the Manchester's location—as a starting point.

With that in mind, a good week before boarding the plane to New York, I poured myself a cup of coffee and sat down to plan a walking tour.

IX

I soon realized I could see much of her Manhattan if I simply walked along Riverside Drive. Heading toward Harlem from the Manchester, I could start with Father Dougherty's place, though all I knew was that it was located off 108th. From there, I could pass by the home of her friends from Milledgeville, George and Barbara Beiswanger (410, near W. 113th), then finish with journalist Phyllis Meras's place at 425 Riverside (near W. 115th). Leaving from the Manchester and going in the other direction, I could walk to the apartment of Iowa housemate Ruth York (244 Riverside, near W. 97th), followed by the home of Jack and Dilly Thompson (214 Riverside, near W. 94th).

Yes, 214 Riverside was the same address mentioned in the mysterious notation, and Jack was the same person as John Thompson. By this point in my research, I knew that Thompson was a writer and that he had been good friends with Lowell and Macauley (they'd all met at Kenyon).

But I was still no closer to deciphering what happened on June 19.

X

And then I stopped, pen in hand, gobstruck.
I realized that I was going to be in Manhattan on June 19.
Not in 1948, of course. Sixty-nine years later.
But I would be there all the same.

I looked at the flight information. I would be arriving at LaGuardia around 3 P.M. I wouldn't have time to make it to Christ Church by 4 P.M., but as luck would have it, I would have time to check into the hotel and arrive at 214 Riverside by 5 P.M.

I'd be decades late for a party I was not invited to, that was not taking place in my lifetime, and whose purpose I was not privy to. But it mattered not.

I was excited. I was going.

XI

And when I arrived at that two-star hotel on June 19, I unpacked my raincoat because the skies were gray and heavy. I threw my suitcase into the closet. I charged out of that tiny room, out of that cramped hotel, and crossed Broadway, heading for the Hudson River. Once I got to Riverside Drive, I turned left and kept walking. According to Google Maps, I wasn't too far from the Thompsons' home. It was a straight shot from there, a seventeen-minute walk.

I was walking, walking. Trees were all around me. Every now and then, I caught a view of the river. But the straight shot seemed suddenly not so straight. I didn't know it then, but I was learning firsthand that there are two Riverside Drives or, rather, two sides with Riverside Park between them. I was walking on the side closer to the river. I should have stayed on the side closer to Broadway.

I kept walking. I noticed the octagonal brick below my feet when I got to West 105th. When I was past West 103rd, I could see the river. When I arrived at West 100th, the skies opened. Fat splashes pummeled my hooded head. I snapped a photo of a monument flanked by statues and decorated with the image of charging horses. In the rain, the horses looked utterly mad, and this left me a little unsettled.

I turned around and headed back, my skirt clinging to my legs and my knockoff Keds squishing with every step.

XII

I sought refuge in a taqueria across from the Manchester. While I waited for the rain to end and for my clothes and shoes to dry, I sipped a margarita (on the rocks, no salt). To my right was the open door. To my left were a man and a woman, in their forties perhaps, who chatted about online dating experiences. When they left, another couple replaced them. Over drinks, the man tried to talk his companion into learning how to ride a bicycle.

I ordered a second margarita and dinner.

I did more than just drink and eavesdrop, of course. Looking at Google Maps, I could see that I had made it eight blocks from where I had started and had stopped six blocks shy of my destination. I learned that the monument that had seemed so disturbing in the downpour was the richly symbolic 1913 Firemen's Memorial. The horses were not mad. They were heroic.

After dinner, I crossed Broadway and headed down 107th to Ascension for Mass. After the great deluge, I needed all the blessings I could get.

I attempted my trip to John's and Dilly's place again the next day. Under clearer skies, I could take my time and stop to admire the Firemen's Memorial, walking around it before continuing to 214 Riverside Drive—a beautiful, seven-story building called the Chatillion. I paused there, imagining party guests walking through the door.

Soon enough, I would learn that O'Connor had not been among them.

XIII

Summer 2019. In the two years that had passed since my last visit to Manhattan, I learned much as I researched each entry in O'Connor's address books. I also realized that I had occasionally misinterpreted entries. The scratch-outs, arrows, and marginalia were sometimes confusing, and sometimes, I would discover that my original reading of an entry had been incorrect. And it was for that reason that I spent that summer scouring the photos on my smartphone to examine each alphabetical section of the brown address book, the one O'Connor had used in the late 1940s.

By this time, I could pause over a listing and remember having walked by the address, or at least thereabouts. For example, as my eye passed over the entry for the Lowells in the *L* section, I recalled the afternoon I had walked down 104th toward Central Park, only to find that their particular building number no longer existed. On my way back to the hotel, I stopped in a little shop and bought some crocheted, green beaded earrings to remember the fruitless walk-by; shaped like decorative wreaths, they were an ironic souvenir of a door that no longer exists.

Swiping my thumb along the screen of my smartphone, I moved from *L* to *M*. The Midtown East listing for Edgar Moran appeared, immediately followed by information on Miss M. T. Maxwell, who had taught at what is now known as Georgia College. Directly underneath that was the address of Mrs. Hank Messick in Iowa City. For my purposes, this information was of no interest except that it included the Manhattan phone number and address of Miss Anne Draper.

I stopped there. It was not the first time this entry had given me pause. Of course, Draper was Macauley's fiancée, but I had found no mention of Draper visiting him in Iowa in all my readings of O'Connor's letters. How would she have met Faye if she had not been to Iowa? Macauley, of course, knew Hank Messick through the workshop, and it stood to reason that he knew Faye through social gatherings. So, if Faye had needed a place to stay in Manhattan, it's plausible that Macauley had offered that she could stay with Draper. Still, I wondered, if Faye were to stay with Draper for a spell, why would O'Connor need to make note of this temporary address? More curious still were the notes that came at the end of the listing (see Figure 2).

Truro
Cape Cod
Mass

There were many X's—one through Messick's Iowa address, one through Draper's New York address, and one through the three lines of that added information. These X's were distracting.

At least, they had been until that moment, for it was then that I noticed the heavy black ink that was used in this secondary listing.

And I suddenly noticed that a black line, the sort one makes when one wants to distinguish between what is already there and what is about to follow, separated the Iowa address from the New York address. All this time, the phone number WAtkins 40538 diverted my attention and kept me from truly seeing that black line. All this time, I had interpreted Mrs. Hank Messick's entry as flowing from the Iowa City address to a phone number that could have belonged to either the Iowa address or Anne Draper's home.

But now, I saw it all with clear eyes. The phone number (and the address, and the *in care of*) that followed were not part of the Mrs. Hank Messick listing as I had thought all along. It was related to the large single *R* floating to the left.

Before that moment, I had no idea what to make of that big R, but suddenly I knew that it stood for "Robie," just as I now realized that the June 19th notation on the following page, the one that had stirred my curiosity years before, was not a stand-alone note. Instead, it was a continuation of the information O'Connor had recorded near the R.

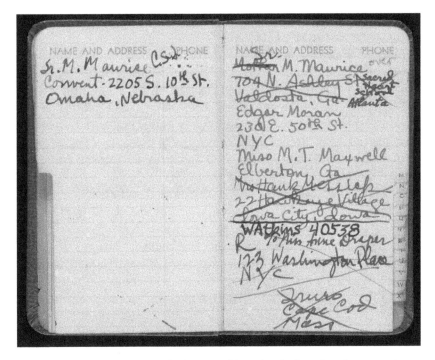

FIGURE 2: Another page in the brown address book. (Used with permission from Flannery O'Connor Papers, Stuart A. Rose Manuscript, Archives, and Rare Book Library, Emory University.)

I pictured O'Connor standing at a hallway phone, leaning against a wall, cradling the receiver of a black rotary between her ear and shoulder as she took down information.

I'll be at Anne's, I could imagine O'Connor hearing Macauley say over the phone. *Here's how you can contact me.*

I can imagine him adding one detail and another and another—each detail being the unwelcome kind that floats around a head as that head is dealing with thoughts of its own.

Here's where we're going on our honeymoon. I can see her writing obediently, quickly, her letters a little large. I can see her pause as she reaches the end of the page.

And, Flannery, of course you're invited to the wedding, Flannery and I hear him say.

It will be a small affair, just close friends. Flannery . . . Flannery? You still there? Are you writing this down? And with that, she dutifully turned the page to record the time and location of both the June 19, 1948, wedding and the reception that followed at John Thompson's home.

You'll come, won't you?

XIV

In letters to Regina written in 1948, O'Connor mentions one thing and another. She states that her short story is to be published by *Mademoiselle*. She acknowledges the trouble she is having with Rinehart editor John Selby. In one letter, she mentions that Robie has married and that he and Anne were honeymooning in Cape Cod.[7] In another still, she tells of visiting the offices of Rinehart and meeting the publicity director, none other than Anne Draper Macauley. O'Connor notes that she found her to be quite nice.[8]

In these letters, O'Connor does not mention that she had skipped the wedding. Nor does she give a reason as to why she would want to. For that, we turn to Sally Fitzgerald.

In "Flannery O'Connor: Patterns of Friendship, Patterns of Love," Fitzgerald states that, for O'Connor, the act of Macauley's betrothal was painful. She confirms that, though invited, O'Connor did not attend. She mentions that O'Connor shared with Clyde McLeod her intention to miss it.

The friend was sympathetic. "Sorry you didn't attend the Robie nuptials, but I sorta understand how you feel," McLeod wrote.[9]

Fitzgerald never comes out and tells us what O'Connor did instead of going to the wedding. Still, in a way, she shows us.

Of all the correspondence at her disposal, Fitzgerald chooses O'Connor's first letter to Elizabeth McKee as the one to begin *The Habit of Being*. In this letter, O'Connor introduces herself, saying that Paul Moor had recommended McKee's services.

O'Connor mailed that letter from Yaddo. It was dated June 19, 1948.

XV

I do not know if Flannery O'Connor ever set foot in Christ Church. I know for a fact that she didn't do so on June 19, 1948. Still, that church is a part of her Manhattan as much as Ascension Church in Morningside Heights is, St. Patrick's Cathedral (which she first saw in 1943), and even St. John the Divine. I don't know if she ever entered the latter, but I know she must have passed it on the way to or from a meal taken at Columbia University in the summer of 1949.

And though O'Connor did not enter the Thompsons' home on that particular summer evening—an evening surely filled with cheers and toasts and love—I know she was a guest there at least once and felt welcome enough to drop by to see if Jack and Dilly were home. This I know from what O'Connor wrote to her mother.

But even had O'Connor not gone on to know the Thompsons, to see the layout of their place, to drink a cup of coffee at their table or balance a martini in her hand as she chatted from her perch on the sofa, 214 Riverside Drive would still be a part of her Manhattan.

For all I know, she never stepped up to the Lowells' apartment door (back when it still existed), yet their apartment is part of her Manhattan.

Her Manhattan is made up of more than the names and the places that you will find listed in this book. Her Manhattan is made up of what happened and what didn't. Of what she experienced and what she merely thought about—if the thinking about it was strong enough to be remembered later on.

Remembered, perhaps, one morning while at home at Andalusia, while sitting in her bedroom, at her desk, at her typewriter, her hands on the keys. Or recalled, maybe, one afternoon on the porch, an open letter in her hand and the countryside visible beyond it, the black line of trees catching her flickering eye.

Flannery O'Connor's Manhattan

Introduction: The Tour Begins

The tour of Flannery O'Connor's Manhattan begins now.

Since this is an imaginary tour, we can imagine the perfect bus for such an outing. Say, a peacock-hued bus that yowls, as needed, rather than honks, one that is ringed by the image of a black line of trees and features, somewhere, a large, blood-soaked sun.

You board. You sit. The seat is padded, and the air, cool. The person in the next seat turns to you and asks: "Would Flannery be amused or horrified by all of this?" Your answer leads to a brisk and enjoyable debate.

The bus eases into traffic, and you're on your way.

The tour does not include all of Manhattan but a good bit of it, starting with a swing through Harlem. From there, you move on to the Upper East Side. This is followed by a drive through Gramercy Park and Murray Hill, the latter being where O'Connor lived "for a handful of anxious weeks."

That's the tour guide talking. The guide wears a black hat, and some passengers find this amusing. The guide also wears a fox-colored T-shirt, *The Good Guide* in big letters across the back. Some passengers get the allusion—the ones who don't turn to their smartphones.

The bus zips along. You refer to your map. The Lower East Side is next, followed by a blink of a stop in Lower Manhattan.

Greenwich Village and SoHo: check. The neighborhoods of Clinton and Chelsea: check. Finally, an exploration of the Upper West Side, notably Morningside Heights, ends the tour, if only for sentimental reasons.

"In the summer of '49," the guide says, "when she was twenty-four, O'Connor stayed in the Manchester, located on the corner of Broadway and 108th. O'Connor was there to work on her first novel, *Wise Blood*."

With a sweep of the arm, the guide indicates the twelve-story Beaux Arts beauty as the bus rumbles toward Columbia University.

"O'Connor often took her lunches at a cafeteria located on campus—a walk of mere blocks from the Manchester. As the cafeteria entrance was closer to Amsterdam Avenue, one can easily imagine O'Connor walking along that thoroughfare on her way back home, a stroll that would have taken her right past St. John the Divine Cathedral, which is unfinished to this day."

And it is there, in front of the cathedral, that the bus pauses, hazard lights flashing. You and the others dismount. The cathedral dwarfs everything. You climb the many steps to the impressive, carved doors and enter the massive sanctuary, footsteps echoing.

"Today's visitors to the cathedral are likely to notice its American Poets' Corner," the guide says, leading you to the Arts Bay on the north side of the nave. "It was modeled after the Poets' Corner of Westminster Abbey."

You stand shoulder to shoulder with the others to admire the engraved stone slabs honoring poets, playwrights, fiction writers, and essayists.

"Dedicated in the 1980s, the American Poets' Corner was not a part of the cathedral in O'Connor's lifetime. She was inducted fifty years after her death."

"In 2014," someone mumbles.

"O'Connor is recognized there among writers she particularly admired, such as Edgar Allan Poe and Nathaniel Hawthorne, and writers she knew, such as Katherine Anne Porter and Elizabeth Bishop. Most fittingly, O'Connor is honored there with her friend Robert Lowell, who in 1949 introduced her to Manhattanites who would prove most influential in her life and career."

Your group streams out of the cathedral and gathers on the steps, oblivious to the cars and taxis flowing by.

"There is no way O'Connor could have foreseen all this," the guide says. "There is no way O'Connor—as she typed away at *Wise Blood*, as she wondered whether a publisher would take her book, as she questioned how she would make enough money to live—could have imagined that she, one day, would be honored *here* for her contribution to American literature."

As if reading your mind, the guide looks you in the eye. "She could not have imagined that because, in 1949, writers were not honored here."

You nod.

"But picture Flannery O'Connor, dressed in a simple skirt and sensible loafers. Picture her strolling past the cathedral in the early days of her career with no idea of the honor to come. No idea of all she would achieve in only fifteen years."

"No idea that she would be dead in fifteen years," you say. And when you see the way the guide stops at this comment, you wish you had phrased it differently.

But the guide continues. "And that makes the recognition at St. John the Divine all the more fitting and profound."

And thus, the tour ends, the guide handing out pamphlets from the Cloisters museum, the American Museum of Natural History, St. Patrick's Cathedral, and Radio City Music Hall.

"Flannery O'Connor enjoyed going to these places," the guide says. "You will, too. Make a day of it. And don't forget to include Rockefeller Plaza—she was interviewed on NBC back in 1955."

O'Connor is so strongly associated with rural Georgia that a book focusing on her connections to urban Gotham is odd. Still, these connections are important in attaining a fuller understanding of her life and career. Though she never lived in New York again, there is more to her recollection of the borough than her experiences of 1949. To consider these later acquaintances, friends, and places in context, some knowledge of her life is helpful.

But in all probability, if you were drawn to this book by its title, you already know the basic story of Flannery O'Connor, or at least enough to get by while discussing the subject at a cocktail party.

Flannery O'Connor 101

If you've read a biography or two, you know that she was born in Savannah and left the coast as a teen to live in Milledgeville—located in the same state but oh-so different in every way. You know that she lived in the Cline mansion (formally known today as the Gordon-Porter-Ward-Beall-Cline-O'Connor-Florencourt House) in the heart of town. The Clines were her mother's people; her mother was Regina, and O'Connor called her by that name.

You probably know that O'Connor's father, Edward F. O'Connor, died of lupus when his daughter was fifteen. You absolutely know that after graduating from Georgia State College for Women (now Georgia College), she attended the University of Iowa Writers' Workshop, where she wrote the stories that made up her thesis and started working on the novel *Wise Blood*. And that she was a guest at Yaddo, a retreat for artists in Saratoga, New York, for a while after that, and then lived for a year or two with Robert and Sally Fitzgerald in Connecticut before being diagnosed with disseminated lupus erythematosus—these days recognized as systemic lupus erythematosus—the autoimmune disorder that had taken the life of her father.

In time, she walked about on crutches, not because of lupus but because bone softening was one of the side effects of the treatment for lupus: regular injections of adrenocorticotropic hormone (ACTH), which was extracted from the pituitary glands of pigs.

Lupus signaled the end of independent life. She was forced to move back to Milledgeville to live with her mother for the last fourteen years of her life, the two of them passing their days on a farm with peacocks and ducks and geese and cows (but especially, for O'Connor, peacocks).

And despite all this, or maybe because of it, she wrote beautifully, so beautifully, with a God-given talent and God-centered purpose. Then, at the age of thirty-nine, three books behind her and a fourth one on the way, she died.

That much, you know already. (And if you didn't, you certainly know it now.)

What you might not know is that, for a piece of time, she lived in Manhattan. Hers was not the typical story of a young talent seeking the bright lights; rather, it was the cocktail of paranoia and fear known as the Red Scare that led her to Manhattan to live in March 1949. Weeks later, the fear of running out of money encouraged her to leave. Though she would come back for brief visits, they were always of the purpose-driven variety.

Her time in Manhattan was important to her development as both a person and a writer. It would give her a working knowledge of the city that was the heart of the publishing world, a place she would experience briefly through its tall buildings and crowded streets and remotely through the writers, agents, editors, and others she corresponded with, people whose names were recorded in hand-held, handwritten address books.

These books, these palm-size, multipage lists of people and businesses O'Connor knew quite well or just barely, are important documents that, when combined with her correspondence, can shed light on a fairly unexplored corner of Flannery O'Connor's life: the Southern midcentury writer's time in and connection to Manhattan.

Overview

First, there is the general geography to consider: The book is called *Flannery O'Connor's Manhattan* rather than *Flannery O'Connor's New York* because not all of New York City is included. While her address books include a few Bronx and Brooklyn addresses, they are not included here, as Manhattan was associated with the publishing world.

Second, there is the matter of structure. While starting at the beginning and reading through to the end is the logical way to read nearly any book, one can jump directly into any chapter in Part II and simply dig in. The entries are designed so that each one will refer to related listings regardless of where they fall in the chronology of pages. For example, the entry for Arabel J. Porter in Chapter 10 does not assume that the reader remembers what was written about Catharine Carver, whose entry appears in Chapter 6; it does not presume that a reader has even read that chapter.

PARTS I AND II

The book is divided into two distinct parts. Part I acknowledges and explores O'Connor's physical relationship to Manhattan: where she stayed, where she went, and what she did during her visits to or time she lived in the city.

Chapter 1 considers her first trip to the city in 1943, while Chapter 2 details the time she actually lived in, or near, Manhattan (which is, incidentally, the last time she was able to live independently of her mother). Chapter 3 details her trip to promote the book *A Good Man Is Hard to Find*.

Chapter 4 describes a stop in Manhattan as part of a pilgrimage to Lourdes, France. It is especially interesting in that its information is derived from Regina O'Connor's travel diary, which Flannery herself typed. Chapter 5 considers O'Connor's conversations about the city through correspondence with her close friend Maryat Lee.

Part II provides biographical material on the people and places O'Connor listed in her five address books. Chapters 6, 8, and 10 explore and explain the who and what of the Manhattan address book entries. Chapter 7 introduces readers to writers and artists listed in her address books. Chapter 9 delves into the lives of three not-famous but quite interesting correspondents, each a writer who initially reached out to O'Connor as a fan.

About the Listings

The addresses are generally reproduced as O'Connor recorded them; the exception to this is whether the city is listed, and how. O'Connor would fluctuate between writing "New York City," "New York," "NYC," and "NY," and she did not always list the postal zone. Because all addresses listed here are in Manhattan, the city will not be identified unless she included the postal zone code in her address book; if she did, the code will follow the abbreviation "NYC" regardless of what she wrote.

TELEPHONE NUMBERS

Andalusia did not get a phone (or a phone number: 2-5335) until the summer of 1956.[1] O'Connor described how the device's arrival led Regina to change how she conducted her farming affairs, now talking to everyone from the seed-and-feed man to the veterinarian from her desk in the back hall.[2] What O'Connor does not mention, though would have been taken for granted at the time, was the expense of long-distance phone calls—a reality that caused many to rely on letter writing.

While O'Connor did record telephone numbers, most of the entries in her books include address(es) only. Also interesting is that the appearance of these numbers changed over time. Phone numbers in the first two books (the brown and the black Elite) note either the exchange name (TRafalgar) or the primary letters of that exchange (TR), followed by numbers (TR 7-0200). By the time she used the red book, O'Connor recorded a few seven- or ten-digit sequences that were coming in to use by then. What was once TR 7-0200 had become 877-0200 or, if long distance, 212-877-0200.

Phone numbers are reproduced here as she recorded them.

SPELLING GLITCHES

Spelling was not O'Connor's strong suit, a fact she readily acknowledged and often took delight in exploiting. Because it feels inaccurate, if not inauthentic, to ignore this aspect of who she was, her original spellings have been preserved in the listing title (accompanied by *sic*). The entry itself features the correct spelling.

The accompanying biographies are meant to give only a brief overview, not a complete biography, of well-known people and places. More attention is given to those who were not famous.

APPENDIX

Finally, an appendix is included for those who would like to consider O'Connor's Manhattan in clusters. The listings are gathered by parts of town as determined by zip code, starting with Harlem and winding its way to the Upper West Side.

Five Little Books

In 2014, the Stuart A. Rose Manuscript, Archives, and Rare Book Library (MARBL) at Emory University acquired more than thirty boxes of letters, writings, and other personal effects from the Mary Flannery O'Connor Charitable Trust, the literary estate of the author. In addition to correspondence and memorabilia, this trove includes five small personal address books that belonged to O'Connor, each sized to fit a woman's hand easily.

In this day of the electronic and digital, of instant and immediate, a paper address book seems quaint. But in the way that historians lose much as personal, handwritten letters are replaced by texts and emails, we experience a similar loss in that these once-common progressive chronicles have been replaced by electronic recordkeeping. Address books do more than simply coordinate, in a loose alphabetical order, the addresses and phone numbers of people and businesses known. Long after their usage has ended, they provide a peripheral history of location and relocation. If one knows what to look for, they infer beginnings (of jobs or friendships) and ends (of lives or relationships). Each book is a chronicle of that which touches a life.

THE BOOKS

For the sake of identification, the individual books will be referred to as the brown, the black Elite, the red, the small black, and the white. The black Elite is called such because of what is printed on the title page: *The Elite Address Book and Telephone List*.

Of these, the brown, black Elite, and red were the most heavily used by O'Connor. These three contain not only the most entries, but also the most scratch-outs, add-ins, and directional arrows to lead the eye from an old address to a new one.

Each book contains addresses from all over the United States: forty states and the nation's capital. In addition, there are entries from two territories (one American, one British) and fifteen foreign countries (spread over four continents).

Of the Manhattan addresses listed (with some repeated from one book to the next, or even within the same book), there are 51 in the brown, 74 in the black Elite, 55 in the red, 11 in the small black, and 12 in the white, coming to a total of 203 Manhattan entries.

Since O'Connor's life has been written about at length, and because much of her correspondence has been preserved, it is possible to use the names listed (whether there are Manhattan addresses attached or not) to roughly date each book.

The brown, circa 1945(?)–1950

Of the five books, the brown was used first, possibly as early as 1945.

In this book, we have addresses of people O'Connor knew either while attending the Iowa Writers' Workshop, staying as a guest at Yaddo, or living, albeit briefly, in New York City and then Redding, Connecticut. True, while some of these individuals are mentioned in later address books, it is in the brown book where there is the highest concentration of such early connections.

The brown book offers a look at the people O'Connor met and the friends she made as she began her pursuit of the writer's life.

IOWA, THEN YADDO

Among those she knew while at Iowa (1945–1948), there is a listing for Anna Guzeman, who ran the boarding house where O'Connor stayed her post-graduate year.

There are entries for workshop director Paul Engle, visiting lecturer Andrew Lytle, and instructor Paul Griffith. Of her friends, Carolyn Nutter is included, as are those O'Connor lived with in Currier House, either as suitemates (Gloria Bremer and Barbara Tunnicliff, the latter hired to type O'Connor's graduate thesis) or roommates (Sarah Dawson, Louise Trovato, and Martha Bell).[3] Bremer is not to be confused with the similarly named Gloria Bremerwell, whom O'Connor met in the workshop.

Among the workshop participants, there are entries for Robie Macauley, Clyde McLeod, Jean Williams (later Wylder), and the Messicks (Hank was in the program; wife Faye was, coincidentally, a GSCW alumna).

O'Connor scribbled what one assumes are four-digit telephone numbers for McLeod, Williams, and the Messicks on the inside back cover.

Many of the names in the brown book associated with O'Connor's time at Yaddo (summer 1948 to early 1949) indicate she was widening her circle of acquaints as a writer. However, with the exception of poet Robert Lowell, known to his friends as Cal, and painter Clifford Wright, these connections were short-lived, and their names were not carried over into later books: Elizabeth Hardwick, Edward Maisel, Evelyn Seide, Irene Orgel, Patricia Highsmith, and Vivienne MacLeod (later Koch).

Once-listed as well is Elizabeth Ames, the first executive director of Yaddo, who had come under the scrutiny of the FBI and the press while O'Connor was there. The inclusion of her name is particularly interesting because of the role Ames played in O'Connor's time at Yaddo, both in allowing her a second stay in the fall of 1948 and for being the reason for O'Connor's sudden, not to mention dramatic, departure.

At a special meeting of Yaddo's board of directors held Saturday, February 26, 1949, Lowell led fellow guests Hardwick, Maisel, and O'Connor in allegations that Ames had harbored a known Communist. This meeting was precipitated by a *New York Times* article linking journalist Agnes Smedley (a Yaddo guest from 1943 to 1948 working on a biography of Communist revolutionary Zhu De) with a Soviet spy ring. Though the *Times* returned days later, stating there was no proof regarding Smedley, the damage had been done.[4]

O'Connor had intended to stay through July, but this plan was no longer viable as Yaddo closed temporarily to settle the issue.[5] Shaken, Lowell, Hardwick, and O'Connor headed for Manhattan.[6] O'Connor stayed with Hardwick in her apartment, 28 East 10th Street, for a few days before taking a room at Tatham House, 138 East 38th Street, recording both addresses in the brown book. Lowell booked a room in a hotel off Washington Square but would not be there for long.[7]

The issue was settled weeks later with an admonishment from the board. As many in the arts community rushed to Ames's defense, Lowell himself suffered a bit of a public black eye. Most who knew him saw what came to be known among the Yaddo crowd as "the Lowell Affair" as the beginning of the disturbing unraveling he would experience over the next few weeks as he bounced from one place to another. After a few days in Manhattan, he spent a week in a Rhode Island Trappist monastery, then briefly returned to New York before heading to the Midwest to visit friends. Before long he was sent, though not by choice, to a small, private mental hospital north of Boston. Diagnosis: manic depression.

O'Connor's first listing for Lowell is sparse, with no last name given (see Figure 3). It is somewhat shakily written, perhaps reflecting

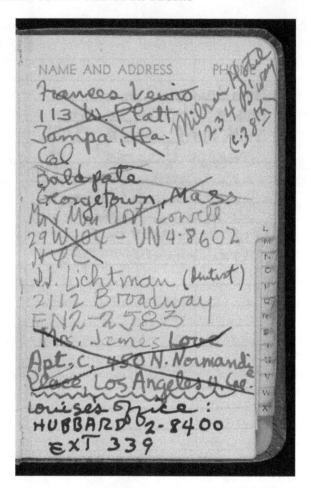

FIGURE 3: From the brown address book. (Used with permission from Flannery O'Connor Papers, Stuart A. Rose Manuscript, Archives, and Rare Book Library, Emory University.)

O'Connor's mood after learning that her friend had been subjected to shock treatments.

> Cal
> Baldpate
> Georgetown, Mass

Lowell stayed there from April to July of 1949.[8]

Upon leaving Baldpate, he married Hardwick on July 28, 1949. Though the couple had planned to live in a rented home in Redhook, New York, for a year, Lowell entered Payne Whitney Clinic on the Upper East Side for psychiatric treatment mere weeks after the ceremony. During his stay, Hardwick moved into the West 104th apartment that O'Connor listed under an entry for Mr. and Mrs. Robt. Lowell. Once he completed treatment, the couple would reside there until leaving for Iowa in January 1950.[9]

O'Connor does not record the Iowa address in the brown but in the black Elite, listing it under R. Lowell. Hardwick, though still married to Lowell during O'Connor's lifetime, would never again figure in her address books. That can't be said of four other names that would first appear in the brown book, however, and these are of people Lowell introduced to O'Connor: Caroline Gordon, Robert and Sally Fitzgerald, and Robert Giroux. Their importance in O'Connor's life and career cannot be overemphasized.

GORDON, FITZGERALD, FITZGERALD, AND GIROUX

To be fair, Lowell did not directly introduce O'Connor to Gordon (who is recorded in O'Connor's brown book under her married name, Caroline Tate). Rather, he introduced the name of the promising writer to Gordon late in 1948 when he wrote to ask if there were any openings at Columbia University. However, two years later, when Robert Fitzgerald asked Gordon to read a draft of *Wise Blood*, she became O'Connor's writing mentor and friend. After much correspondence, the two finally met in person years later.

Lowell brought O'Connor to the Fitzgeralds' York Street apartment upon arriving in Manhattan. Lowell went there intending to discuss the Yaddo upheaval, but time would prove this visit to be significant to O'Connor's life and career. In introducing her to the Fitzgeralds, he was presenting the people she would share a home with and who, more importantly, would be the future stewards of her writings, image, and reputation. Some sixteen years later, Robert Fitzgerald would compose what might be considered O'Connor's first biography in the form of the introduction to *Everything That Rises Must Converge*, which was published after her death. He also served as her literary executor and, with Sally, edited *Mystery and Manners* (1969).

As discussed in the Preface, Sally Fitzgerald also wrote about her friend and gathered and edited O'Connor's writings for publication.

Within a day or so of meeting the Fitzgeralds, Lowell introduced her to his Harcourt, Brace editor, Robert Giroux. Not only would Giroux, in time, become her editor during her life, but he would also retain that role after her death. In addition to seeing *Everything That Rises* through to publication, he put together *Flannery O'Connor: The Complete Stories*. The collection, published in 1971, won the National Book Award; it was the first time the award was given posthumously.

The black Elite, about 1950–1962

The black Elite is the next book used. Interestingly, this book starts at about the point when O'Connor, whose health has demonstrably weakened, is forced to return to Georgia.

Again, we can turn to Lowell and his relocations for chronology. In January 1950, he moved to Iowa to teach at the Writers' Workshop, and this address is listed in the book. Lowell's Iowa address is scratched out in favor of a Cincinnati address; he was the George Elliston Poet in Residence at the University of Cincinnati in 1954. When that address is scratched out, the words "Duxbury Mass" are squeezed in, but no official address follows. While the notation indicates her knowledge of Lowell's intention to move there in 1953, he and Hardwick never ended up there.[10]

At the top of the next page is a listing for Robert Lowell at 239 Marlborough, an address he and Hardwick would share for years (this address is repeated in the red book and in the white).

As for the Fitzgeralds, the black Elite starts with their Connecticut address, but this listing would not be good for long. Under their name in this book comes a series of scratch-outs and directional arrows that go on for several pages, indicating several addresses in Italy, where they relocated in 1953.[11]

While the family was to live there over the next ten years, Robert would occasionally return to the States to teach. O'Connor includes an entry for him with a University of Notre Dame address; she visited him (then Chair of Poetry) there in 1957.[12] A Levanto, Italy, address was in use when O'Connor and her mother visited the Fitzgeralds the following year on their way to Lourdes.[13]

Perhaps one of the more interesting correspondents to follow address-by-address is Caroline Gordon. Gordon was married to poet Allen Tate and, therefore, is found under *T* in O'Connor's black Elite.

To say Gordon moved around a lot is an understatement (see Figure 4). In this book alone, O'Connor lists her as living in St. Paul, Minnesota; Minneapolis (two addresses); Lawrence, Kansas; Princeton, New Jersey (three); and Rome. Gordon lived in these locations from 1952 to 1962.

Other entries in this book represent people significant to O'Connor's 1955 trip to New York to promote *A Good Man Is Hard to Find*. O'Connor

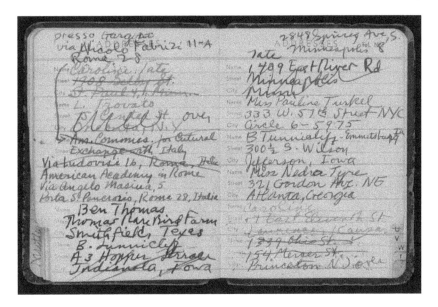

FIGURE 4: From the black Elite address book. (Used with permission from Flannery O'Connor Papers, Stuart A. Rose Manuscript, Archives, and Rare Book Library, Emory University.)

records the contact information of W. G. Rogers of the Associated Press, who interviewed her when she was in town. In addition, Rochelle Girson of the *Saturday Review* is listed.

The black Elite is where we first see listings for two women who would be important friends to O'Connor, Betty Hester (known as "A" in *The Habit of Being*) and Maryat Lee. They entered O'Connor's life in July 1955 and December 1956, respectively. Their addresses would continue over into the red book.

The red, 1962–1964

The red book appears to be O'Connor's final address book, and it features the contact information of people she knew or corresponded with during the last two years of her life.

Details from the life stories of the Fitzgeralds and Caroline Gordon support this assumption. The Fitzgeralds' Levanto address is recorded and then scratched out; the address for the farm in Perugia, which they moved to in 1962, takes its place.[14]

Gordon's addresses range from homes she inhabited from the fall of 1962 to the spring of 1964.

It is in this book that the addresses of O'Connor's later correspondents are recorded. For example, Janet McKane, who began correspondence with O'Connor in 1963, is included, as is editor Rust Hills, who featured the unfinished *Why Do the Heathen Rage* in a special issue of *Esquire* in 1963.

HELLO, ZIP CODES

More than just simple changes in residences and friendships are obvious in this particular book. Some details reflect how the ways people communicated were in flux. Through scratch-outs and additions in both lead and ink, we see the beginnings of the move from two-digit postal zone codes to five-digit zip codes.

The small black and the white

As the books were produced by different manufacturers, and they were years apart, it is difficult to compare the physical books themselves. To discuss these comparisons, remembering the terms *recto* and *verso* when speaking of the pages is helpful.

If a review is needed, a recto page is always odd-numbered and will lie to the right in an open book. Chapters traditionally begin on recto pages, which is true of the alphabetical sections of the address books.

When the recto is flipped or turned, the verso follows on its back and lies to the left. Versos are even-numbered.

The brown, the black Elite, and the red have anywhere from thirty-six to forty-eight versos, while the small black and the white have twenty-eight and twenty, respectively. That said, the white and the small black are clearly smaller books and perhaps not intended for heavy usage. There simply was not as much room for entries.

In addition to having fewer pages to write on, the small black and the white have fewer pages filled out. O'Connor's entries often appear only on the recto, or maybe the verso, but not both.

Taking this into consideration, these were likely the books O'Connor did not use regularly. Perhaps these were books she took with her when traveling, or maybe even when in the hospital. Or perhaps these were books she bought to have on hand when she had neglected to bring her address book with her.

In looking at the small black and the white, a mix of entries also appear in either the black Elite, the red, or both. But the entries that are peculiar to these lesser-used books, entries that appear nowhere else, are of particular interest.

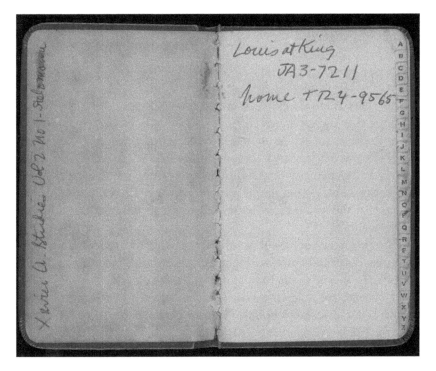

FIGURE 5: Inside the cover of the red address book. *Left*: If O'Connor was looking for a place to record information that she could find in a hurry, the inside cover of her address book was a good choice. *Right*: O'Connor's uncle, Louis Cline, lived in Atlanta during the week and worked at King Hardware Company. (Used with permission from Flannery O'Connor Papers, Stuart A. Rose Manuscript, Archives, and Rare Book Library, Emory University.)

Because the white book includes Caroline Gordon's 1956 address and an entry for W. G. Rogers (whom O'Connor met in 1955), O'Connor likely used this book around the time she used the black Elite.

The small black, as is true of the red, features a few listings with zip codes. It also lists writers she was in touch with during the last years of her life, which is when she was using the red. One such writer was Robert Drake, who reviewed *The Violent Bear It Away* in 1960 and met her in 1963.[15] Another is journalist Phyllis Meras, who may well be the last person to interview O'Connor. The interview took place in March 1964, in between hospital stays.

The correlation between black Elite/white and red/small black is not clearly cut. The small black, for example, shares a few addresses with the black Elite, one being the address of Brentano's bookstore in

Manhattan, a store O'Connor relied on as there was nothing comparable in Milledgeville.

MORE CLUES

Still, other details align the small black, time-wise, with the red book while not sharing any actual entry.

For example, an article about O'Connor's first three books appeared in a Black, Southern, and Catholic university's journal. The author, Rainulf A. Stelzman, sent the issue her way. O'Connor quickly responded with enthusiasm, noting that it was the best she had read on her work, adding that she would refer interested parties to Vol. 2, No. 1 of *Xavier University Studies*.[16]

O'Connor scribbled the journal's identifying information on the inside cover of the red book (see Figure 5). And while there is no listing for Stelzman in the red book, there is one in the small black.

Of course, speculation aside, one can't really know the purpose behind these lesser-used books, just as a person can't know for sure if there were only five address books. Truth be told, there was likely at least one more because there is no mention in any of the five books of Richard Stern, a Chicago writer she corresponded with from 1959 to 1963; her letters to him appear in both *The Habit of Being* and his collection of miscellanies, *The Books in Fred Hampton's Apartment* (E. P. Dutton, 1973).

While another book (or more) would undoubtedly help to more fully answer the question of who O'Connor knew and when, it is undeniable that the known five books do much to show the writer in a fresh light if, as the saying goes, a person can be judged by the company she keeps.

Part I: New York City

1 / The Education of Mary Flannery O'Connor

> I am not only having a fine time here in New York, I am also becoming educated at a very rapid rate.
>
> —MARY FLANNERY O'CONNOR TO KATIE SEMMES,
> JULY 29, 1943[1]

Many assume Flannery O'Connor first saw New York either when she lived there in 1949 or when she was a guest at Yaddo the year before. It seems, however, that O'Connor's first visit took place in 1943 when she was still introduced as Mary Flannery.

The braces on her teeth were giving her trouble.[2]

1943: The United States was two years into fighting World War II. Enrolled in GSCW's wartime three-year program, O'Connor, eighteen, was about to start her junior year.[3] Her father had died two years earlier, and she and Regina were living in the Cline mansion with the latter's sisters: one called Sister (that is, Mary Cline) and the other nicknamed Duchess (Katie, a clerk in the post office).[4]

It was a summer of travel for both mother and daughter. In May, Regina left to visit her cousin, Mary Catherine Flannery Semmes of Savannah, whom both mother and daughter called Cousin Katie. Regina stayed there for the better part of a month before coming home, only to return to Savannah while O'Connor was out of town.[5]

O'Connor would be gone much of that summer. For three weeks in August, she was scheduled to stay in Arlington, Massachusetts, with her aunt, Agnes Cline Florencourt, and her four cousins.[6] To get there, O'Connor would take a train with family friend Lydia A. Bancroft.[7] Miss Bancroft, as O'Connor referred to her, was an art instructor at GSCW and sometimes a boarder in the Cline home. Having earned her Bachelor's and Master's degrees at Columbia University, Bancroft knew her way around New York.[8]

The plan? The two would leave mid-July for a few weeks' stay at the Montclair, New Jersey, home of Bancroft's sister, Grace Stone, and niece Helen. While there, Bancroft (at the time, sixty years old) and Helen (forty-eight) would show O'Connor the sights of New York City, at times joined by artist (and former GSCW instructor) Margaret Sutton (thirty-eight). At the end of the month, O'Connor would board a train to Massachusetts while Bancroft headed to Delaware to visit family. The two would meet up three weeks later for a brief second stay with the Stones before making the trip back home to Milledgeville.[9]

O'Connor was a regular letter writer even at a young age and, as such, wrote many letters to Regina during their separation. She also wrote to Cousin Katie on occasion and, in one letter, made a point of saying how she appreciated the trip to New York and enjoyed every moment of it.[10] It's the sort of comment one makes to someone paying for an excursion, which might well have been the case here; after all, Semmes was a very wealthy woman who acted as a benefactor to the O'Connor family on more than one occasion.

While such a journey was certainly exciting and fun, an almost cheeky emphasis was put on its potential to inform, with a few references in letters of the New York trip being "educational."

It was. And then some.

All Aboard

Travel *is* educational, down to the physical act itself. In a letter to Regina, O'Connor enclosed a cartoon chronicling the realities of public transportation for Cousin Katie's amusement: With the handwritten caption "Cool, comfortable, accommodating cars" setting up the joke, O'Connor draws herself, saddle oxfords and all, as an exhausted and cramped passenger whose comfort is challenged by both the lowered seat (to the front of her) in her lap and a sailor's foot pressing into her seat from behind.[11] (See Figure 6.)

Not only is there the physical discomfort of travel, but also the unease a person, particularly an unseasoned traveler, might feel when in the presence of those unlike oneself. While the sailor's presence was a wartime regularity, in one letter, O'Connor makes mention of public transportation being filled not only with soldiers but also with Jews and Blacks.[12] In her solo train ride to Massachusetts, she was shocked at how a middle-aged White woman chatted amiably with a Black (and, one assumes, off-duty) porter who subsequently put his feet up and napped.[13]

Cool, comfortable, accomodating cars.

FIGURE 6: O'Connor's cartoon shows the conditions she experienced while traveling in 1943. (Used with permission from Flannery O'Connor Papers, Stuart A. Rose Manuscript, Archives, and Rare Book Library, Emory University.)

Also educational are the attractions one finds in big cities. The destinations that her guides chose were indeed informative: the Metropolitan Museum of Art, the American Museum of Natural History (where O'Connor was drawn to the mounted ducks), and the Planetarium.[14] In addition, there were visits to Radio City Music Hall, where O'Connor attended performances of the City Service Concert Orchestra and, on another occasion, of the Don Cossacks.[15] Because her charge was a devoted Catholic, Bancroft made sure to include a visit to St. Patrick's Cathedral; O'Connor commemorated the event with the purchase of a postcard picturing the Our Lady of New York altar in the Lady Chapel, which she sent to Regina.[16] This altar, consecrated the year before, was still relatively new when O'Connor viewed it.

A Requiem Mass in O'Connor's honor would be given in the Lady Chapel twenty-one years later, a few days after her death.[17]

In a letter to Regina, O'Connor talks of receiving word from Sutton about an upcoming Sunday afternoon venture that would include taking a ferry.[18] If that ferry was the one to Staten Island, the boat ride does not seem to have taken place, as O'Connor does not mention it in her letter describing the day. But plenty else occurred that O'Connor was quite affected by.

The afternoon started with dinner at the Stones', followed by a trip to the zoo.[19] (Considering their time spent on the subway, she likely saw the Bronx Zoo rather than the one in Central Park.) O'Connor mentions going but gives no details of the experience, saving her words for the events that stood out in her mind. After the zoo excursion, Sutton led the group by way of public transportation to the Pell Street Inn at 18 Pell Street in Lower Manhattan's Chinatown district.[20] While the restaurant name may have seemed Western enough, one glance down iconic Pell Street would have told O'Connor otherwise, and when she entered the building, her nose twitched uncomfortably at the new and literally foreign aromas.

Young O'Connor did not want to eat there, much less be there. She thought it fortunate that her cold (which she later determined was actually hay fever) spared her from having to actually taste the objectionable food (though, to be polite, she declared it superlative).[21] In the end, she says, the food did seem clean, an important detail to note as it points to the idea that there was more to her reluctance than squeamishness. O'Connor was perhaps acting as many Americans of that time would, a time when a common name for soy sauce was bug juice.

O'Connor grew up at a time when people experienced the Yellow Peril, that existential dread suggesting that East Asian people were dangerous. At the time of O'Connor's visit, the Chinese Exclusion Act of 1882 was still in place, though it would be repealed by December of that year; China was, after all, on the side of the Allies. By the war's end (and only two years after O'Connor's visit), Chinese cuisine would be more commonly accepted and enjoyed in this country.[22]

Segregated

Finally, travel holds the power to broaden one's outlook, of course, and perhaps that is the sort of education O'Connor's guides had in mind. Bancroft and Sutton had experienced firsthand what it was to live in Milledgeville when they moved there to teach at the university. Likely, they wanted to show O'Connor that the rest of the country did not live the way she did.

That is to say, segregated.

As they sat at the Pell Street Inn, the foursome took time to dash notes on a single postcard to Regina. After Bancroft's basic greeting that announced their location, Sutton took the pen to say she had "seen to it" that O'Connor had ridden through "the dirtiest subways and 'L's in New York, through all the dirty ugly sections," adding that, as she saw it, O'Connor had never had "so much fun and so much pain at the same time in all her life."[23] Stone wrote that they were enjoying taking O'Connor to see unfamiliar things, "thus broadening her education."[24]

O'Connor, her mind on the foreign fare she did not want to eat, simply commented on the state of her digestion. But in private correspondence to Regina, she expressed her extreme discomfort in Blacks and Whites sitting near one another on public transportation, adding that she was not ready to, or interested in, doing so herself.[25]

And she saw that this mixing was happening beyond the subways. While still in Montclair, she wrote to her mother about her visit that day to Columbia University—shocking because Black and White students sat together in the classrooms and, more disturbing, used the same restrooms.[26] In another letter, O'Connor commented that Bancroft deemed a trip to the automat as part of her "education" (again, that word), an outing that caused O'Connor's ice cream to go down the wrong way when she saw a young Black woman, tray in hand, make her way to go sit with three White people.[27]

It's that down-the-wrong-pipe reaction that shows how truly limited her worldview was, at that time, as a life-long resident of the Jim Crow South, one whose viewpoint was formed not only by her community but also by her privileged position within it. As offensive as some of her comments would be found today, they are typical of one who had never differently known, had never differently seen, had never been differently shown. She was genuinely shocked by what she saw, and what she saw was indeed educational.

O'Connor's description of a young Black woman choosing to sit with three White diners ends with the observation that the three "didn't know the difference, however."[28] Perhaps this comment shows that education was starting to take effect.

Indeed, the "dirty ugly" sights and sounds she experienced would emerge a few years later in "The Geranium," which was O'Connor's first literary publication (not to mention the unveiling of her writer's name, sans "Mary") as well as the lead story in her MFA thesis. She describes the subway rides Old Dudley takes with this daughter, excursions where people of different races are mixed as though they are the bubbling contents of a soup pot that finally boils over. The ugly building where his daughter lives is just one in a row of many where people leaned out of their windows, looking at each other. That the daughter takes him on an overhead train she calls "an 'El'" is mentioned, as well.

After her visit with the Florencourts, O'Connor met with her three guides at Pennsylvania Station in New York. From there, they headed for a Swedish restaurant. Arriving at 6:15 and leaving at 9:00, O'Connor happily reported that most of the time was spent eating.[29] As they had done at the Pell Street Inn weeks before, the party scribbled cheery notes to Regina on a postcard. If the image on the card—St. Patrick's Cathedral—was a hint to where they dined, they ate at the Swedish Rathskeller (201 E. 52nd Street).

These two book-end visits to New York comprise a collective moment of independence for O'Connor from her mother; they also mark a time in her life when she was directly shown how others lived, perhaps for the first time. The education, conceivably, had paved the way to growth.

Two years later, she left Georgia for the University of Iowa Writers' Workshop, a little over 900 miles away from home. In a few of her daily letters to Regina, O'Connor mentions Gloria Bremerwell, a young Black poet also enrolled in the program (at the time, fiction writers and poets were not separated). In a letter from October 1945, O'Connor makes a point of telling her mother that she went to dinner with Bremerwell and two White friends, Ruth Sullivan and Miriam Johnson, being sure Regina understood that Sullivan and Johnson were White and Bremerwell was Black.[30] In this letter and others, O'Connor makes it clear that she enjoys Bremerwell's company. Though we can tell by O'Connor's written response that her mother warned her of the dangers of interracial associations, O'Connor firmly puts the older woman in her place and more or less tells her to mind her own business.[31]

One can imagine a crowded cafeteria, students wearing bright sweaters, and Bremerwell, dinner tray in hand, approaching the table where Sullivan, Johnson, and O'Connor chatted. And, much like the trio in the automat years before, one can hope that they, too, didn't know the difference.

2 / City Life

The years 1948 through 1950 marked a time in O'Connor's life when she lived either in New York City or near it—first in Saratoga Springs and then in Redding, Connecticut. This proximity to Manhattan was important at the beginning of her writing career as it allowed her the opportunity to meet face-to-face with people in the business (editors, agents) and gave her a beyond-tourist knowledge of the city itself.

This chapter considers her life in and visits to Manhattan during that period.

Saratoga Springs: A Train Fare Away

After her time in Iowa, O'Connor was a resident at Yaddo Artists and Writers Colony in Saratoga Springs, New York. One cannot underestimate the effect this stay would have on her career and life if not so much in terms of the work she did there, but in the people she met. She arrived on June 1, 1948.

She was there to work on the novel *Wise Blood*, a book that already had the interest of Rinehart & Company publishers. This interest came in the form of the Rinehart-Iowa Award—a $750 advance for a book written by an Iowa Writers' Workshop student with an option, upon the book's acceptance, for an additional $750.[1] At this point, the ball was clearly in the publisher's court. John Selby, editor-in-chief of Rinehart, wanted to see a first draft before moving forward.

Perhaps spurred on by the seasoned writers she was meeting at Yaddo, O'Connor searched for an agent to help navigate the publishing waters.

Elizabeth McKee came recommended by fellow writer Paul Moor and, in June, became O'Connor's agent.

HARD TO PLAN

Having an agent on board and a possible publisher in the wings was a sign to O'Connor that her career was moving in the right direction. But with such progress came a new level of complication in her life, one added because she did not live in New York City. Her permanent address on West Greene Street in Milledgeville, Georgia, was some 870 miles away from Manhattan.

Fortunately, O'Connor was "only" 185 miles from the heart of New York when she was staying at Yaddo. Unfortunately, her time there was ending in July. For that reason, O'Connor tried to schedule a meeting between herself, McKee, and Selby for early August. If she could make that happen, O'Connor told her mother, she would likely stay at the Hotel Pennsylvania or some other hotel near the train station.[2] Not living in New York, she was learning, was not only inconvenient but expensive, particularly for a full-time writer in need of an advance.

With McKee leaving for Europe at the end of July, O'Connor left the state without the benefit of speaking about her book in person. But as O'Connor had been awarded another stay at Yaddo, this one starting in the fall, she was able to schedule a mid-September stop in Manhattan. O'Connor reserved a room at the Woodstock Hotel.[3]

The brief trip bristled with activity. O'Connor arrived on a Sunday and had cocktails with McKee and husband, Ted Purdy, after which friend Margaret Sutton took the three to dinner. The next day, O'Connor had lunch with Selby and McKee at the Ritz Carlton and toured the Rinehart offices afterward. While there, she was introduced to Anne Draper Macauley, publicity director of Rinehart and newlywed wife of her good friend, Robie. One wonders if that meeting was perhaps a little awkward for O'Connor, who had been invited (by Robie) to the wedding but did not attend. Still, O'Connor told her mother she liked Anne.[4]

O'Connor dined again with Sutton, this time with Yaddo friend (and Rinehart author) Elizabeth Fenwick. The dinner was followed by a visit to another Yaddo acquaintance, artist Evelyn Seide.[5]

With "The Capture" coming out in the November issue of *Mademoiselle*, associate editor George Davis invited her to lunch.[6]

Her meeting with Selby had been productive in that O'Connor had a better sense of what was expected of her. O'Connor returned to Yaddo knowing she needed to submit six chapters to be considered for an advance.[7] In truth, she had already written twelve chapters that she was not ready to show anyone; after meeting with Selby, however, she began rewriting from the beginning.[8] At this point, she was not confident that Rinehart was the right publisher for her book, especially with new Yaddo friends talking up Harcourt, Brace.[9] Still, she was grateful to be able to work at Yaddo through July. Working steadily through the fall and into winter, in December, she told McKee that she might come to New York in January.[10]

However, the happy atmosphere that fostered her creative work abruptly evaporated with the onset of a scandal involving Yaddo's director (to read about that, see Introduction). O'Connor and other shaken guests left abruptly for New York. On the one hand, the controversy was upsetting, particularly to O'Connor as she was scratching her way through *Wise Blood*. But on the other hand, the unforeseen disruption solved a major problem for her.

For the moment, at least, that problem was solved. Scheduling meetings in New York was no longer difficult. O'Connor was in New York.

IN NEW YORK CITY

Much has been said of O'Connor's obvious affection for Lowell while at Yaddo.[11] Knowing of this, naturally, one might assume that O'Connor followed Lowell, who wanted to discuss the Yaddo situation with friends Robert and Sally Fitzgerald, to Manhattan.[12] And he was already in a leadership position, having championed the charges against the Yaddo director that led to him and O'Connor (along with writers Elizabeth Hardwick and Ed Maisel) choosing to leave Saratoga Springs. But O'Connor had already made plans to go to Manhattan, plans she now had to amend.[13] She wrote to McKee in late February to cancel a scheduled March 1 appointment with Selby. She would be traveling that day, O'Connor explained, but she would call her the next morning.[14]

Already, life was more convenient.

O'Connor spent that first night of her new, if temporary, New York residency at Elizabeth Hardwick's apartment.[15] She soon found other lodgings. She was on her own.

Murray Hill, Tatham House

O'Connor moved into a furnished room at 138 East 38th Street, a YWCA property in Murray Hill known as Tatham House.[16] (The building's name is pronounced the way O'Connor records it in her address books: *Tatum*.) Her room was one of 250 in a building dedicated to safely housing women in various occupations, from secretaries, teachers, and nurses to journalists, actresses, and models. Such women-only hotels and apartment buildings were popular in New York City from the 1920s to the 1970s.

Tatham was a location with many conveniences for the single gal. O'Connor paid two dollars a day and, as a resident, could buy breakfast in the building. She also frequented a co-op cafeteria on 41st Street, located between Park and Madison.[17]

Lowell would leave a few days after coming to Manhattan, making his way to a Trappist Monastery in Rhode Island for a weeklong retreat before traveling elsewhere. Still, before he did, he introduced O'Connor to people who would prove to be not only lifelong friends, but also influential and supportive allies.

She met Robert Giroux, Lowell's editor at Harcourt, Brace, on her second day in town, though their paths had crossed already. In 1946, Giroux, Macauley, and Robert Penn Warren had chosen a story by O'Connor as the winner of a college fiction contest.[18] Lowell then introduced her to Robert and Sally Fitzgerald, figuring the three would hit it off as they were all passionately Catholic.

After meeting Giroux, O'Connor soon had lunch with his colleague Ted Amussen.[19] She also met with a lawyer who told her she was not obligated to Rinehart.[20]

There were other social gatherings. She had dinners with Hardwick and Fenwick. She attended her first ballet with Jack and Dilly Thompson.[21] She got together with Margaret Sutton and met her friends.[22] And Lowell and Hardwick took O'Connor to a dinner party at the home of Mary McCarthy and Bowden Broadwater. It was there that O'Connor famously expressed vehement disdain over McCarthy's comment that the Eucharist was a good symbol.[23]

Interestingly, years later, O'Connor, in a list of people to send *Wise Blood* for promotional reasons, included Mrs. Bowden Broadwater.[24]

Despite its advantages, O'Connor didn't like her room at Tatham House; she even disliked its smell, as she told Iowa classmate Jean Williams Wylder.[25] She felt she had no real reason to stay in New York as she had yet to firm things up, one way or another, with Rinehart.[26] Though financial reasons certainly played a part in her wanting to leave, there was likely more to it. She was reeling from both the event at Yaddo and the negative response of the Yaddo community toward those who had testified at the board meeting. To make matters worse, a special meeting of the Yaddo Board to discuss the charges was scheduled for later that month.

Also, Lowell's apparent unraveling was likely troubling. At Yaddo, Lowell had rediscovered his Catholic faith and, before leaving for Manhattan, attended Mass with O'Connor for the first time in over a year.[27] His finding religion was more than just a matter of seeing the light, as it were. Lowell was experiencing what he (and his friends) would come to recognize as a sort of revving-up period that always preceded a manic episode—a storm before the storm, so to speak.[28] These manic behaviors found an outlet in his new religious purpose, although in troubling ways, such as declaring March 3 as the Day of Flannery O'Connor and taking an ice bath as he prayed fervently to her patron saint, Thérèse of Lisieux.[29]

O'Connor's approaching twenty-fourth birthday provided a good excuse to go home, particularly as she struggled to figure out her next step. O'Connor wrote to her mother to say she'd likely come home March 17.[30]

But that she'd likely come back to Manhattan in April.

Morningside Heights, the Manchester

In the Emory archives, there is a small and yellowed page tucked in with the address books. Its perforated edge indicates it was ripped from some notepad. The information is written in pencil.

Flannery O'Connor
255 W—108th St
Apt 12 C—
New York N.Y.
phone MO2-1494

This is the address of the Manchester, where O'Connor stayed, from some point in early to mid-April, all the way through to the end of August 1949. The same address and phone number can be found in O'Connor's brown address book, but with one difference: It's not listed under O'Connor's name, but Elizabeth Fenwick's.

And thus, we come to the first of a couple of mysteries surrounding O'Connor's stay in Morningside Heights. Had O'Connor stayed in New York rather than pop back home for a few weeks, the who-and-what of her next living arrangement would likely be found in a letter to Regina (had the letter been kept).

But O'Connor, frazzled by both what had happened at Yaddo and what was not happening with Rinehart, went home for a handful of weeks. As a result, we do not know the details behind this quickly made living arrangement, a set-up deemed important as it marks a critical step in the young writer's life and career.

As one can surmise from reading the *Habit of Being*, O'Connor was a habitual letter writer. Because she lived most of her life with her mother, Regina, there was no need to write to her unless she was away, but when she was, she did almost daily. Most of her letters were written in longhand.

The letters written while at Tatham House stand out as though to represent her state of mind. They are typed on lined sheets torn from a small notebook. On one such sheet, O'Connor mentioned her plans for returning to New York.[31] She says "here" (presumably Tatham House) was an option, but there was also the possibility of a room that might become available in April. The room, she explains, was "Margaret's present one; she is thinking of moving into someone's apt. while same is in Europe."[32]

The situation wasn't quite that.

WHICH MARGARET?

In O'Connor's letters to Regina, "Margaret" (that is, with no last name or other identifier added) sometimes referred to cousin Margaret Florencourt. However, in 1949, Florencourt, a graduate of both Radcliffe and Massachusetts Institute of Technology, resided in Massachusetts.[33]

Again, in her letters to her mother, O'Connor also (often) referred to family friend Margaret Sutton by first name only. Sutton lived in Manhattan but was well past the "furnished room" stage and had been residing at 210 West 14th Street since 1939. So, if one goes by the wording of O'Connor's brief, typed letter, this Margaret is not Sutton.

However, if one takes other facts into consideration, we see that she likely is.

By 1949, Sutton had been living in the same apartment for ten years, but it was not, technically speaking, her apartment. She lived with her friends, painter Alfred Levitt and his wife, attorney Gertrude Horowitz. The couple, married since 1930, had lived in the apartment since at least 1935 (perhaps earlier).[34]

Levitt went to Europe regularly to paint (some of his works are owned by the Met). In particular, though, he often photographed cave paintings in France and Spain, important and extensive documentation for which he was knighted.[35] That said, the couple left for an extended stay in Europe on April 13, 1949.[36]

Six days before their departure, O'Connor was preparing for her move back to New York.[37] For all we know, she had already unpacked by the time the Levitts boarded the Queen Elizabeth.

It is evident that O'Connor did not take Sutton up on her offer, and it's possible (based on her wording in her letter) that she didn't understand Sutton's living arrangement when that offer was made. Her friend, after all, planned not so much to move into her friends' apartment (she was already there) but into their (likely larger) room. Maybe the Levitts didn't want Sutton using their room, or maybe Sutton, for whatever reason, reneged.

Most likely, O'Connor herself decided against living in the Greenwich Village location. The building was a five-story walk-up, and she could have balked at the idea of climbing so many flights daily. (Her short story "A Stroke of Good Fortune" comes to mind.) Even while in her early twenties, O'Connor complained about lacking energy.[38]

Whatever the reason, we know O'Connor didn't take that room—which is a shame: Marcel Duchamp lived in the building, and Levitt himself said the man was an odd character who greeted him with "good morning" in the evening and "good evening" in the morning.[39] One can only imagine O'Connor's reaction to that or how exchanges with the French artist would have slipped into her fiction.

WHERE'S ELIZABETH?

In the chronology provided in *Collected Works*, Sally Fitzgerald stated O'Connor found a furnished room to rent with the help of Elizabeth Fenwick.[40] In *The Habit of Being*, Fitzgerald states that the apartment was not far from where Fenwick lived.[41] In a letter included in that book, O'Connor tells a friend that she had lived next door to Fenwick.[42] In an earlier letter, O'Connor tells her agent that she had received her correspondence only because Fenwick, who had then lived next door, sent it her way.[43]

That O'Connor rented a furnished room in the Manchester is of no debate. That she was led to the apartment by Elizabeth Fenwick is also not questioned. But if Fenwick lived next door, why wasn't another address recorded under her name in the address book? If by "next door" O'Connor meant the room next to hers in the same apartment, that would have been mentioned.

C/O MISS DUNCAN

Mystery aside, thanks to Hardwick, O'Connor rented a room from Mary B. Duncan, a naturalized citizen from Canada who was sixty-four in 1949. She, at least at that point, had never married.[44]

Miss Duncan, as O'Connor referred to her, rented living space to four tenants at a time. She occasionally advertised vacancies in the *Furnished Room—Upper West Side* section of the classifieds, as she did in April 1950.

108th 255 W (cor Broadway). Small
sunny room, bath; business woman; no
cooking. MO 2-1494.[45]

Another classified ad, this one from 1951, describes an available room as being "pleasant" and having both cross ventilation and water.[46]

As is true of many Manhattan apartments of its time, the apartment as it was configured in 1949 no longer exists.

Manhattan Life

The New York that O'Connor lived in was a place that was experiencing growth. The July 1949 issue of the Manhattan Telephone Directory contained 1,646 pages, which was 56 pages longer (an increase of 23,000 listings) than the November 1948 volume.[47]

Despite the general excitement that often accompanies population growth, O'Connor kept her mind on her writing. The spring and summer of 1949 was a period of serious and consuming work. But while she devoted her days to following fictional characters Hazel Motes, Enoch Emery, and Sabbath Lily Hawks as they rumbled around fictional Taulkinham, Tennessee, O'Connor's nights were spent with New York friends such as Fenwick, Hardwick, Sutton, and the Fitzgeralds.

Her daily life had a pattern, a pleasant predictability.[48] She went to Mass daily at Church of the Ascension, located around the corner on 107th. She dined regularly at the Columbia University student cafeteria, which was within walking distance from the Manchester. When destinations were farther away, she rode the subway or caught a bus. She declared the public library as too overwhelming. She did not see any plays but did visit the American Museum of Natural History (as she had done in 1943). Of particular enjoyment were two trips to the Cloisters, a museum of medieval art and architecture located in Washington Heights; in particular, she was delighted by a specific statue of the Madonna and infant Jesus, one she would remember in later correspondence, each figure happy and seeming to laugh.[49]

O'Connor also had visitors. She met with her Iowa roommate, Louise Trovato, who planned to be in town for two weeks.[50] Though visits are not mentioned in her letters, she was in touch with Lydia Bancroft, who was apparently up North that summer.[51] Cousin Margaret Florencourt was scheduled to come in August, but Cousin Louise Florencourt got there first, arriving in June for a three-day stay and sleeping at night on a pallet on the floor. O'Connor, who liked to stick to writing during the day, found the visit too disruptive to her routine, not to mention her household. O'Connor describes Duncan becoming upset because Louise failed to clean up water on the bathroom floor. (Hardly world-shattering, this, but as Duncan was suffering from trench mouth at the moment, one gathers that even the most minor incident would be perceived as upsetting.)[52]

Louise Florencourt (who, four years later, would become one of Harvard Law School's first female graduates[53]) was not without her own amusements. She spent time with Harvard-educated Lyman Fulton, who was completing a residency in internal medicine at New York Hospital. When he came by the apartment, O'Connor played hostess by offering him tap water and goat cheese.[54] Before O'Connor moved, Louise would come back for another visit, but O'Connor told her mother she hoped her cousin could entertain herself, as she didn't have another three days to spend entertaining guests.[55]

In addition to her progress on the novel, O'Connor had other worries as health issues plagued her. She saw Dr. John P. West about a pain in her side and was comforted when he told her she could call him at any time.[56] In a later letter, she noted that the doctor was treating her for trench mouth.[57]

LASTING EFFECT

With the end of summer, or thereabouts, came the end of O'Connor's life as a New York resident, however brief and temporary it was. But the value of that parcel of time when her feet hit the New York sidewalks every day cannot be underestimated. She came to know the city the way an occasional visitor could not and understood it far differently than if she had merely popped in occasionally from Yaddo. By living in the city, whether in Tatham House or the Manchester, she was able to form her own everyday impressions of the city that was the hub of the publishing world.

Years later, in reflecting upon her time there, O'Connor said that there is a definite emphasis on setting, if not location itself, in New York, an observation that seems rather obvious. But she took this observation past the mundane by adding that the great Northern metropolis was not linked to memories of wartime defeat as were the cities and towns of the South.[58] Because of that, she said, such a city could not touch as deep an emotional place in its people. It's a comment made all the more thought-provoking when one considers that her story, "A Late Encounter with the Enemy," mocks the Lost Cause ideology.

And a conclusion made all the more interesting knowing, for nearly five months, O'Connor lived but a mile away from Grant's Tomb.

Connecticut

By September 1949, O'Connor had moved in with the couple she had met in the first days of March, the Fitzgeralds, who had purchased a house in rural Redding, Connecticut, with a post office address listed as nearby (and larger) Ridgefield. With O'Connor renting a space over the garage and taking her meals in the main house, the living arrangement was seen as a way to both help the young writer stretch her uncertain dollars as she continued to work on *Wise Blood* and, as a babysitter, give Sally Fitzgerald breaks from the children.

Initially, O'Connor was not to be the only boarder. There was talk of including Lowell and Hardwick.[59] Interestingly, the purchase of the property more or less coincided with the couple's marriage, which neither the Fitzgeralds nor O'Connor attended.[60]

O'Connor could, and did, go to New York as needed. For example, she spent two days there, likely November 3 and 4, to tend to breaking away from Rinehart.[61] She would return again, though she didn't leave the train station, on her way home in December 1949 for the Christmas holidays. While at the station, she visited with the Lowells—it was their first gathering since the couple's marriage, not to mention the first since Lowell's stays in two separate mental facilities.[62]

O'Connor's plans to see the couple again upon returning in the new year were dashed by an unplanned surgery to correct a "floating kidney" (otherwise known as Dietl's Crisis, a severe form of nephroptosis).[63] While O'Connor would joke that the surgeon had hung her kidney on a rib, the actual procedure would have involved attaching the kidney (which, due to a weak ligament, drops into the pelvis upon standing up) to the abdominal wall.

Her New York acquaintance, Dr. Lyman, would later wonder if the surgery was the first indication of lupus.[64]

When she returned to Connecticut in March 1950, O'Connor was set to get back to the task of finishing *Wise Blood*. Having recovered from the surgery, she was feeling well enough to make the occasional trip into the city, even writing to a friend that she would be willing to meet her in New York should her friend come out that way. She added that she went to the city occasionally to visit.[65]

But her health would continue to be a concern. Before she left in December 1950 for a holiday trip back home, she was tentatively diagnosed with rheumatoid arthritis by a local doctor. When Sally Fitzgerald saw her off at the New York train station, O'Connor walked stiffly. By the time O'Connor reached Georgia, she was seriously ill.[66]

CONNECTICUT, PART TWO

In 1951, O'Connor believed she had rheumatoid arthritis. She believed that because the truth—that she had lupus—was withheld from her under orders from Regina, who feared upsetting her daughter. (Today, it is difficult to imagine a physician not sharing such information with an adult patient directly. More difficult to digest is that Regina shared the diagnosis early on with the Fitzgeralds.[67]) Still, O'Connor looked forward to getting well enough to move back to Connecticut. To help in the process of recovery, the two moved into Andalusia, a family-owned farm on the outskirts of Milledgeville, leaving both the Cline Mansion and life in the heart of town behind.[68]

O'Connor saw the move to Andalusia as temporary. She lived there for the rest of her life.

In June 1952, after Wise Blood's release, O'Connor traveled to Connecticut for an open-ended visit, returning to the studio apartment over the Fitzgeralds' garage. Robert was away teaching in Indiana, and Sally was pregnant with their fifth child.

The house was brimming. In addition to the two women and (now) four children (one of whom developed chicken pox during her stay), there was a Slavic nanny on board and a twelve-year-old Black girl visiting through a program that provided vacations to underprivileged New York children.[69] The house was, naturally, chaotic. Adding to O'Connor's unsettled feeling was Fitzgerald's revelation that her ailment was not arthritis but lupus. O'Connor was shocked and relieved at the same time, having had her suspicions all along.[70]

But the trip was not a total wash. While there, O'Connor finally met Caroline Gordon in person. O'Connor rode out to New York to treat her to lunch as a thank you for not only Gordon's valuable criticism on drafts of Wise Blood but also her blurb for the book cover.[71] Not only was this a significant visit for both, but it also represented O'Connor's last day trip to New York, the kind of quick in-and-out one is afforded only by proximity. It was a luxury she had enjoyed for only a few years—a luxury she was now losing.

Though she had planned on an open-ended stay, O'Connor's visit ended after six weeks due to contracting a virus. Though ill, she accompanied the twelve-year-old on the train ride to New York City. From there,

O'Connor flew to Atlanta, where she would learn that the virus had reactivated her lupus.[72]

Once home, she sent for items she had left in Connecticut. From then on, O'Connor knew that living in Connecticut, or New York, or anywhere other than her mother's home was no longer possible. Still, occasional visits would occur, just as travel to different places would eventually resume. In 1953, for example, following a trip to Tennessee to visit friends, O'Connor spent three pleasant weeks with the Fitzgeralds.[73]

On her way back to Milledgeville, O'Connor went to New York and saw Giroux. Over lunch on September 2, he suggested she gather her short stories into a collection. This collection would become her second book, *A Good Man Is Hard to Find.*[74]

3 / *A Good Man Is Hard to Find*

On May 30, 1955, O'Connor traveled to Manhattan to publicize *A Good Man Is Hard to Find*, scheduled for an early June release. This trip marks the one time that O'Connor visited New York as an established author for the purpose of promotion.

The highlight of the visit was her appearance on the television show *Galley Proof* on May 31, hosted by Harvey Breit, a poet and playwright who reviewed books for the *New York Times Book Review*. Television was still a new enterprise at that time, thus doubling the thrill (not to mention the anxiety) of being interviewed on the air.

O'Connor was scheduled to stay at the Woodstock, the same hotel where she stayed in September 1948.[1]

A New Editor

What should have been a moment of celebration for O'Connor was marred by the recent resignation of Robert Giroux from Harcourt, Brace. Therefore, he was not involved in the release of the book he had both suggested and edited. However, he had left O'Connor in good hands. In planning the visit, a series of letters flew between O'Connor and her new Harcourt, Brace editor, Catharine Carver, covering details that nowadays would be handled by email.

It was initially to be a brief but busy visit: dinner with Harcourt, Brace editor Derek Lindley and his wife Monday night, lunch with Breit on Tuesday, followed by the show's filming starting promptly at 1:30. Wanting to be added to the list of appointments was Arabel Porter of Signet

Publishing, whose *New World Writing* was featuring "You Can't Be Any Poorer than Dead" that year. With so much going on, Carver suggested that O'Connor stay at least until Wednesday, June 1.[2]

On May 18, O'Connor wrote to tell Carver that she would stay through Friday, June 3, but she did not expect the publisher to pay for the extra days.[3] Carver replied that she would meet O'Connor on the tarmac, adding that several more people were interested in seeing O'Connor during her visit, both socially and otherwise.[4]

A few days later, O'Connor needed to change the plan slightly. She had been to see her doctor, and he had concerns. She said that while for the past few months she had been able to get around without a cane, the doctor feared too much walking would reverse the progress she had made. If she stayed at the Woodstock, O'Connor knew she would be tempted to walk the three or four blocks to the Harcourt, Brace office rather than hail a cab. That said, she asked Carver to book a room at a hotel closer to Grand Central Station instead.

On a lighter note, she added that she was interested in seeing Tennessee Williams' play on Broadway.[5]

With O'Connor's departure only days away, Carver sent a telegram saying she made a reservation at the New Weston at 49th and Madison.[6] She said the accommodations would be nicer (and quieter) than hotels near Grand Central and had the added advantage of having a couple of lobbies perfect for meeting with people.[7]

New York, New York

Though accommodations had been switched and a couple of appointments had been changed, the beginning of her visit began as planned, with Carver there to greet her at the airport on Monday, May 30. Two representatives from the television program met them for dinner at the Weston at 7 P.M.; Breit did not show up until 10 P.M., as he was returning from his wedding trip with his third wife, poet and playwright Patricia Rinehart.[8]

It was raining when O'Connor wrote to her mother Tuesday morning, using hotel stationery. The blue dress had gotten rather wrinkled, she wrote, but all the other clothes had fared well. How she wished she had brought her raincoat rather than the fur. It was unfortunate that she had not remembered to pack a toothbrush; she would have to go buy one. Luckily, she did remember to pack the Gevral.[9]

With the week she had planned, she would need all the energy she could muster.

A Week in the Life of a Writer

At 1:30 on Tuesday afternoon, O'Connor appeared on NBC's *Galley Proof*, which was broadcast over a 135-mile radius.[10] This show is important because it provides a rare glimpse not only of O'Connor speaking, but of her bantering with an interviewer.

After filming the television show, she had tea with Giroux at the hotel. Though the two were undoubtedly happy to see each other, the meeting took on greater importance as Giroux spoke to her regarding her dealings with Harcourt, Brace. Specifically, he advised her about a stipulation to include in her upcoming book contract. And in general, he let her know that if she ever chose to leave Harcourt, Brace, her work would be welcome at Farrar, Straus & Cudahy.[11]

Wednesday was busy. O'Connor had breakfast with *Harper's Bazaar* fiction editor Alice Morris, who had chosen "Good Country People" for the June issue. Coincidentally, Morris was Breit's second wife.

O'Connor had lunch with her agents and was then interviewed by W. G. Rogers of the Associated Press. She dined with Carver that evening and then attended a performance of *Cat on a Hot Tin Roof*.[12] The play had opened ten weeks before and featured the original cast of Barbara Bel Geddes, Ben Gazzara, and Burl Ives. Years later, playwright Maryat Lee noted that her friend had seen only one professionally produced play in her lifetime.[13] If that is true, then Williams' very Southern and very sexual work was the one play O'Connor saw. She didn't like it.[14]

Thursday's activities included a late morning interview with Rochelle Girson of the *Saturday Review* Syndicate, followed by lunch with the editor of *Harper's Bazaar* (who, while not named, was likely Carmel Snow). After viewing the kinescope of *Galley Proof*, O'Connor met up with "the Signet lady" (Arabel Porter), who took her to meet the head of Signet Books, which had published the second edition of *Wise Blood*.[15]

Finally, at 7 P.M., O'Connor met with painter Margaret Sutton, who had shown her around New York in 1943, for dinner.[16] Perhaps Friday morning was set aside for her session with photographer Erich Hartmann, set up by Harcourt, Brace.[17] Though the details are unknown, it seems that W. G. Rogers had suggested to O'Connor that she needed an up-to-date headshot.[18]

A Walk to the Park

There were two correspondents that O'Connor had tentative plans to meet with during this trip: Beverly Brunson and Fred Darsey (for more on both, see Chapter 9). Both had admired O'Connor's work to the point where they had felt inspired to write the author—Brunson in 1953 and Darsey early in 1955. While O'Connor did not end up seeing Brunson, she did spend time with Darsey one afternoon.

Darsey first wrote to O'Connor while residing in what was then called Milledgeville State Hospital, a mental facility known as the world's largest. To say the hospital was infamous was in no way an exaggeration: thousands of Georgians had been sent there with either a vague, unnamed condition or disabilities given as the reason for committal, and the resident/staff ratio was, in the 1950s, 100 to 1.[19]

Darsey and O'Connor were three months into their correspondence when her latest letter was returned because he had "eloped"—the term the hospital used for those who escaped.

Darsey had hitchhiked to New York, and after a few nervous weeks spent worrying he would be apprehended, he continued the correspondence.[20]

And just in time, too: she was coming to New York and he had just enough time to zip off a letter to her before she left Milledgeville. He told her he hoped to spend a good deal of time with her.[21]

He said he had to work during the week but was available that weekend. He envisioned showing O'Connor the sights: Saturday would be a full day that started with a Staten Island ferry ride and a boat trip around the island of Manhattan; they would then go to Central Park, the Empire State Building, and Chinatown before heading back to the Bronx Zoo (as he had never been there); Sunday's itinerary would include St. Patrick's Cathedral, and then, who knows? There was so much that the two of them could do together. If she wanted to see a play, he could make that happen. They could even take a spin on the carousel if that wouldn't make her too dizzy.[22]

And she was welcome to stay at his place. His roommate would turn over his bedroom to her (he would sleep on the divan).[23]

O'Connor wrote back to him on May 25 and took the time to explain her health issues would make it impossible to do all that he had suggested. She could not stay with him because the publisher was paying for her hotel so she could be where they could find her easily. And to that end, so much was already planned for the week that she was unsure when she would be available. As for the weekend, she already had plans with friends.[24]

Carver informed her that Darsey had called to ask that time be set aside expressly for him.[25] It was. According to Darsey, he and O'Connor met at her hotel and walked up Fifth Avenue. They went to Central Park, where they sat on a bench for nearly two hours, basking in the sunshine and talking.[26]

In September, O'Connor's doctor would deliver the disappointing news that she was to begin using crutches.[27] But in early June, O'Connor was able to walk without aid, making this stroll with a friend particularly memorable—though one can't help but wonder if she took his arm.

Honored

O'Connor capped off the week with a train trip, accompanied by activist Pauline Turkel, to Tory Valley, New York, to attend a party given in her honor. The gathering was hosted by Caroline Gordon and Sue Jenkins Brown in the latter's home, known to many in the literary community as Robber Rocks.

In a letter to Sally Fitzgerald, O'Connor recounted how, when asked to read a story at the gathering, both Gordon and Brown loudly suggested she read a short one.[28] While she did end up reading "A Good Man Is Hard to Find," she started with (but didn't finish) "Good Country People," which led a party guest, writer Malcolm Cowley, to ask if she had a wooden leg.[29]

The next day, O'Connor and Gordon attended Mass together.[30] O'Connor soon returned to New York and then left for home.[31]

Disappointments

The week had been an exciting one. It was the sort of experience that would make many writers feel like they had arrived. But in her correspondence to Darsey, written upon her return home, O'Connor made it clear that much of the experience had made her uncomfortable. For example, watching the kinescope of her TV appearance was far from pleasant. Describing herself as looking like a "very tired, very disgusted, very sleepy, very impatient moron," she was even more disappointed in the heaviness of her accent, which she found came across more Southern than usual among the "more normal sounding ones."[32]

Her concerns weren't limited to televised interviews. In a letter to AP columnist W. G. Rogers, she stated that interviews were usually a terrible experience for her, one that she thought should require anesthesia to get through (though her conversation with him, she assured him, had been enjoyable).[33] He responded that he was sorry "interviews have been a problem. They shouldn't be." He said that most of the book press he knew would have been happy to talk to her.[34] His comment makes one wonder if the problem had been in convincing O'Connor to grant the interviews, or if there weren't many people asking to speak to her to begin with. Either way, she does not seem to have enjoyed the spotlight.

And there was the matter of lifestyle, too. In a letter to Regina, one in which she mentioned changing her plane reservation, she spoke of a slight fever she had, blaming it on the "long hours between meals around here." Eating so late gave her "the headache."[35]

Finally, she came home to Milledgeville, knowing that life in New York did not interest her. In response to the letter she found waiting for her upon arriving home, she told Darsey that she had given him the wrong impression if he thought she would enjoy living in New York. Yes, she would like the intellectual stimulation of people she would know there, but the lifestyle itself would not be to her liking, noting that one had to be "geared to a very high pitch just to cross the street." Furthermore, she found the city depressing.[36]

Back in her world now, a world that was scheduled and secluded, she was glad to be home with the chickens. They didn't know, nor did they care, that she was a writer.[37]

1957

Two years later, she was still none too eager to return to the city.

In 1957, the National Institute of Arts and Letters awarded her a grant worth one thousand dollars and asked that she be in New York on May 22. O'Connor told Denver Lindley she would be there, but the idea of trying to fight her "way in and out of New York on these crutches" was worrisome.[38] Lindley told her that, although the committee would be disappointed, she didn't have to attend.[39]

O'Connor, having just come home from delivering a talk at Notre Dame, was relieved.[40]

Perhaps one of the most interesting accounts of a New York visit comes from the travel diary of Regina Cline O'Connor. The chronicle describes a trip undertaken by Regina and her daughter to Lourdes, France, the place where St. Bernadette experienced multiple visions of the Virgin Mary in 1858.

In 1958, Cousin Katie Semmes offered to send mother and daughter on a Centennial Pilgrimage to Lourdes organized by the Diocese of Savannah.[1] Perhaps "offered" is not quite the right word; in truth, she insisted they go. For O'Connor, the idea of participating in an immodest group bath was especially unappealing.[2] But it was the potential and probable rigors of travel that almost got her out of her commitment to go, with her doctor saying visiting seven places in seventeen days was out of the question.[3]

Semmes persisted, and, as a result, it was decided that the O'Connors would split from the pilgrimage group after crossing the ocean and then travel on their own to Milan to meet up with Robert Fitzgerald. After a few days at home with the Fitzgeralds, the two women, joined by Sally, would rejoin the group to see Lourdes and Rome.[4]

In return for her generosity in paying the $2,100 in fees, Semmes asked each for an account of her travels, even supplying them with leather-bound diaries to capture their memories. O'Connor spent so much of the trip in bed with a bad cold that she didn't write anything (though she did tell friend Maryat Lee that she felt one day she would). But she did type up Regina's diary, which includes information about their time in New York before heading overseas.[5]

Before Leaving

With Catharine Carver having left Harcourt, Brace a mere nine months after being assigned to O'Connor, Derek Lindley had taken her place. In planning the trip, O'Connor wrote to Lindley, saying she would like to show her mother the new Harcourt, Brace offices, but soon found out, and not from Lindley, that he had left for Viking Press. With this news, and feeling not much in the way of loyalty to the publisher, O'Connor began the process of breaking from Harcourt, Brace and accepting Giroux's offer to publish with Farrar, Straus & Cudahy.[6]

The timing, lodged in the middle of trip preparations, could not have been worse. Harcourt, Brace editor John McCallum and colleague George L. White traveled to Andalusia to discuss the matter with her face-to-face. She held firm in her decision to leave. Afterward, White wrote to invite O'Connor and her mother to see the offices and be treated to lunch.[7]

Arrival

On April 21, 1958, mother and daughter flew from Atlanta on a Delta 121, stopping in Washington before landing in New York around 3 P.M. Anne Brooks Murray, Giroux's assistant, met them at the airport in a limousine. Giroux was not in town for the visit but had offered the limo—if only to prove that a publishing house did not need to have a Madison Avenue address to be top-notch. For her part, O'Connor was grateful for the transportation, as she had never before attempted getting around New York on crutches.[8]

Arriving at the Manger-Vanderbilt Hotel (Park Avenue at East 34th) around 6 P.M., the two women found their friend Lydia Bancroft waiting in the lobby. In addition, two notes were waiting for Mary Flannery (as her mother calls her throughout the diary, and O'Connor dutifully types): one from Caroline Gordon and another from Maryat Lee. After dropping off their luggage, they were happy to find that Margaret Sutton had arrived. The four enjoyed dinner in the hotel dining room. After Bancroft and Sutton left, Gordon joined Regina and O'Connor, following them to their room and staying until 10 P.M.

The next day, after breakfast in the hotel coffee shop, Regina went shopping while O'Connor met with her publishers, Sheila Cudahy and Roger Straus, and agent Elizabeth McKee. When Regina returned to the hotel, she met McKee for the first time. O'Connor, Regina, and another from the pilgrimage tour had lunch at Altman's Charleston Garden—a restaurant on the top floor of the B. Altman & Company department store on

Fifth Avenue. The restaurant featured an actual plantation façade on one wall, while the other walls were covered by murals depicting an outdoor garden.

O'Connor and Regina arrived at Idlewild Airport (now John F. Kennedy International) that evening.

Because Sally Fitzgerald convinced her to do so, O'Connor did bathe with other pilgrims in the spring water at Lourdes.[9] She did see the Sistine Chapel while in Rome. Because she was sick, she received a special blessing from Pope Pius during an audience that included her pilgrimage group. O'Connor was home by May 9.

The Lourdes journey proved to be O'Connor's last visit to New York City. Travel was getting harder, her health was getting worse, and the difficulties of getting around on crutches were a major consideration. A time or two in her diary, Regina noted how her daughter was the only person she saw on crutches and how the simple act of walking from one point to the next was complicated, if not nearly impossible at times, in places that did not offer alternatives for disabled travelers.

When she was back home, O'Connor wrote to McCallum (now her former publisher) to thank him for the books he had sent her way, adding that she was still recuperating from the trip. Her "capacity for staying at home (had) now been increased to 100%," she said, mentioning that she had spent most of her time looking through hotel windows because of her bad cold.[10]

George White scribbled a note to McCallum on the letter itself. "This is painful," he wrote. "I'm very sorry for her."[11]

5 / New York, O'Connor, and Lee

O'Connor and playwright Maryat Lee were introduced in 1956. Their friendship lasted to O'Connor's death; in fact, what has been accepted as O'Connor's last letter was written to Lee. They were very different—in dress, in religion, in politics—and much has been made of their correspondence about race. (For more on the playwright, see Chapter 7.)

Another interesting (and unexplored) thread that winds through their letters is the issue of O'Connor visiting New York. Lee lived and wrote in New York, and a good bit of their correspondence touches on the subject of O'Connor coming to the city.

Or, rather, O'Connor most definitely *not*.

O'Connor and Travel

Despite O'Connor's declaration as to being done with travel after the Lourdes pilgrimage, she did indeed travel, mostly to speak at universities, participate in symposiums, or receive an honorary degree.

In 1959, she spent five winter days in Chicago, followed by four that spring in Nashville, staying with good friends Brainard and Francis Cheney.[1] In 1960, she spent a week in Minnesota, and in 1961 delivered a talk to Benedictine nuns in St. Louis.[2] In the spring of 1962, she visited the Carolinas, Illinois, and Indiana in separate trips.[3] That November, she spoke at four colleges in Texas and Louisiana during a six-day trip.[4] In 1963, she traveled to Smith College in North Hampton, Massachusetts, and, in October, spoke at Hollins College in Virginia, Notre Dame of Maryland in Baltimore, and Georgetown University in Washington, DC.[5]

Throughout these later years, more than just a general difficulty in mobility increased; her pain and discomfort escalated as certain joints disintegrated because of the steroids used to control the lupus. By 1959, the act of chewing had become painful to the point that Maryat Lee eventually, and as a surprise, sent O'Connor a Waring blender. (The blender, though now a common household appliance, was considered such a marvel that O'Connor invited the managers of her favorite restaurant, the Sanford House, to see it. The two did not own a blender themselves.[6]) In 1961, O'Connor asked about receiving a hip replacement but was reminded that surgery could trigger the lupus.[7]

In 1960, O'Connor told writer Richard Stern that she would never visit New York (or, for that matter, his hometown of Chicago) again.[8] She mentioned to Janet McKane, a New York school teacher who became a valued correspondent in the final years of O'Connor's life, that she actually tried to avoid going to New York in her travels.[9] But it is in the correspondence with Maryat Lee that the possibility of New York visits comes up, or is asked about, most often.

Going, Not Going

Lee, originally from Kentucky, was a playwright who, in 1951, wrote and produced the first American street play, *Dope!*[10] She lived at 192 Sixth Avenue (now Avenue of the Americas) in a third-floor apartment that comprised five rooms, with a bathtub in the kitchen.[11] O'Connor met Lee when the latter came to Milledgeville in 1956 to visit her brother, who was then the new president of GSCW. In 1957, Lee married Australian artist and furniture designer David Foulkes Taylor (see Figure 7). Having met initially in London and married in Japan, they each chose to live in their respective countries.[12]

In her letters, Lee often asks O'Connor about coming to New York to either visit her or stay in her (unoccupied) apartment. The first time Lee offered her place came a scant few months after the two had met. Although she had already planned to sublet her apartment to another friend while out of the country, she let O'Connor know that the place could be hers for about three months if that plan fell through. O'Connor appreciated the offer, but she said she didn't think she was up to navigating the city on her own now that she was using crutches.[13]

It didn't help that the building didn't have an elevator.

Lee, hopeful that perhaps she had misread the letter, asked again: Crutches or no crutches, did Flannery want to come? O'Connor answered quickly: Thank you, but no.[14] As it was, she was having a hard time getting

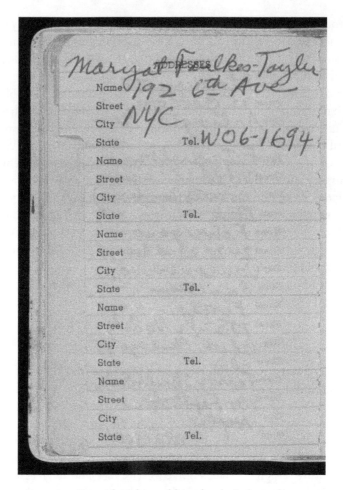

FIGURE 7: From the white address book. In her other address books, O'Connor records her friend's name as Maryat Lee. (Used with permission from Flannery O'Connor Papers, Stuart A. Rose Manuscript, Archives, and Rare Book Library, Emory University.)

to the University of Notre Dame for an upcoming reading: She was, she said, the sort of person who might want to visit a place but, in reality, not want to make the effort to get there.[15] As she seemed willing enough to travel when she was younger and in (relatively) good health, one can assume that the realities and difficulties of travel for one with a disability were what held her back.

Still, upon running into O'Connor in Milledgeville a couple of weeks later, it was almost comical when Lee's brother asked if she was going to make the trip to Manhattan "for atmosphere, and all that," adding that he thought it nice of his sister to make the offer. O'Connor said she would have to make do with the local atmosphere.[16]

Before Lourdes, after Lourdes

The next mention of New York came when O'Connor announced that she and Regina would stop there before heading to Lourdes. When O'Connor wrote to tell Lee that they would be there April 21 and 22 (though neither was a full day), Lee asked if the two could come in a couple of days earlier. She also spoke of her own commitments on the second day, what with a seminar planned from 5:30 to 7:30 and the possibility of a rehearsal. Still, she offered to take O'Connor and Regina to the airport as she had her mother's car.[17] O'Connor responded that they could not change their plans and that this trip would likely not work for a visit.[18]

Lee wrote a letter while her friend was in Europe, saying how O'Connor's idea of a "little vacation" in New York would be a good thing, describing the city as a "port in the storm" where O'Connor could "get away from the cares and worries of Milledgeville."[19]

O'Connor (and Regina) did make a brief landing in New York on the way back home, but her efforts to call Lee from the airport were thwarted when the phone refused her dime. Still recovering from seeing Europe through hotel windows (having had a bad cold during much of the trip), O'Connor declared she would never again leave Baldwin County, adding, "You will not see me in New York. I knew there would be something final about that trip and that's it."[20]

O'Connor took a lighter tone the following week. After reading that Lee doubted that she herself would ever enter Baldwin County again because of a falling out with her brother, O'Connor offered a compromise: If Lee would come to Milledgeville again, she would likely visit her in Manhattan.[21]

A New Approach

In 1959, Lee used a new tactic to convince O'Connor to come to New York. She told her friend that as she could travel to one Southern college or another to give talks, she could surely make her way to New York.[22] In another letter, she asked if O'Connor would be coming to sign copies of *The Violent Bear It Away*. If so, she and Regina could use her apartment "free and unencumbered."[23] But O'Connor replied she would not come to New York unless paid to do so, which wasn't likely, especially since she hated such events.[24]

In another nod to her diminishing mobility and stamina, O'Connor spoke of an upcoming trip to New York that was to include Regina. She wrote to say they would be in New York to attend a Ford Foundation conference for grant recipients and would stay at the New Weston from August 29 through September 1.[25] However, upon learning that the conference had been canceled, she quickly deleted the trip from her calendar.[26]

Medical Care

Lee's interest in O'Connor's coming to New York was more than social; she was concerned about her friend's lupus and felt she could find better care in the metropolis. Lee, unasked, looked into physicians in New York and Rhode Island on O'Connor's behalf. In more than one letter, the Bader brothers—Drs. Richard and Mortimer—are mentioned[27]; O'Connor even listed them in her final address book. Still, O'Connor was not interested in seeing a physician in New York. She said lupus had to be "observed over a period of time."[28]

No, You Come Down South

Meanwhile, O'Connor occasionally suggested that Lee should come down South and wrote to say leaving New York would be good for a couple of reasons. Problems writing? O'Connor said the cure would be to leave New York and head South. Thyroid acting up? O'Connor recommended a trip to Atlanta as "there is no doctor in New York that will be after anything but your money."[29]

In the summer of 1963, O'Connor once again avoided spending time in New York. Knowing she would have a layover in Idlewild coming back from a reading in Massachusetts, she told Lee ahead of time that she would not be stopping for a visit. It's not as if she didn't have a reason to go to New York beyond Lee's open invitation; O'Connor had already declined an invitation to a cocktail party thrown by *Esquire* for the authors featured in its July issue.[30] It was an honor for all invited, of course, but in O'Connor's case, especially so: She had been placed in the middle of the "red-hot center" of the editor's 1963 Literary Establishment chart.

But the glitz and the glamour of such an event did not appeal to O'Connor. It never did, just as the fast pace of the New York lifestyle never appealed to her. She had been to Manhattan, had lived in Manhattan and, in the end, couldn't be bothered. Her sights were set on bigger things.

Bigger, even, than New York City.

Part II: The Listings

Mrs. Cyrilly Abels Weinstein
14 Fifth Ave., NYC 11
Cyrilly Abels (1903–1975) was the managing editor of *Mademoiselle* (see *Mlle* entry) for fifteen years before forming her own agency. At *Mademoiselle*, she changed the magazine from a fashion publication targeting young women to one featuring up-and-coming writers. As such, she presented the works of O'Connor as well as Carson McCullers, Katharine Anne Porter, Truman Capote, and others. In one issue, she introduced readers to Dylan Thomas by publishing his play, *Under Milkwood*.[1]

In a 1958 letter to writer Cecil Dawkins, O'Connor mentions that she had received notice from Cyrilly Abels asking for a story. O'Connor suggested to Dawkins that, as she herself didn't have anything to offer at the moment, she would recommend Dawkins' story instead.[2]

This was her home address.

James Agee
17 King St.
This name and address did not appear in any of O'Connor's address books. However, O'Connor did supply both to Robert Giroux (see entry) before he left Harcourt, Brace (see). In a letter dated April 26, 1955, O'Connor asked that Agee be sent an advance copy of *A Good Man Is Hard to Find*.[3]

Agee, on his way to a doctor's appointment, suffered a fatal heart attack twenty days after that request was made.[4]

James Rufus Agee (1909–1955) was a poet, critic, novelist, and activist. He wrote the screenplays for *The African Queen* (with John Huston) and

Night of the Hunter. His account of tenant families, *Let Us Now Praise Famous Men*, is considered by many to be his masterpiece. His final book, the posthumously published *A Death in the Family*, won the 1958 Pulitzer.[5] O'Connor, while a fan of his other work, admitted to not being able to get through his final novel.[6]

Alfred A. Knopf Inc.
501 Madison Ave., NYC 22

Though the company Alfred and Blanche Knopf built did not publish O'Connor's work, its books would have been known to her. In the 1950s, Knopf published *The Diary of Anne Frank* and Julia Child's *Mastering the Art of French Cooking*. In 1959, son Alfred Knopf, Jr. left the company to start Atheneum Books (see entry).

Ellis Amburn
156 E. 52nd St., NYC 22 / PL 5-2566

After writing for *Newsweek*, Amburn (1933–2018) worked as an editor for several publishers, including Coward-McCann (see entry), and as such, edited various authors, including Muriel Spark and John Kerouac. He was a ghostwriter with Zsa Zsa Gabor, Peggy Lee, Priscilla Presley, and Shelley Winters. Writing a biography of Roy Orbison led to authoring other books on various actors, writers, and singers.[7] His last book, published weeks before his death, was a biography of Olivia de Havilland.

His name appears in the red book under *The Transatlantic Review* listing.

Ted Amussen
383 Madison Ave., NYC 17

Theodore S. Amussen (1915–1988) was an editor at Harcourt, Brace (see entry) when he met O'Connor. His insight was invaluable to her because he had previously worked at Rinehart (see). His later résumé included stints as editor for National Geographic Society special publications, editor-in-chief at Henry Holt (see), and chief of the National Park Services books division. He was working at the National Gallery of Art before he retired.[8]

In a letter to her agent, Elizabeth McKee (see), O'Connor mentions wanting to come to New York to discuss, with McKee and Amussen, leaving Rinehart for Harcourt, Brace.[9] Her relationship with him went beyond seeking professional advice: She turned to Amussen and his wife for a physician recommendation when she feared she had appendicitis.[10]

This is the address of Harcourt, Brace. O'Connor lists Amussen's name under the publisher's listing in the brown book.

Adda H. Anderson (*sic*) (silversmith)
887 First Ave./PL 5-9130
Following Ann Orr's (see entry) address and phone number in the brown book is an office phone number, an address, and then Andersen's name followed by the word "silversmith."

Adda Husted-Andersen (1898–1990) of Denmark came to New York after World War II and set up both a workshop and a retail outlet. A proponent of the Modern craft technique, she was a well-regarded artist and teacher. She also served on the editorial board of *Craft Horizons Magazine*. Husted-Andersen's work was exhibited in several places, including a highly touted 1946 exhibition at the Museum of Modern Art.[11]

Appleton-Century-Crofts
35 W. 32nd St., NYC 1
The press started in 1825 as Appleton & Co., a general store that sold many items, including books. A few years later, the owner, Daniel Appleton, started to publish books and eventually merged his company with Century Co. D. Appleton-Century consolidated with F. S. Crofts in 1948, the year O'Connor met editor-in-chief Ted Purdy (see entry), husband of her agent.[12]

In 1960, Appleton-Century-Crofts was bought by Meredith Publishing (the name stayed the same). Prentice Hall purchased it in 1973.[13]

Mr. Gino Ardito
344 E. 9th St.
Gino Ardito (1935–2001) wrote a screen adaptation of "The Life You Save May Be Your Own" in 1963, for which he held the copyright with Leonard Melfi.[14] He reached out to O'Connor about possibly turning the story into a film. She referred him to her agent, Elizabeth McKee, who referred him to an attorney named Rembar (perhaps Charles Rembar, a lawyer who also acted as an agent). Both were vague about the short story's availability. The ambiguity only urged Ardito to pursue the idea further, the film he had in mind becoming all he could think about.[15]

He typed a fifteen-page adaptation, which he sent to O'Connor.[16] She described it as basically her story but in script form. He also sent her photographs to visually show her what he had in mind. She returned the photos and said the house he had chosen for the Crater home was nothing like the one she had in mind when she had written the story.[17] A few years after her death, he wrote to editor Robert Giroux (see entry) about the rights and was told he would have to, once again, speak to McKee.[18]

Ardito directed the occasional play and appeared in movies and television shows in bit parts, such as "policeman at rally" in *Taxi Driver* (1976).

Associated Press
50 Rockefeller Plaza, NYC 20

When O'Connor was in New York in 1955 to promote *A Good Man Is Hard to Find*, she was interviewed by W. G. Rogers (see entry) of the Associated Press.

"AP" is noted under Rogers' listing.

Atheneum Pub.
162 E. 38th St., NYC 16

Atheneum Books was a publishing house established by Alfred A. Knopf, Jr., Simon Michael Bessie, and Hiram Haydn (see entry). Atheneum, which was housed in a four-story brownstone at this address, was founded in 1959 when Knopf broke away from his family's publishing house to form the company with Bessie (from Harper & Row) and Haydn (from Bobbs-Merrill). In 1978, Atheneum merged with Charles Scribner's Sons to form Scribner Book Companies.

The company is listed under Hiram Haydn's name.

Drs. Richard & Mortimer Bader
1050 Fifth Ave., NYC 28

Richard and Mortimer were twin brothers. According to separate wedding announcements (which list the brothers as each other's best man), in 1955 Richard (1922–2013) was on the staff of Mount Sinai Hospital, studying cardio-pulmonary disease, and, in 1960, Mortimer (1922–2003) was co-chief of the Cardio-Pulmonary lab.[19] A 1982 wedding announcement lists Mortimer as a clinical professor of medicine at Mount Sinai Medical School.[20]

In a couple of letters, Maryat Lee (see entry) mentions various New York doctors regarding lupus treatment. The Bader brothers are among those mentioned.[21]

The Beiswangers
410 Riverside Dr., Apt. 132, NYC 25 / MO 3-7395

George W. Beiswanger (1902–1993) and Barbara Page Beiswanger (1901–1985) joined the Georgia College for Women faculty at the beginning of the 1944–1945 academic year. The married instructors came to be known as Dr. He-B and Dr. She-B.[22]

George, who, in addition to being a philosophy instructor, was also a dance critic and aesthetician, saw great intellectual promise in O'Connor, a student who would often challenge him in class. He encouraged O'Connor to apply to attend graduate school at his alma mater, the University of Iowa. In addition, he contacted his connections and secured O'Connor a full-tuition scholarship.[23]

Though he retired from the university in 1969, he continued to write about dance, particularly modern. His work as an observer and critic of dance began in 1934, and over the years, he strove to connect developments in choreography (and other art forms) to philosophy.[24]

Barbara taught at the university for nineteen years, leaving her stamp with the creation of Modern Dance Group.[25]

Brentano's
586 Fifth Ave., NYC 36

Brentano's got its start in 1853 when August Brentano, a native of Austria, asked to set up a newsstand in front of a New York hotel. This idea was considered quite an innovation, as newspapers and magazines were sold door-to-door then. With the help of his nephew, Arthur, the business grew over the years to include multiple stores and, with its stock of rare books, privately published pamphlets, and foreign periodicals, Brentano's received orders from around the world. At one point, the company operated a publishing department.[26]

In 1985, Waldenbooks acquired Brentano's; in 1994, Waldenbooks merged with Borders. In 2011, what was, by then, the independent Borders Group filed for bankruptcy, and all stores closed.[27]

In 1959, O'Connor wrote to Maryat Lee (see entry), asking for the address of Brentano's, stating she wanted to start an account because, as she noted, one couldn't buy books in Milledgeville.[28]

Sue Jenkins Brown
108 Perry St., NYC 14

Susan Jenkins Brown (1896–1982) was an author and book editor known primarily for both her early connections to the Provincetown Players, an influential theater collective, and her 1969 book about poet Hart Crane, who lived for a time with her and her husband. Crane lived not at the Perry Street location but in the Browns' home, Robber Rocks, a house well-known to the New York literary circle. It was in the Tory Valley area near Sherman, Connecticut. (O'Connor includes the location in both Perry Street listings.)

In 1955, when O'Connor spent a week in Manhattan to promote her second book, Brown and Caroline Gordon hosted a party in her honor at Robber Rocks. In a humorous letter recalling the gathering, O'Connor states that when asked by a guest to read a story aloud, the hosts screamed that she should choose the shortest one.[29]

While O'Connor and Brown enjoyed a correspondence for a while after, this gathering would mark their first and last in-the-flesh meeting.

In a letter to Maryat Lee (see entry), O'Connor mentions that Brown wanted to dramatize her in-progress novel, *The Violent Bear It Away*, adding that there was no guarantee she would want to do so after reading the completed work.[30] And Brown didn't: While she had seen possibilities in the novel's first chapter when it appeared as "You Can't Be Any Poorer than Dead" in *New World Writing*, she decided she could not dramatize the novel as a whole.[31] She later approached O'Connor with thoughts on dramatizing "A Good Man Is Hard to Find" (Get rid of the baby? Change the ages of the other children?), but the idea never went any further.[32]

The Perry Street address is one that Gordon had lived in during her first divorce from, then later in the early days of remarriage to, poet Allen Tate. The two would transform the kitchen into a combination dining room and study and make a kitchen of a bedroom.[33] As it became clear that the couple was still better off apart, Gordon considered sharing the apartment with Brown.[34] Gordon decided that life in Tory Valley was the answer, and she gave Brown a down payment on three acres of Robber Rocks (land that Tate would surreptitiously sell back) with the agreement that her friend could use the Perry Street apartment.[35]

Beverly Brunson
315 E. 56th St., NYC 22
5 W. 8th St., NYC 11
45 W. 68th St., NYC 23
6 Jones St., NYC 14

Beverly Brunson (1928–2000) corresponded with O'Connor from 1953 to 1955. Her addresses are found in the black Elite, indicating that the correspondence stopped, at least on O'Connor's end. To read about Brunson as well as her and O'Connor's interesting correspondence, see Chapter 9.

The 56th Street address was the first used in their correspondence. The 8th Street listing is the address for the Hotel Marlton (see entry). The Jones Street address is not listed in O'Connor's address books but mentioned in a letter from O'Connor as the location to which she will send Brunson a copy of *A Good Man Is Hard to Find,* adding that if Brunson were to move any time soon, she should let her know of the new address.[36]

Daniel Callahan
232 Madison Ave., NYC 10016

Daniel Callahan (1930–2019) was known to O'Connor as the executive editor of *The Commonweal* (see entry), as it was known from 1924 to 1965. He held the position from 1961 to 1968.

With a degree in philosophy from Harvard University, Callahan was valued as a Catholic intellectual during a period of significant change in the Catholic Church. By the end of the decade, however, he declared himself agnostic.

The intersection of ethics and medicine was of great interest to him and, using money lent to him by his mother-in-law, co-founded what is now known as the Hastings Center, the world's first bioethics research institute, in Garrison, New York.[37]

This is the (then) address for *The Commonweal*.

This is one of the rare examples of O'Connor recording the new five-digit zip code. It is found in the small black book.

Catharine Carver
15 E. 94th St., NYC 28 / ATwater 9-3719
146 E. 89th St., NYC 28
178 E. 95th St., NYC 28

Catharine Carver (1921–1997) was working under Robert Giroux (see entry) at Harcourt, Brace & Company (see) and, as such, edited O'Connor's work. When Giroux left, she was assigned as O'Connor's editor, though this arrangement was to last only nine months before Carver moved on.[38]

O'Connor liked and respected Carver, who, by all accounts, was a conscientious editor; before editing Aileen Ward's biography of John Keats, for instance, Carver reread his work.[39] It was Carver who made all arrangements for O'Connor's publicity trip to New York to promote *A Good Man Is Hard to Find*. In a letter to her mother from that trip, O'Connor described Carver as a nice, bespectacled woman in her thirties who did not wear a hat.[40]

O'Connor respected Carver's opinion so much that she continued to send her work for commentary after Carver left Harcourt.[41]

Catholic Unity League
415 W. 59th St., NYC 19

The organization, composed mostly of lay people, was organized to distribute free Catholic books and pamphlets to non-Catholics, finance lectures to non-Catholics, and provide a library of books to be lent to

Catholics. It was started in 1917 by a priest and three Knights of Columbus members and organized by Paulist Fathers of New York.[42]

Miss Lillian Chiriaka
Newsweek Box 150, Times Square Station, NYC 36

Lillian Chiriaka was an editorial assistant for *Newsweek* who interviewed O'Connor prior to the release of *Wise Blood*. O'Connor, indicating that she felt ineffective as an interviewee, followed the phone interview with a typed letter that included fully fleshed answers to the questions she had been asked.[43] This letter was followed by another in which O'Connor made sure she had stated Andalusia had 1,700 acres, not 17,000.[44]

As O'Connor did not have a home phone until 1956, this interview most likely would have occurred at her family's home, the Cline mansion in Milledgeville.[45]

The Colquitt Girls' Club
141–143 E. 37th St., NYC 16 / MU 4-8351

In 1960, a young unmarried woman staying at the Colquitt Girls' Club could expect to pay between $18.00 and $21.50 weekly for a (shared) room, two meals a day, and "ice-box raiding privileges."[46] Of course, an interview was required before being accepted.

Surprisingly, there is a Milledgeville connection here, which is likely why O'Connor lists this residence under Mrs. Colquitt Koepp's name (see entry).

Columbia Gas System
120 E. 41st St., NYC 17

Despite the address, O'Connor's use of this contact information was as a consumer in Georgia, not New York. In the late 1960s, the company moved its headquarters to Wilmington, Delaware.

The Commonweal
232 Madison Ave., NYC 16

Known in O'Connor's time as *The Commonweal*, the magazine was, and still is, the United States' oldest and lay-edited, independent Catholic journal. To quote its website, *Commonweal* "has an ongoing interest in social justice, ecumenism, just-war teaching, liturgical renewal, women's issues, the primacy of conscience, and the interchange between Catholicism and liberal democracy."[47]

O'Connor enjoyed the magazine and not only subscribed to it but also recommended it to friends. In one letter, she asks new friend Betty Hester about whether she (as is said in the South) takes the magazine and mentions how, if Hester doesn't, she would gladly pass along her copies, once read.[48]

Coward–McCann, Inc.
210 Madison Ave., NYC 16

The publisher was acquired by G. P. Putnam's Sons in 1936 and later re-named Coward, McCann & Geoghegan. It ran as an imprint until the 1980s.

O'Connor notes the publisher in Theodore M. Purdy's listing.

Criterion Books, Inc.
257 Fourth Ave.

Criterion, a publishing firm, was acquired by Abelard-Schuman, Inc. in 1960.[49] By 1974, both were acquired by Thomas Y. Crowell & Company, which, in turn, was taken over by Harper & Row.[50]

The address would soon be changed in 1959 after the New York City Council changed the name of Fourth Avenue (running from 17th Street to 32nd Street) to Park Avenue South.[51]

O'Connor lists the firm in Murray McCain's listing.

F. Darsey
129 E. 10th St. / AL 4-2375
178 Stanton St., NYC 2
1218 E. 31st St., NYC 16
904 Park Ave.
212 E. 12th St.

Fred Darsey (1922–1980) corresponded with O'Connor from 1955 to 1962. To read about him, see Chapters 3 and 9.

Of these listings, the Stanton address was where Darsey lived when he invited O'Connor to stay with him (and his roommate David) in 1955 when O'Connor was in town to promote *A Good Man Is Hard to Find*.

The 12th Street listing was the address he shared with his wife, whom he married in 1962.

Mr. George Davis
122 E. 42nd St. (*Mlle*)
305 E. 48th St. / MUrray Hill 8-0565

George Davis was associate editor at *Mademoiselle* (see *Mlle* entry) when "The Capture" was published in 1948.[52]

Davis, who had lunch with O'Connor in September 1948 and March 1949, was known around town for more than just being an editor.[53] Davis's first and only novel, the critically acclaimed *The Opening of a Door,* was published in 1931 when he was twenty-four. In 1936, he became literary editor of *Harper's Bazaar* (see) and, as such, brought in the writing of Carson McCullers, W. H. Auden, and others. Based on that alone, one would assume his position as editor was secure. But Davis was arrogant and at times disruptive. He was rarely at his desk before noon. As a result, he quit the position in 1940 because he feared he'd be fired for his behavior.[54]

He quit, but he also thought that he would be invited right back. When that didn't happen, he moved to *Mademoiselle,* where he wore both associate editor and fiction editor hats.[55]

He was still arrogant, gossipy, occasionally disruptive, and often absent. This time, though, he was aware of the political clashes among staff, particularly his own with managing editor Cyrilly Abels (see). In 1947, he quit the fiction editing position but continued as associate editor. In resigning from that post, he said he was not interested in the conversation about who would take his place. His resignation was honored, and assistant fiction editor Margarita G. Smith (Carson McCuller's sister) was promoted without consulting him. One year later, he wrote to complain about Smith's incompetence and, once again fearing he would be fired, resigned. And even after that, he wrote again to complain about Abels' ultra-Left-leaning politics and how they affected the work environment.[56]

Though Davis claimed to be against McCarthyism, in 1953 he took it upon himself to report all he knew of Communist infiltration in the publishing industry.[57]

Davis was known for both the parties he threw and his bohemian lifestyle. He borrowed money from burlesque entertainer Gypsy Rose Lee to rent, with McCullers, 7 Middaugh Street in Brooklyn. They rented out the rest of the space to Auden and other authors, poets, painters, and circus performers who lived and loved (loudly) in the Brownstone. In 1945, the house was razed to make room for the Brooklyn-Queens Expressway.[58] When he moved to the Upper East Side, the parties continued spectacularly (and were paid for by the magazine).[59]

Though he was known by all as a homosexual, he married widow Lotte Lenya. He worked to revive both her singing career and *The Threepenny Opera* (by her deceased first husband, Kurt Weill).[60]

In O'Connor's brown book, *Mademoiselle's* address is X'd out under his name. A notation ("Sat—1"), likely indicating one of the lunch dates, is scribbled by the listing.

Desclee Co., Inc.
280 Broadway, NYC 7
Desclee was a Catholic book publishing company. The main office was in Tournai, Belgium.

The publishing house was started by Henri (1830–1917) and Jules (1828–1911) Desclee, Belgian brothers who founded the Maredsous Abbey, which was built to house exiled Benedictine monks. In the 1870s, the brothers established the Society of St. John the Evangelist and then later the Society of St. Augustine, both of which worked to restore Christian art to liturgical publications.[61]

Candida Donadio
145 E. 49th St., NYC 22
Perhaps best known as the agent who sold *Catch-22*, Donadio (1929–2001) also came to represent John Cheever, Bruce Jay Friedman, William Gaddis, Michael Herr, Peter Matthiessen, Jessica Mitford, Mario Puzo, Thomas Pynchon, Philip Roth, Robert Stone, and Richard Stern.

Donadio began her career with the McIntosh & McKee agency (see entry) as a secretary. In that position, though, she was well-known for her hard work and diligence while working with represented authors. Herbert Jaffe, already representing actors, playwrights, and screenwriters, hired Donadio when he decided to expand his agency to include novelists.[62]

This was the address of Herb Jaffe Associates (see), which is mentioned in the listing.

Fr. Dougherty
Riverside Drive off 108th / AC 2-1211
O'Connor likely met Fr. Daniel Dougherty (1900–1978) while she was living in Manhattan. According to the 1949 Catholic Directory, he was, at that time, on leave from the Archdiocese.

In the 1940s, Dougherty was on the faculty of Cathedral College in New York, becoming pastor of St. Patrick's Church in Verplanck, New York, in 1954. By the time of death, he had attained the title of Monsignor.[63]

Miss Anne Draper
123 Washington Pl. / WAtkins 40538
Anne Draper was engaged to Robie McCauley (see entry), a writer O'Connor met in 1947. While at Yaddo, O'Connor mentions, in a letter written to her mother, that Draper and Macauley had married.[64] Though

she was included in the handful of those invited to the ceremony and reception, she did not attend.[65] (For more information, see Preface.)

In a September 1948 letter to her mother, O'Connor mentions meeting Draper (by then, Mrs. Macauley) for the first time while visiting John
Selby (see) at Rinehart (see), adding that she liked her very much.[66] Draper
was publicity director at Rinehart and would later work as director of
Kenyon College's publicity department. Draper died in 1973.

Esquire
488 Madison Ave., NYC 22

Esquire started in 1933 as a men's magazine that emphasized style, so-
phistication, and drawings of immodestly dressed women; in time, it
dropped the latter. The magazine became known for featuring unconven-
tional articles and topics and showcasing the work of upcoming fiction
and nonfiction writers.[67]

"Why Do the Heathen Rage?" appeared in the July 1963 issue; an accompanying article placed O'Connor in the middle of the "red-hot center" of the Literary Establishment chart.[68] That summer, though she would
be touching down in New York on the flight home from a reading, she
declined the invitation to the cocktail party given in honor of that issue's
contributors.[69]

O'Connor's final story, "Parker's Back," was published posthumously
in 1965.

Under this listing, she notes that Rust Hills (see entry) is the fiction
editor.

Farrar, Straus & Cudahy
19 101 Fifth Ave., NYC 3 / OR 5-3000
Union Sq. W, NYC 3

Farrar, Straus & Company was started in 1945 by John Farrar and
Roger W. Straus (see entry). Farrar was editor-in-chief of George H. Doran
Company at the age of twenty-five. He started the Breadloaf Writer's
Conference in 1926 and was named director of Doubleday, Doran after
the two firms merged. In 1929, he joined forces with Stanley Rinehart,
forming Farrar & Rinehart. After World War II, Farrar started Farrar,
Straus & Company with Roger Straus, a journalist from a well-to-do
family.[70]

After a shaky start, the company renamed itself Farrar, Straus & (Stanley) Young. Having acquired the Chicago firm of Pellegrini & Cudahy in
1953, it became Farrar, Straus & (Sheila) Cudahy when Young resigned.
Robert Giroux (see) joined in 1955, bringing with him seventeen authors

from Harcourt, Brace—among them, Thomas Merton, Robert Lowell, Jack Kerouac, and (eventually) O'Connor.[71]

Books were stamped with the Farrar, Straus & Giroux label starting in 1964. It was noted in Straus's 2004 obituary that the firm was "the last surviving representative of the age of independent houses owned privately by gentlemen of literary taste."[72]

Elizabeth Fenwick
255 W. 108th St., Apt. 12-C / MOnument 2-1494
Office: HAnover 2-3754

Fenwick was a novelist O'Connor met while at Yaddo. To read about her, see Chapter 7.

She also is listed in O'Connor's address books by her married name, Mrs. D. J. Way.

Robt. Fitzgerald
27 W. 44th St.

Fitzgerald (1910–1985), a poet, translator, and professor, was indeed a friend to O'Connor: He was one of the few people with whom she would discuss her father's death.[73] He was also an accidental influence. She read Fitzgerald's translation of *Oedipus Rex* as she was writing *Wise Blood* and, as a result, added the self-blinding as a penance element.[74]

She named Fitzgerald as her literary executor in the will she filed before her 1958 trip to Lourdes. He wrote the introduction to *Everything That Rises Must Converge*.

This is the (then) address of the Harvard Club (see entry), which she lists under his name. See also *The Fitzgeralds* entry.

The Fitzgeralds
1737 York (at 91st) Ave. / SA 2-3833

In March 1949, Robert Lowell (see entry) brought O'Connor around to meet his friends Sally (1917–2000) and Robert Fitzgerald (1910–1985), the latter a poet and translator. Lowell thought O'Connor might find much in common with the devoutly Catholic couple.[75] When Lowell left Manhattan, O'Connor continued to gather with the couple on her own; by that summer, she would tell her mother she was going to move to Redding, Connecticut, with them. O'Connor lived in the apartment over their garage until her health failed. Though they saw each other a handful of times after O'Connor moved back to Georgia, they continued their friendship through correspondence. O'Connor dedicated *A Good Man Is Hard to Find* to them.

Sally spoke of the sixteen months that O'Connor lived with them, sharing meals and Masses and lively conversations, as filled with joy and productivity.[76] After O'Connor's death, both Fitzgeralds wrote about O'Connor and published her work. Robert served as her literary executor.

The Ford Foundation
477 Madison Ave., NYC 22

The charitable organization was established in 1936 by Edsel Ford, son of Henry Ford. In 1959, the foundation awarded O'Connor an $8,000 grant for her accomplishments as a writer. She planned, after the purchase of an electric typewriter and comfortable chair, to make the money last over a ten-year period.[77]

W. McNeil Lowry's name is included with the listing.

Lyman A. Fulton, MD
#54 New York Hospital, 525 E. 68th St., NYC 21

Tennessee-born and Harvard Medical School–educated, Fulton (1925–2011) was completing a residency in internal medicine at New York Hospital when he met O'Connor through his friend Louise Florencourt, O'Connor's cousin. O'Connor mentioned in a letter to Mary Virginia Harrison (who also knew Fulton) that Louise had brought him by a couple of times during her visit in the summer of 1949.[78] Fulton later recalled that O'Connor served her guests faucet water and goat's milk cheese, and the simple fare became something of a joke between them.[79]

Though he did not maintain a correspondence with O'Connor (which he admits to regretting in later years), he noted she wrote to him shortly before leaving New York to tell him she had been diagnosed with Dietl's Crisis, commonly called a floating kidney. In later years, Fulton thought the condition to be among the first in a series of health battles leading up to the lupus diagnosis.[80]

It's interesting to note that O'Connor uses the "Dr." title before physicians she saw (or might potentially approach) as a patient. It seems the addition of "MD" to the medical resident's name was an indication of education, as opposed to a doctor whose services she would seek.

This is the address of what was then New York Hospital (see entry).

Richard Gilman
47 E. 88th St., NYC 27
377 Park Ave. S, NYC 16

Richard Gilman (1923–2006) was a critic who spent three days with O'Connor in 1960. They came to know each other after he reviewed

A Good Man Is Hard to Find for the Catholic magazine *Jubilee*. After her death, he narrated and wrote the script for an episode of *Directions '65*, a broadcast sponsored by the National Council of Catholic Men that honored the writer. In 1969, he wrote a piece about his visit to Andalusia (and the newly released *Mystery and Manners*) that appeared in *The New York Review of Books*.[81]

In the East 88th Street listing, the 27 postal code seems to be a mistake. It likely was 28.

The Park Avenue address was originally written as "Fourth Ave," but was corrected to reflect the 1959 name change.

Robt. Giroux
383 Madison Ave., NYC 17
101 Fifth Ave., NYC 3 / OR 5-3000
19 Union Sq. W
219 E. 66th St.

On March 2, 1949, poet Robert Lowell (see entry) brought his friend Flannery O'Connor to meet his editor Robert Giroux (1914–2008).[82] Although she was, at that time, already committed to Rinehart (see) and editor John Selby (see), it was in Giroux that O'Connor would find a mentor, confidant, and lifelong friend. After it became clear to O'Connor that Rinehart was not the place for her first book, she signed with Harcourt, Brace & Company (see).

Giroux was her editor for both *Wise Blood* and *A Good Man Is Hard to Find*, after which he left to join Farrar, Straus & Cudahy. O'Connor's third and (posthumously published) fourth books were published by this company that would eventually become Farrar, Straus & Giroux.

Besides O'Connor and Lowell, Giroux worked with T. S. Eliott, Thomas Merton, Bernard Malamud, Randall Jarrell, Jack Kerouac, Susan Sontag, Carl Sandburg, Virginia Woolf, Isaac Bashevis Singer, Elizabeth Bishop, Katherine Anne Porter, Walker Percy, Derek Walcott, and others.[83]

The Madison Avenue location is the address of Harcourt, Brace; O'Connor lists Giroux's name under the publisher's listing. The East 66th Street address was Giroux's home in Lenox Hill.

Miss Rochelle Girsen (*sic*)
25 W. 45th St.

Rochelle Girson (1915–2002) was the *Saturday Review*'s book review editor. To read about her, see Chapter 7.

Elaine Gottleib (*sic*)
212 W. 11th St. / CH 2-5183

Elaine Gottlieb (1916–2004) was a fiction writer. To read about her, see Chapter 7.

John Simon Guggenheim Memorial Foundation
551 Fifth Ave., NYC 17

While still at Yaddo, O'Connor applied for a Guggenheim with a respectable bevy of supporters: Philip Rahv (see entry), Paul Engle, George Davis (see), Ted Amussen (see), Robert Penn Warren, and Robert Lowell (see).[84] With all that support, however, she was not chosen. She applied again ten years later, this time with two published books under her belt and the support of Robert Giroux (see), Denver Lindley (see), and Andrew Lytle, but was denied yet again.[85]

7 / Writers and Other Artists

As one might expect, O'Connor met or knew of writers and other artists who lived in New York. Here is an exploration of the lives of some who were recorded in her address books.

For their contact information, consult the applicable alphabetical listings chapter.

Elizabeth Fenwick

Elizabeth Fenwick (1916–1996) was already an established writer of detective stories and psychological thrillers when she met O'Connor at Yaddo in 1948.

Born Elizabeth Jane Phillips in St. Louis, Missouri, she was the daughter of a former Ziegfeld Follies performer (who, bowlegged, was hired to play boys) and a man from a prominent family who was unsuccessful in business and, eventually, disabled by an experimental medical treatment.[1] Fenwick's childhood was, in a word, chaotic: "her parents divorced, her little sister died [in the final days of the 1918 flu pandemic], her stepfather died, and her parents remarried."[2] To make matters worse, Fenwick's father was dominated by his widowed mother, who often supported the family.[3]

Listed as Betty Jane Phillips in the 1930 Detroit census, young Fenwick lived in several different states before coming back to St. Louis.[4] While working as a secretary to support her parents, she joined the St. Louis Poets Workshop in 1936. Other members of this group included poet Clark Mills McBurney, future poet laureate William J. Smith, and playwright Thomas Lanier Williams (later known as Tennessee).[5]

Despite the protests of her (dependent) parents, Fenwick moved to Manhattan in 1941 where she found work "as a secretary, but was lonely."[6] As a result, she relocated to Cornell and married McBurney. Soon she was "writing detective novels under the name E. P. Fenwick to disguise that she was female."[7] The name "Fenwick" was chosen as a tribute to her recently deceased and much-loved uncle, John Fenwick Nicholson.[8]

Her first marriage not so much ended but evaporated. During World War II, Clark McBurney worked in counterintelligence and moved on to the newly created Central Intelligence Agency afterward. When he unaccountably ceased communication and abandoned her, the marriage was annulled in 1946.[9]

In 1950, she married David Jacques Way (1918–1994), who, at the time, was a printer. "He was a protégé of the typographer Bruce Rogers," Way's daughter, Jessica, said. "He was designing and printing the catalog to the Frick Collection, and he ran the publishing company Clarke and Way with his friend Burt Clarke just after his marriage to Elizabeth."[10] Way had been struck by a photo of Fenwick that appeared in *Life* in 1947.[11]

According to the family, Fenwick accepted his proposal with the understanding that she wanted children right away; the two welcomed daughter Deborah early on. Though their marriage lasted twenty years, it was far from harmonious. The two often lived apart, sometimes within the same apartment building.[12] After their eventual divorce, she left the East Coast for the West as she "followed her 16-year-old daughter (who had graduated a year early) to college in California, and then to Colorado after Deborah got her residency and started a family there."[13] It was there that, after publishing fourteen mysteries, three mainstream novels, and one children's book over thirty years, Fenwick stopped writing for publication in 1973. She died of Alzheimer's disease in 1996.[14]

Though O'Connor would mention that she and Fenwick were as different from each other as could be, the two shared a deep friendship.[15] It was Fenwick who led O'Connor to the furnished room in the Upper West Side in 1949; six years later, O'Connor asked that an advance copy of *A Good Man Is Hard to Find* be sent to her.[16] As seen in *The Habit of Being*, in the final years of O'Connor's life, the two discussed various treatments for lupus, a condition that O'Connor believed plagued her friend. (It turned out to be Raynaud's syndrome.)[17]

Scholar Curtis Evans notes that, while domestic suspense novels by female midcentury writers fell in disfavor after popular tastes changed, the work of Fenwick has suffered "greater neglect than most" despite her books' initial popularity.[18] Perhaps the tide is turning: In 2022, Fenwick's

Make-Believe Man (1963) and *A Friend of Mary Rose* (1961) were reprinted in one volume by Stark House Press.

Rochelle Girsen (*sic*)

Rochelle Girson (1915–2002) was the *Saturday Review* book review editor from 1958 to 1973. Before that, she wrote the syndicated columns "Among Books and Authors" and "This Week's Personality" for the *Saturday Review* Book Service. An enthusiastic traveler, she wrote about her travels to more than sixty countries on four continents in the 1967 *Maiden Voyages: A Lively Guide for the Woman Traveler.*[19]

Girson interviewed O'Connor when the latter was in New York to promote *A Good Man Is Hard to Find.* In the address book listing, O'Connor notes that Girson is with the "Sat Re Syn."

Elaine Gottleib (*sic*)

Elaine Gottlieb's (1916–2004) address is listed in O'Connor's brown book, and it is directly followed by the address and phone number of Gottlieb's mother's Long Beach, New York, home. Interestingly, on a separate slip of paper kept with O'Connor's address books in the MARBL archive, there is a notation for *M.F. O'Connor,* likely in Regina's handwriting, followed by Gotleib's (misspelled) name, Manhattan address, phone number, and the date July 1, 1949.

Gottlieb was a short story writer, novelist, translator, and teacher whose own story was a page-turner. A New York native, she moved to Manhattan at the age of twenty-five, determined to become a writer. Staying in Mexico in 1946, she quickly fell in love with a handsome, older man, author and flying ace Elliott Chess (1898–1962). The two were engaged within two weeks of meeting each other and, to celebrate, caught a bus to Guadalajara. Their joy was soon challenged when gunmen attacked the bus. Chess saved Gottlieb's life. The two lived together for two months but were never legally married. Gottlieb boarded a train for New York, and although Chess promised to meet her there, they never saw each other again. Gottlieb gave birth to their daughter, Nola, the following year.[20] She notified Chess of the birth of the little girl with a brief letter, her last to him.[21]

On Nola's fifth birthday, Gottlieb married the poet and novelist Cecil Hemley (1914–1966). The two had two sons, Jonathan and Robin. The married couple met and fraternized with various writers, including Isaac Bashevis Singer. The Hemleys translated and edited several of his works from the original Yiddish.[22]

When Hemley died because of heart failure, Gottlieb traveled from university to university, teaching to support her family. Nola battled schizophrenia her entire life before overdosing at the age of twenty-five. Robin would go on to write *Nola: A Memoir of Faith, Art, and Madness*, a book about his sister and their lives growing up.[23] Gottlieb died at eighty-eight.

Considering the date included with Gottlieb's contact information, on Friday, July 1, 1949, Nola would have been two days shy of her second birthday. One can't help but wonder if O'Connor had been invited to a small party in her honor.

Elizabeth Hardwick

Elizabeth Hardwick (1916–2007) was known for her essays and fiction, her tortured relationship with Robert Lowell (whom she married in 1949 and divorced in 1972), and starting (with others, including Lowell) *The New York Review of Books*.[24]

After leaving Yaddo abruptly in 1949 (with Lowell and O'Connor), she returned to her apartment and allowed O'Connor to stay for a few days. The doorman, O'Connor stated, seemed to think the two were sisters, a resemblance O'Connor saw as physical while Hardwick attributed to their (dissimilar) Southern accents.[25]

For more on Hardwick and her marriage to Lowell, see the entry for Mr. & Mrs. Robt. Lowell.

Pat Highsmith

Novelist Patricia Highsmith (1921–1995) wrote books that were not so much whodunits but, as it's been said, whydunits. The most famous was *Strangers on a Train* (1950), which Hitchcock turned into a 1951 film. Also successful were her books about a murderous character named Tom Ripley. She left the United States in the early 1960s to live in Europe. She was known as someone who preferred the company of cats to people and smoked two packs of cigarettes a day.[26]

Highsmith was encouraged by author Truman Capote to apply for a Yaddo residency, and it was there that she worked on *Strangers on a Train*, (re)starting from scratch after the book had had several rejections. In her diary, she names the writers and artists gathered there (ending the list with O'Connor's name) and describes them as dull, with no big names among them.[27]

Highsmith and O'Connor had little in common beyond their craft. While O'Connor went to daily Mass with some of the Yaddo employees,

Highsmith was more likely to go drinking with other Yaddo residents. O'Connor was far from a teetotaler: in one letter, she speaks of going to and enjoying a gin party.[28] Still, from this critical perceived difference—one that O'Connor noted about herself compared to the Yaddo guests in general—springs a rather questionable anecdote Highsmith shared a good forty years after the Yaddo stay.

As the story goes, one stormy evening, Highsmith returned from a night of merriment. Lightning showed O'Connor on the porch, on her knees and pointing to a knothole she said resembled the face of Jesus. Highsmith did not like O'Connor after that, but she seemed not to have been crazy about her before the storm, dismissive of her for being part of the Iowa Writers' Workshop and being from Georgia.[29]

While the story of O'Connor acting like a character from her own fiction is questionable, one piece of the story does emerge as true: the powerful storm. O'Connor composed a letter to her mother one rain-soaked evening, saying she was writing by candlelight because the power had been knocked out.[30]

Despite whether Highsmith liked O'Connor, she was quite helpful to the budding writer. In a letter dated July 12, 1948, Highsmith wrote from her parents' Hastings-on-Hudson, New York, address to share the name and contact information of her agent, Margot Johnson. Johnson had asked about O'Connor because Highsmith had mentioned her in a letter. In referring to O'Connor's situation with Rinehart publishers, Highsmith relayed that it was difficult to get an advance based on the strength of an outline and one chapter. Highsmith added she would be in Hastings-on-Hudson for about a month and shared her Manhattan address and telephone number in case she had not already done so. (She had.)[31]

When Capote recommended Highsmith for a Yaddo residency, he agreed to do so if she would allow him to sublet her apartment while she was gone. It was in this apartment that Capote finished *A Tree of Night.*[32]

Mr. Dudley Huppler

Dudley Huppler (1917–1988) was an ink-and-paper pointillist and a writer of surreal prose.

A self-taught artist, he had already had a few shows in Minneapolis, Chicago, and his native state of Wisconsin when he visited New York City in 1950. He became involved in the art scene there, and the friendships he made encouraged his return. In 1955, he was part of Andy Warhol's entourage.[33] (Interesting side note: Both O'Connor and Warhol came to Manhattan to live in 1949. O'Connor got there first, but Warhol, of course, stayed.)

Huppler lived at 39 First Avenue from mid/late 1955 to mid-1956.[34] According to Addy Sage, his great niece-in-law and owner of the Dudley Huppler website, "Fame was at his fingertips in the 1950s, only to get cut out of the art scene a decade later. His momentum was lost and perhaps his motivation had changed so he never made a name for himself even though many of his friends' fates were different."[35] Huppler soon left the Northeast.[36]

He made his living as an English professor until 1985, teaching first at the University of Wisconsin–Oshkosh, then at the University of Colorado–Boulder. Some say he was an artist who should be better known, but his strong personality got in the way.[37] Still, his New York connections did not disappear after he left. For example, he wrote the libretto for a 1979 one-act opera buffa, Lee Holby's Something New for the Zoo.[38]

In an unpublished letter to Huppler from 1961, O'Connor mentions guinea hens, referring to a drawing he had sent her. She also refers to the person who may have introduced them: Caroline Gordon, whom O'Connor refers to here as Mrs. Tate.[39] It is entirely possible that Huppler was in attendance at the June 1955 party Gordon threw in O'Connor's honor (see Chapter 3). With Huppler having just completed a spring residency at Yaddo, the two would have had plenty to chat about.

Regarding the drawing of the guinea, one would be tempted to assume that it was a copy of his 1949 "Guinea Hen: The Tragedy of Incomplete Beauty." But, the following passage from The Antiquerie, an unpublished book manuscript written after O'Connor's death, puts the drawing in context. It also hints that Huppler had heard stories about her time at Yaddo, likely from Clifford Wright (see entry).[40]

Once I wrote to ask Flannery O'Connor could I draw her if she came up North. She answered that she didn't come to N.Y. very often and actually she'd rather have me draw her peafowl, "only they come even more seldom." Now [that] she's gone, the two stories told me about her at Yaddo pop again into the mind. How behind the drawn shades of her room in the upper reaches of the "castle," she heard one workman on a ladder say to another: "They got one here now called Flannery O'Connor." To which the other snorted, "Yor hor hor." Then how she, after the ordeal of the trip into town, dropped the gin on the marble steps as she passed upstairs—and kept on going![41]

(Interestingly, the dropped gin incident is referenced in correspondence between Lowell and O'Connor. O'Connor was quick to remind Lowell that the Yaddo steps had been slick and added that what had been dropped was not gin but an unopened bottle of rum.[42])

Later in life, Huppler switched from pointillism to working with colored pencils. His last exhibition, which took place in 1981, featured drawings of tattooed men and boys. A few years later, he would find himself coming back to Warhol. "Between 1986 and up until his death in 1988," Sage said, "he made a series of homage shoe drawings to Andy Warhol." During that period, not long after Warhol's 1987 passing, Huppler came across a book that paired two similar drawings for comparison: his own "Young Man with Rose" and Warhol's "Boy Portrait: Boy with a Rose." "The side-by-side images illustrated Huppler's influence on Warhol," Sage said. It was the first time Huppler had seen his work in a book, and his impact noted.[43]

Huppler never learned to drive and rode a bicycle everywhere. He was riding a bike when he died of a heart attack not far from his home in Boulder.[44]

Carol Johnson

Known as Sr. Marya when she first came to O'Connor's attention, poet Carol Johnson (1928–2015) is the rare example of a correspondent O'Connor approached first with a fan letter rather than the other way around.

O'Connor mentioned Johnson's poetry to friends, urging them to check out the latest issue of *The Commonweal* (see entry) and the like to read her work. In addition to the letters the two exchanged, they spent time together when Johnson visited with mutual friend Ashley Brown.[45] In 1955, O'Connor asked that a copy of *A Good Man Is Hard to Find* be sent to Johnson.[46]

At the time of her retirement, Johnson was a professor at the University of Victoria in British Columbia.[47]

Miss Maryat Lee

When Georgia College welcomed its new president, Dr. Robert ("Buzz") E. Lee in 1956, O'Connor had no way of knowing his arrival would signal the coming of a deep and influential friendship with his New York playwright sister.

While scholars have focused on the correspondence between the two, particularly for its consideration of race, Mary Attaway Lee (1923–1989) is more than just a well-known O'Connor correspondent. Lee was an avant-garde playwright, and by the time O'Connor met her, she had already had success in New York with the one-act *Dope!*. She later formed the Soul and Latin Theater (SALT) and the Ecotheater, which used local residents as actors.[48]

To read more about their friendship (and the part New York plays in it), see Chapter 5.

Ed Meisel (*sic*)

Edward Maisel (1917–2008) and O'Connor met at Yaddo, and their meeting would, in the long run, play a part in O'Connor becoming acquainted with Robert Lowell (see entry) and her coming to Manhattan earlier than anticipated. In a letter to her mother, O'Connor noted that it was Maisel who encouraged Yaddo director Elizabeth Ames to allow her to stay during the retreat's off-season. With that special permission granted, O'Connor said she now considered Maisel a good friend.[49]

Knowing that Maisel and Ames were close, it is difficult to fathom he was part of the "Yaddo Four," a group led by Lowell and including Elizabeth Hardwick (see) and O'Connor which denounced Ames as a Communist sympathizer.[50]

Maisel's *Charles T. Griffes: The Life of an American Composer* was already published by the time O'Connor met the musicologist; the same book would be revised in 1984 to include documented details of Griffes' homosexual life, material that would have never appeared in a book by a reputable publisher in 1943, the date of its original publication.

By the time of his death, Maisel was an internationally recognized writer on music and Tai Chi. His *Tai Chi for Health* was the first American manual published on the classic form of Chinese exercise.[51]

A notation of 226 in the margin might refer to an apartment number.

Vivian McCleod (*sic*)

Though she wrote under Vivienne Koch, her name is recorded as Vivian McCleod in O'Connor's brown address book. The two writers met at Yaddo in 1948.

New York-born Vivienne C. Koch MacLeod Day (1912–1961) was the daughter of Hungarian immigrants. Her father was a drama critic for Hungarian-language newspapers in the United States before founding Eagle Regalia Company.

First studying drama, Koch soon turned her attention to literature and philosophy. Before working as an instructor at Mount Holyoke and, later, New York University, she was a social worker for several years in Harlem. Her first book, on William Carlos Williams, was published by New Directions (see entry) in 1950; a book on W. B. Yeats followed in 1951. The year before her death, her novel *Change of Love* was published by McDowell-Obolensky (see).[52]

She divorced poet and educator Norman Wicklund Macleod in 1946 and married CBS vice president for news John F. Day, Jr. in 1955.[53] They were married in the home of Mr. and Mrs. W. McNeil Lowrey (see).[54]

Phyllis Meras

The career of journalist Phyllis Meras (b. 1931) spans seven productive decades and illustrates how women initially had difficulty entering the then male-dominated field.

Upon graduating from Columbia School of Journalism in the 1950s, Meras was told that, as a woman, she would never find work as a reporter in New York. As a result, she applied for a position with the Rhode Island *Providence Journal*. The paper was interested in interviewing the talented applicant until someone realized the name was not Phillip but Phyllis. Regardless, she boarded a train to Providence, where perseverance and a bit of odd luck (the assistant to the woman's page editor called in sick and never returned) led to a job.[55]

Over the years, her work appeared in the Paris-based *International Herald Tribune*, the *New York Times*, *Ladies Home Journal*, the *Nation*, the *Saturday Review*, and *Vineyard Gazette*. Books on travel, crafts, and food complete the list of publications. She is currently writing a memoir.

Meras is most known for her work as a travel writer, starting as a staff member of the *New York Times* travel section and, for many years after that, serving as the *Providence Journal* travel editor. Despite the emphasis on travel, the list of famous authors she has written about is long and impressive. Leaving the *Journal* upon receiving a Swiss Fellowship to study International Affairs in Geneva, she was writing book reviews when, at the suggestion of her father (and the help of a French cousin in the publishing business),[56] she interviewed writers who were either living—or traveling—abroad. These writers included Simone de Beauvoir, Somerset Maugham, Doris Lessing, Francois Mauriac, and J.R.R. Tolkien. In time, with the help of a Pulitzer Fellowship in Critical Writing, she expanded the list to include American authors such as Truman Capote, Kurt Vonnegut, Carson McCullers, Katherine Anne Porter, and O'Connor.[57] Meras interviewed O'Connor in May 1964, fewer than three months before the writer's death; it is likely the last interview the author granted. While Meras did not mention lupus in the article, she did include that O'Connor found her daily morning writing sessions exhausting.[58] By May 31, the date that Meras's article appeared in *The Providence Sunday Journal*, O'Connor was back in the hospital.[59]

O'Connor frequently gave peacock feathers to friends and visitors, and Meras was no exception. However, after the interview, a fellow traveler who offered Meras a ride balked upon seeing the feathers and declared them bad luck.[60]

"The evil eye in peacock feathers is believed to be the eye of the female demon Lilith," Meras said. "I am superstitious enough to have promptly given the Flannery O'Connor peacock feather gift away as soon as I got home."[61]

Edgar Moran

Charles Edgar Moran (1892–1972) was listed in the first of O'Connor's address books. That he was born in Milledgeville is likely why O'Connor knew him, but he had left town long before she moved there, so perhaps it is that she only knew of him.

There are no mentions of Moran in O'Connor's biographies. Nor is there any correspondence (if there ever was any) preserved. However, if every completed government form tells a story, a collection of forms gathered over decades can suggest an intriguing tale. In this case, it's the tale of a musician who left the Small Town South for the Great White Way, only to eventually give up the dream.

Moran's early years are documented by a 1900 U.S. census form for tiny Gumm, Georgia (which would eventually be absorbed into Milledgeville). Moran's father, Charles L. Moran, was the census district enumerator and, as such, listed eight-year-old Edgar as the first of five Moran children.[62] By the next census, the Moran family was part of Milledgeville proper, with Edgar now listed as the first of nine kids.[63]

The Milledgeville *Union-Recorder* mentioned Moran, then a cadet at Georgia Military College, for his classical piano performances. Of particular interest here is that he performed with Katie Cline, O'Connor's aunt (who likely gave her Manhattan-bound niece Moran's address some forty years later).[64] His musical prowess was mentioned upon his moving to Atlanta in August 1909.[65] He was back in Milledgeville in time for the 1910 federal census, though not before first briefly residing in Georgia towns Griffin (October 1909) and Cedartown (January 1910).[66]

By 1916, at the age of twenty-four, he had moved to New York and was working as a musician. According to his June 4, 1916, draft registration card, he was married and listed his wife as a dependent.[67] In February 1918, he claimed supporting his wife as a reason for service exemption.[68] Whether he had a change of heart or the government changed it for him, Moran enlisted in the Navy five months later and was discharged in 1921.[69]

However, this is at odds with an article in the April 24, 1918 issue of the Milledgeville *Union-Recorder,* which describes a church event in which twenty-seven young men were honored for their service. The group includes Moran and his brother Emmett.[70]

When the U.S. entered World War II, Moran reenlisted at the age of fifty. He was unemployed, and there was no mention of a wife. The person he listed as one who would "always know [his] address" was his brother Jay in Florida.[71]

People get divorced, of course, but in the 1930 and 1940 censuses, he was listed as single (as opposed to divorced). In 1950, he claimed having never married.[72]

According to the Census

Moran may not have been married, but he was hardly alone, according to federal census reports that listed him as living with family over the years. The reports also document what was either his tendency to shave years off his age or his aunt's inability to remember how old Moran was. In 1930, while living in Morningside Heights with his aunt Ida M. Moray (listed as household head) and a cousin, his age was given as thirty-two, though he was thirty-eight.

Ten years later, now living with Aunt Ida, the cousin, and another cousin (listed as head) on East 35th Street, Moran's age was recorded as thirty-three; he was actually forty-eight. In 1950, fifty-eight and now head of a household that includes dear Aunt Ida and a work colleague, Moran was listed as forty-two. At that point, he was living at the address listed in O'Connor's brown book. It was the same address listed on his 1942 enlistment card, and he would live there until at least 1963.

Of course, government forms do more than record marital status and age. They can also indicate profession—and, sometimes, the twists that occur along the path of a dream.

There's No Business Like . . .

In 1916, Moran was employed by the United Booking Office as a musician at the Palace Theatre. In 1918, he was still employed at United and listed his job as a vaudeville artist. While his stint in the Navy likely kept him from performing, he made up for lost time in 1921 by collaborating with Jack McGowan on the song "Birds of a Feather." There were other compositions, both with McGowan (1923, "Turn Homeward") and on his own (1921, "Help Me").

In 1927, he was one of two pianists in the road company of *Queen High*, a musical comedy.[73] The switch to musical comedy indicated the change in theater: Vaudeville was dying, as were silent films, another employment source for professional pianists. This change is reflected in his 1930 census, where he lists his occupation not as a musician but, like his cousin Mona Moray, a dramatic artist.[74] While his cousin continued acting on stage and, later, on radio, Moran kept on with music, though the work wasn't always steady. In 1939, he worked as a musician for a total of fourteen weeks.[75]

There were some songs written by an Edgar Moran in the 1940s, and one even recorded by the DeCastro Sisters, but it is not certain if this was the same person. What is for sure is that Moran, by 1950, had taken a job in a tie factory as a silk inspector.[76]

He was finally recorded as head of the house.

In 1957, Moran began collecting Social Security at the age of sixty-five. He lived his retirement years in Stamford, Connecticut; Aunt Ida died in nearby Ridgefield in 1966 at the age of eighty-two.[77]

When Moran died in 1972, there was a funeral service in Stamford before his body was interred in Milledgeville. While much of what he achieved may have been forgotten over the years, an obituary summed up his life's work succinctly. It mentions that Moran had lived most of his life in New York. It states he had worked as a musician and a composer and had been an accompanist for top performers of the vaudeville era. It claims that he had written the music for several Broadway shows, though none, unfortunately, were named.[78]

He, like O'Connor, is buried in Milledgeville's Memory Hill Cemetery.

Smith Oliver

Standing 6 feet 7 inches tall and exceedingly handsome, Smith Robertson Oliver, Jr. (1920–1992) made a striking impression before he opened his mouth, and once he did, it became all the more memorable. Though it is unknown how O'Connor knew or met Oliver, she had likely read his work in *Sewanee Review*.

Born in Birmingham, Alabama, Oliver was one of nine children living in, at one point, a two-bedroom, one-bathroom, no-basement house.[79] The children grew up to lead interesting lives (among them: a chemist, a nurse, a civil rights activist, a French teacher, and a missionary), and this held true for Oliver. Having learned the dry-cleaning trade from his father, he found work as a clothing presser after graduating from high school. He left Alabama for Detroit, but during World War II, he joined the Merchant Marines, a decision that opened the world to him.

When the war ended, he went to New York and found work as a chef in a Greenwich Village restaurant. The restaurant, perhaps, was the Calypso Café, where he spent late evenings with friends James Baldwin (who worked there as a waiter) and painter Delaney Beauford.[80] It was Oliver who introduced Baldwin to manager Helen Strauss.[81]

Recovering from a failed romance, Oliver left New York for Chicago, where he met Marguerite Lamounia (née Spencer) Jennings (1918–2014). They married in March 1948.[82] "Marge" described her courtship with Oliver while attending the University of Chicago as "the best days of her life." Upon marriage, the couple moved to a charming loft in New York; after a few months, they separated permanently (leaving no legal proof of divorce). Despite going their separate ways, their "friendship and admiration remained strong."

Distinctive Speaker, Free Thinker

Oliver traveled a lot; he saw the world. Though he occasionally lived with relatives and kept in touch with his siblings, he generally didn't see much of his family. For that reason, he remained a man of mystery to his nieces and nephews. "If I knew him the total of a week," nephew Claude Oliver said, "that was a lot."

But that didn't stop Oliver from making a strong impression on the sons and daughters of his siblings. He didn't mince words, which were beautifully and properly uttered: He spoke, as niece Lois Benjamin noted, "the King's English," and he expected the same of her and her cousins.

He was also a free thinker who had grown up in a devoutly religious household (two brothers attended Bible college). As a result, Oliver suffered periods of ostracism throughout his lifetime. In addition, coming from a family that claimed not only African but also significant Scottish, English, and Native American ancestry, Oliver faced both racism and colorism. As Lois Benjamin and Claude Oliver noted, Oliver "never wanted to hear the word 'Black,'" having been taught by his parents that people were more than the color of their skin. But in recognition of the turbulent times he witnessed firsthand, Oliver understood that "America was in the middle of a family fight," Claude Oliver said. It was a fight that bore fruit in some of Oliver's final writings, particularly the book he was finishing at the time of his death. Called *Literary Alternatives to the Negro Protest Novel*, it's a work that his nephew would like to see published.

He sometimes wrote poetry under the name Melquiades, a moniker borrowed from a character in the novel *One Hundred Years of Solitude*. Mostly, though, his work was published under the name Smith Oliver, with pieces appearing in *Zero Anthology, Prairie Schooner, Sewanee Review,* and *Phylon.* A book-length poem, *God-Child,* written in Sao Paulo, Brazil, was published in Madras, India, in 1965 and republished by H. Wolff in 1967. (The republishing merited a small mention in *Jet* magazine.[83]) In addition, Oliver published a book of poetry called *A Poet in San Francisco.*

Oliver lived his final years in Dallas with his brother Douglas. Before dying from a heart aneurysm in 1992, Oliver put together two books that were published in limited editions by the Fort Sumter Group in Dallas: *Several Exemplary Stories* and *A Christmas Tale.*

Two books remain unpublished: *Family Honor and Other Allusions* and *Literary Alternatives.*

Irene Orgle (*sic*)

Irene Orgel (1922–2016?) was born in London. She wrote fiction, poetry, and literary criticism. Her work appeared in *Mademoiselle, Harper's, Chelsea Review, American Scholar,* and other publications. Her book of short stories, *The Odd Tales of Irene Orgel,* was published in 1966.[84]

Orgel came to the United States in 1939 and by 1946 was a graduate student at Columbia University.[85] Like O'Connor, Orgel was at Yaddo in 1948.[86] In 1949, Orgel's story "God and Puppet" appeared in *The Tiger's Eye,* a widely read independent magazine produced in Manhattan that emphasized visual art as much as literature. A few years later, Orgel attended the MacDowell Colony, where she met composer Irving Fine (1914–1962). Their meeting resulted in a 1959 musical score, *Mutability: Six Songs Based on Poems by Irene Orgel,* and, some say, an affair.[87]

In her correspondence to her mother while at Yaddo, O'Connor referred to Orgel as an English girl. In answering her mother's question, the next letter explained that "the English girl was already in this country."[88]

Lettie Rogers

Lettie Logan Hamlett Rogers (1917–1957), born in Soochow, China, was the daughter of missionaries. Her first two novels, *South of Heaven* and *The Storm Cloud,* were about life in China in the 1920s. Her third book, *Landscape of the Heart,* considered the relationship between a psychiatrist and a patient. Her final tome, *Birthright,* explored desegregation in the American South. It was published shortly before she died of cancer.

Along with Peter Taylor, Randell Jarrell, and Robie Macauley (see entry), she taught creative writing at the Women's College of the University of North Carolina (now UNC Greensboro).[89]

While maintaining a permanent North Carolina address, Rogers moved to Manhattan to start cancer treatment at Mt. Sinai Medical Hospital. She first stayed at the Allerton House women's residence but eventually settled into the Hotel Dover. Early in January 1957, she wrote to O'Connor about how she had been told only months before that there was no chance of winning her second bout with cancer. Refusing to accept that conclusion, she sought the help of New York physicians who told her she could live another two years at least with the help of Cobalt—a (then) revolutionary, not to mention expensive, treatment that involved directing a beam of gamma rays to kill tumors.[90]

As Rogers had found hope through New York doctors, she encouraged O'Connor to find better treatment in New York herself. She even went as far as to offer O'Connor (with whom Rogers had, by her own admission, only a brief acquaintance) a place to stay if needed.[91]

As Rogers fought for her life, *Birthright* came out in March 1957. In April, the novel was spotlighted by the Literary Guild, a mail-order book club. Despite her efforts, Rogers died in May of that year at the age of thirty-nine. Coincidentally, O'Connor herself would die at that age.

Though a wavy line obscures the Hotel Dover address under Rogers' name in the black Elite, the name itself remained, almost poignantly, untouched.

Margaret Sutton

> I am quite well and enjoying life in my own unique way.
> —MARGARET SUTTON TO FLANNERY O'CONNOR,
> DECEMBER 23, 1963

A constant in Flannery O'Connor's experience of Manhattan over the years was the presence of Margaret Elizabeth Sutton (1905–1990). It was Sutton who saw to it, in 1943, that her young friend saw the gritty side of Manhattan during her first visit (to read about this, see Chapter 1). And it was Sutton that O'Connor always planned to see, usually for dinner, whenever she came to town.

Though not well-known either then or today, Sutton was a prolific surrealist painter. The native of Bluefield, Virginia, spent much of the 1930s in Milledgeville and lived most of her life in Manhattan. Since O'Connor did not move to Milledgeville until 1940, Sutton likely met her through mutual friend (and former colleague) Lydia Bancroft.

The *Bluefield Daily Telegraph*—the Bluefield, West Virginia, newspaper that also covered news from neighboring Bluefield, Virginia—reported regularly on the achievements and whereabouts of the only child of a dentist. Where Dr. and Mrs. A. B. Sutton's daughter was going to school, where she was traveling to or coming from—all this and more was fodder for its aptly titled *Bluefield, Virginia News* column. Sometimes, her name would be added to a story to add interest. For example, a short piece about how the fire station building had once housed the local post office mentions Sutton had been born in an apartment there. She and her parents were the only former residents mentioned.[92]

The editor noted her talent had been evident early on, recalling in both 1932 and 1937 the chewing gum portrait child Sutton had made of her teacher.[93] If one needed more evidence of Bluefield's editorial pride in Margaret Sutton, the proof is in a 1926 headline: "Home Town Is Proud of Dr. Margaret Sutton."[94]

She had not earned a doctorate, but it was of no matter. Women's societal roles were changing at great speed. Perhaps for Bluefield, Sutton was more than just a dentist's daughter, more than a New York artist. Perhaps for Bluefield, she represented change.

Academic Pursuits

As an undergraduate, Sutton attended State Normal and Industrial School for Women at Radford (now Radford University, located in Virginia) and State Teachers College (now University of Mary Washington, UMW) in Fredricksburg, Virginia.[95] After receiving a Master's in Fine Art Education from Columbia University, she taught in North Carolina and Tennessee.[96] Sutton then headed for Milledgeville where, in 1930, both she and Bancroft were welcomed as new faculty.[97] She taught both science and applied arts courses and, according to the *Bluefield Daily Telegraph*, chaired the art department.[98]

While teaching in Milledgeville, Sutton devoted her summers to furthering her education, starting with a course at Columbia in 1931.[99] For six weeks in 1932, she and other artists visited industrial art schools, art studios, and shops in Paris, Stockholm, and Amsterdam, as well as in a few select German cities through the Art Alliance of America.[100] Sutton attended the New York School of Interior Decorating in 1934.[101]

Her studies were not limited to summer months. Sutton spent the 1936–1937 academic year enrolled in the Art Students League in New York City, learning under abstract expressionist Hans Hofmann.[102] Before returning to Milledgeville, she spent time working on her craft in Providence, Massachusetts.[103]

Sutton came back to the university, but not for long; in September 1939, the GSCW *Colonnade* announced her resignation.[104] Back home, the *Telegraph* reported she was opening an art studio.[105]

During World War II, Sutton attended drafting and engineering classes at Columbia, an education that allowed her to work at Grumman Aircraft Engineering Corporation in Long Island. After the war, she worked as a technical illustrator until she retired.[106] Through it all, she continued to create colorful surrealist paintings and lively abstract ink drawings, most of which were untitled.

Of interest to O'Connor enthusiasts, Sutton often featured peacocks in her work.[107]

In 1936, Sutton lived with a family named King on East 11th Street near University Place.[108] At some point after, O'Connor recorded a West 112th Street address in her brown book. That address was scratched out in favor of 210 West 14th Street, a five-story walk-up known as the Pompeo Coppini Studio. Sutton lived there for the rest of her life.

She spent those years with Ukrainian-born cubist painter and photographer Alfred Levitt (1895–2000) and his wife, attorney Gertrude (Jerry) Horowitz (1898–1983). Like Sutton, Levitt also studied under Hofmann, which is likely how they met.[109] Levitt and Sutton weren't the only artists in the building. Marcel Duchamp (1887–1968) had a studio on the top floor from 1942 until his death. After Horowitz died in 1983, Sutton continued to live with Levitt until her own death in 1990.[110] In 1993, Levitt donated over three thousand works of art from his personal collection to UMW, a gift that included not only his work but that of alumna Sutton.[111]

Three's Not a Crowd

The idea of a single person living with a married couple for decades strikes contemporary minds as odd, if not suggestive. While such a living arrangement was not unusual during the Great Depression, it could certainly raise eyebrows after.[112] And of course, there is this: Sutton had grown up as a single child. Perhaps living with a (slightly) older married couple was familiar and comfortable, if not comforting.

Whether it was a desire for privacy or a robust intolerance of government prying, Sutton was inspired to change the truth when answering the 1950 census. For the sake of comparison, the 1940 census states husband and wife (born in Russia and New York) had resided in the apartment in 1935, and Sutton had lived in Milledgeville, all of which is true. While the couple lied about their occupations (real estate and bookkeeping), everything else was in order, with Sutton listed as a lodger and an unemployed art teacher, which she was.[113]

But one has to laugh upon reading Sutton's responses in 1950 (her housemates were in Europe then). Alfred and Gertrude were renamed George and Anna. Levitt was the proprietor of a beauty salon (perhaps a euphemism for his art studio?), and Sutton, described as their sister-in-law, was a hairstylist. Anna simply lived at home. And all three were born in New York, which was true only of Horowitz.[114]

The answers are as imaginative as anything Sutton ever painted, or drew, or created with wads of chewing gum.

Clifford Wright

Memorably, O'Connor spent the Christmas of 1948 at Yaddo rather than returning home for the holiday. When not writing, she spent time with the only residents there that day, painter Clifford Wright (1919–1989) and poet Robert Lowell (see entry).[115] Wright and O'Connor continued an occasional correspondence for the rest of her life.[116]

Wright (1919–1989) was born Oswald Kallunki in Washington; his more American-sounding name was given to him by his adoptive parents. He left Seattle for New York in 1946. He was awarded a Yaddo fellowship in 1947. The following year, he returned as assistant director.

It was at Yaddo that he met his wife, Danish writer Elsa Gress.[117] Years later, in Denmark, Wright and Gress created a colony of their own, *De-center*, for both artists and intellectuals.[118] The name was a mockery of a (then) proposed government-supported "center" of culture. (The proposal was dropped because, as such, a hub was deemed elitist.) The "de-center" took no government funding and was supported by the couple and contributions.[119]

As an artist, Wright was known for "fantastic abstractions and abstract figurative pieces."[120] Much of his work features the use of India Ink. In particular, he liked to use both ink and Indian ink in his oil paintings, leading to an interesting effect because of the way the liquids react to each other. A poet who knew Wright at Yaddo, however, recalled how the artist would mix paint with his own semen.[121]

Wright was known also for his illustrations and book cover designs.[122]

In 1948, Wright sent O'Connor warm and chatty letters in the months between her two stays at Yaddo. In them, he mentioned how she was missed by the guests and included gossip about them.[123] In 1954, Wright suggested that O'Connor could cross the ocean to see him as she was certainly prosperous enough to afford the trip. O'Connor replied that he must have her confused with another O'Connor, perhaps a plumber.[124]

Harcourt, Brace
383 Madison Ave., NYC 17 / EL 5-3610
750 Third Ave., NYC 17 / OX 7-8400

In 1919, Alfred Harcourt and Donald Brace left Henry Holt & Co. (see entry) to form their own publishing firm with Will D. Howe, a former English professor. Within a year, Howe left and the name was changed to Harcourt, Brace & Co. The company quickly gained recognition, publishing Sinclair Lewis's *Free Air* (1919), *Main Street* (1920), and the Pulitzer Prize–winning *Arrowsmith* (1925). As an employer, the company made waves early on by offering women equal employment opportunities.[1]

In 1955, William Jovanovich, who had had been hired eight years prior as a textbook salesman, was named president. Determined to turn the company into a conglomerate, he changed the company name to Harcourt, Brace & World, Inc. upon going public and merging with World Book Company. The company continued to acquire other firms, and by 1970, the name was changed to Harcourt Brace Jovanovich, Inc.

In time, the company's acquisitions grew to include Sea World marine parks and a few insurance operations. But after thirty-six years as chairman, Jovanovich resigned, with the company buckling under a debt of $1.7 billion. In 1981, the company became a subsidiary of General Cinema.[2]

Neither trusting nor liking Jovanovich and fearing the former textbook salesman would change the company from one that was known for literature to one that sold textbooks, executive editor Robert Giroux (see) left Harcourt, Brace in 1955. When he did, many authors followed him to

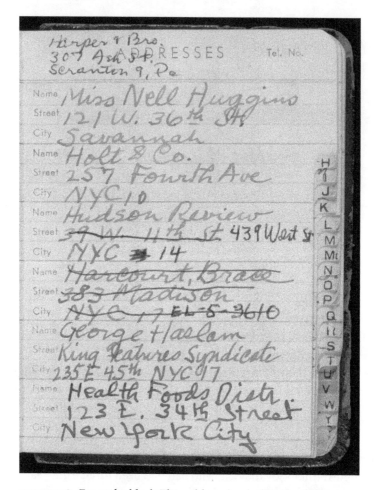

FIGURE 8: From the black Elite address book. (Used with permission from Flannery O'Connor Papers, Stuart A. Rose Manuscript, Archives, and Rare Book Library, Emory University.)

Farrar, Straus & Cudahy (see).[3] When O'Connor came on board, he assured her that a publisher did not need a Madison Avenue address to meet their authors at the airport with a limousine.[4] (See Figure 8.)

Harcourt, Brace published O'Connor's first two books.

Elizabeth Hardwick
28 E. 10th St., NYC 3 / GRamercy 3-7987

Writer Elizabeth Hardwick (1916–2007) allowed O'Connor to stay in her Devonshire House apartment briefly in 1949 after the two, with

Robert Lowell, left Yaddo Artists and Writers Colony. To read about her, see Chapter 7.

For more on Hardwick and her marriage to Lowell, see the entry for Mr. & Mrs. Robt. Lowell.

Harper & Brothers
49 E. 33rd St., NYC 16
The company published *40 Best Stories from Mademoiselle* in 1960. O'Connor's 1948 short story "The Capture" was included.

Harper's Bazaar
572 Madison Ave., NYC 22
The magazine published "A Late Encounter with the Enemy" (September 1953); "A Temple of the Holy Ghost" (May 1954); "Good Country People" (June 1955); and "The Enduring Chill" (July 1958).

The Harvard Club
27 W. 44th St.
O'Connor lists this club's (now former) location under Robert Fitzgerald's (see entry) name.

The club, which allowed only alumni and faculty of Harvard to join, did not allow female members until 1973. With that, the special "Ladies Entrance" (which O'Connor would have used) was removed.[5]

George Haslam
235 E. 45th St., NYC 17
George Haslam (1912–2001) was the high school newspaper advisor when Regina O'Connor asked about her shy daughter being on the staff of the *Peabody Palladium*. When he asked the fifteen-year-old to write something, she told him she was better at drawing. And with that came the pithy one-block cartoons that peppered the pages of the *Palladium* and, later, the GSCW *Colonnade*, which he also advised. Many credit that introduction to publishing as the springboard to her career as a writer.[6]

After three years of teaching history and geography at the college, Haslam worked as a journalist before going into sales, working in Manhattan for King Features Syndicate (see entry) and International News Service. In the late 1960s, he moved to Atlanta, where he inspired the "Uncle George" series of paintings by Savannah folk artist Chris Roberts.[7]

Over the years, they corresponded, his letters initially addressing her as Mary Flannery, then later, the preferred Flannery. After the publication of her second book, Haslam teasingly mentioned he had held on to her first linoleum cut as it would be worth a lot of money one day.[8] Though joking, he would be proven right: In 2014, a signed, first edition copy of *A Good Man Is Hard to Find* fetched over $9,000 in auction (the estimate had been $4,000–$6,000).[9]

O'Connor lists him as being with King Features Syndicate (see).

Robert Hatch
333 Sixth Ave., NYC 14

Robert Hatch (1911–1994) became the film critic for the *Nation* in 1954 and was later that magazine's managing editor and executive editor. Though retired in 1978, he still contributed reviews, including one of the film *Wise Blood* in 1980.[10]

O'Connor lists his name as part of the entry for the *Nation* (see entry).

Hiram Haydn
162 E. 38th St., NYC 16

Hiram Haydn (1907–1973) was a founder of Atheneum Books (see entry) and the editor of *American Scholar*, the literary magazine of Phi Beta Kappa, from 1944–1973.

O'Connor recommended Haydn as an editor to her friend Cecil Dawkins, noting that her own editor Catharine Carver (see) thought highly of him.[11] She suggested Haydn also to Maryat Lee, whose friend Eileen was seeking a publisher.[12]

O'Connor's advice worked for at least one of them. In 1963, at Haydn's request, she sent a blurb for the dustcover of Dawkins' *The Quiet Enemy*, a short story collection published by Atheneum later that year. In the same letter, she added she was also impressed by Eileen's stories (she admitted she didn't remember her last name) and said she had encouraged Lee to send them his way.[13]

This was the address of Atheneum Books, which O'Connor includes in the entry.

Health Foods Distr.
123 E. 34th St.

An ad for All Health Foods Distributors offered that one would find a variety of health aids, ranging from electric juicers to slanting boards to supplements, and a catalog was available for the asking.[14] As O'Connor was initially placed on a salt-free diet when she was diagnosed with lupus, perhaps she was interested in the salt-free foods the company offered.[15]

Even before the lupus diagnosis, O'Connor complained of easily depleted energy and turned to vitamins and supplements. In 1943, while visiting the Florencourt cousins, she reported that she was getting more from her vitamins by taking them with tartar sauce.[16] While at Yaddo, she bought beef iron and wine tonic specifically to give her the boost she needed to work on the book.[17] Years later, O'Connor twice mentioned taking Gevral while in New York.[18]

Even though it was marketed toward the geriatric set, O'Connor touted the benefits of Gevral to writer Cecil Dawkins, saying the supplement didn't increase her hunger as vitamin pills did.[19] To Maryat Lee (see entry), she recommended adding Gevral and a splash of coffee to a glass of cold milk.[20]

Pat Highsmith
353 E. 56th St.

O'Connor met Patricia Highsmith (1921–1995) at Yaddo. To read more, see Chapter 7.

Rust Hills
488 Madison Ave., NYC 22

L. Rust Hills (1924–2008) was the fiction editor of *Esquire* (see entry), serving in that position on and off for nearly forty years. As such, he brought the work of Norman Mailer, John Cheever, Ann Beattie, Richard Ford, Raymond Carver, Annie Proulx, and others to the magazine's readers. He edited Arthur Miller's story "The Misfits," which appeared in the magazine before it was made into a memorable film. In addition, he edited excerpts from novels, including William Styron's *Sophie's Choice* and Richard Ford's *Independence Day*.

He edited several *Esquire* short story anthologies and wrote books of essays. His book on writing, *Writing in General and the Short Story in Particular* (1977), was well received and used as a college textbook. He retired in 1999.

In 1963, Hills put O'Connor in the "red-hot center" in his Literary Establishment chart.[21] At his invitation, O'Connor submitted the unfinished *Why Do the Heathen Rage*, which was excerpted for the July 1963 issue. Later that year, he reached out to O'Connor, saying he felt that writers start out writing short stories but, along the way, turn their attention to novels, of course, but also articles they are paid to write. That said, he had it in mind to pay writers to write short fiction and offered O'Connor that opportunity.[22] It was an offer she politely, even a bit stiffly, refused, noting that she would gladly show him the story she was working on when it was completed but that it could not (and would not) be considered a commissioned piece.[23]

Hills is mentioned under the *Esquire* listing.

H. Stanley Hillyer
21 University Pl.

Hillyer (1887–1955) was the president of the real estate firm Hillyer & Bell and was known for his work in assembling the land for the (then) New York University-Bellevue Medical Center.

The interests of Hillyer, a World War I veteran who had served as an army captain in France, did not stop with land deals. He was president of the Washington Square Association and director of Greenwich House. He was a member of the board for the Washington Square Home for Friendless Girls, a trustee of the West Side Savings Bank, and the vice president of Musicians Foundation, Inc.[24] In addition, he applied for copyrights to three songs: one lullaby and two songs written for a four-man chorus and piano.[25]

O'Connor added a one-word note to the entry in brackets: [chess].

Holt & Co.
257 Fourth Ave.

Henry Holt & Company was founded in 1866 by Henry Holt and Frederick Leypoldt, making this one of the oldest trade publishers in the country. It is now part of Macmillan Publishing (see entry).

O'Connor includes John Woodburn (see) in this listing.

The address itself, which is shared by Criterion Books (see), is worth noting: In 1959, much of Fourth Avenue would be renamed Park Avenue South.[26]

Franz J. Horch, Associates
325 E. 57th St., NYC 22 / PL 3-9810

Franz Horch (1900–1951) was an émigré who had directed theater in his native Austria. Coming to this country to escape Nazi persecution, he found work representing authors and made a name for himself securing foreign rights for both American and émigré writers. Edna Ferber, Thomas Mann, John Dos Passos, E. B. White, and Upton Sinclair were among his clients. Roslyn Targ (1925–2017), an agent for Horch, continued the agency after his death. Specializing in foreign translation rights, she represented Sherwood Anderson, Harper Lee, F. Scott Fitzgerald, and others.[27]

This was Horch's home address.[28]

Hotel Dover
687 Lexington Ave., NYC 22

Built in 1926, the Dover was the location of *pied-a-terres* until World War II. After that, it operated as a transient hotel until it closed in 1982. In 1991, the hotel was reopened by its new owners as The Fitzpatrick.[29]

O'Connor includes this address, and apartment 2G, under Lettie Rogers' entry.

Hotel Marlton
5 W. 8th St., NYC 11

The Hotel Marlton was built in 1900 and became a hangout for writers, actors, and, later, Beat poets. Lillian Gish, Edna St. Vincent Millay, and Jack Kerouac are but a few of the famous people who either stayed or resided in the single room occupancy hotel.[30]

In 1987, the hotel was leased to The New School as the dormitory Marlton House. The historic building was purchased and renovated in 2012, reopening as the boutique Marlton Hotel.

O'Connor listed this hotel as one of three addresses for Beverly Brunson (see entry).

Hudson Review
39 W. 11th St., NYC 11
439 West St., NYC 14

This (then) brand-new, independent literary magazine would have been the talk of the writers at Yaddo when O'Connor was there in 1948. Four years later, O'Connor suggested that a copy of *Wise Blood* be sent to editor Frederick Morgan (1922–2004).[31] (The magazine did not review her book.) Several months later, she asked that her story "The River" be sent for their consideration.[32] They didn't publish it, but *Sewanee Review* did.

Interestingly enough, the editor who did not seem interested in her work was a former student of poet and critic Allen Tate, husband of O'Connor mentor Caroline Gordon. Morgan would sit in the editor's chair for the magazine's first fifty-five years.[33]

Catharine R. Hughes
64 University Pl., NYC 3

In 1961, Catharine Hughes (1935–1987) was publicity director for Sheed & Ward publishers.[34] At the time of her death at fifty-one, she was known as an editor and author as well as a drama critic and theater consultant.[35]

Hughes' name is listed not on its own but under Sheed & Ward (see entry).

Mr. Dudley Huppler
39 First Ave.

Dudley Huppler (1917–1988) wanted to draw O'Connor. To read more, see Chapter 7.

Miss Helene Iswolski (*sic*)
319 E. 91st St.

In a 1955 letter to her friend Betty Hester, O'Connor mentions that an article on Simone Weill had appeared in *The Third Hour*, a journal that grew out of an ecumenical group led by Helene Iswolsky (1896–1975)[36]. A Russian émigré, Iswolsky was the daughter of the last Tsarist Russian diplomat to France; she and her mother escaped during the Nazi occupation of that country. Later, in the United States, Iswolsky became friends with Dorothy Day, the journalist and social activist whose newspaper, the *Catholic Worker*, went on to inspire a movement from which The Third Hour grew.[37] While the focus of the Catholic Worker movement centered on social justice and nonviolence, the purpose of The Third Hour group was to encourage peace between all Christian churches, from Catholic and Orthodox to Lutheran and Anglican and Protestant.[38]

O'Connor became aware of Iswolsky through Erik Langkjaer (see entry). After his first visit to Andalusia in 1953, during which he talked about both Day and his "aunt" (actually, Iswolsky was a family friend), O'Connor took out a subscription to the *Catholic Worker* and ordered back issues of *Third Hour*.[39]

Miss Edith Ivey
23 E. 10th St., NYC 3
119 E. 29th St., #606, NYC 16

Edith Ivey (1911–1970) was born in Milledgeville and returned to the town later in life. In between, she lived in Manhattan as early as 1935 and is listed in the 1940 census as an advertising executive.[40] In 1950, still in advertising, she lived in Atlanta.[41] Later that decade, she introduced O'Connor to poet and novelist James Dickey, also in advertising.[42]

Ivey came to Milledgeville for an extended visit in 1962, dealing with some personal strife and grief. By year's end, she had resettled in Manhattan and wrote to let the O'Connors know; Flannery responded that they were "much cheered" to hear from her.[43] In 1963, at the end of a long, chatty letter about art, Catholicism, and life in New York, Ivey thanked O'Connor for her (and Regina's) warmth and kindness during a difficult time.[44]

She died at the age of fifty-nine after a long illness.[45] Like O'Connor, she is buried in Memory Hill Cemetery in Milledgeville.[46]

Herb Jaffe Associates
145 E. 49th St., NYC 22

Brooklyn-born Herb Jaffe (1921–1991) formed his literary agency in 1957 after working in the film industry, first as a freelance press and talent agent for MCA and then moving on to the studio's television division. In time, he sold his agency and returned to film, eventually heading United Artists worldwide production department. When he was in that position, the studio released such game-changing films as *Midnight Cowboy* and *Last Tango in Paris*. He went on to work as an independent producer on the memorable *Lion in Winter* and on other films.[47]

O'Connor's link to this agency was secretary-turned-agent Candida Donadio (see entry). She lists the agency under Donadio's name.

Robert Jiras
32 E. 35th St.
306 E. 18th St.
50 Riverside Dr.

Robert Jiras (1922–2000) had wanted to be an actor, but a prominent stutter made that unlikely.[48] Instead, he got his start in show business in makeup, working on such films as *A Face in the Crowd* (1957), *Splendor in the Grass* (1961), *Bonnie and Clyde* (1967), and *Shampoo* (1975), and developing the first makeup department for CBS.[49]

Interested in turning O'Connor's stories into film, he contacted agent Elizabeth McKee (see entry), who told him O'Connor would not grant permission. Undeterred, he called O'Connor and set up an appointment to meet with her on August 26, 1956, explaining he wanted to make a film based on "The River."[50] He drove to Milledgeville and O'Connor, who liked him, gave him the green light, even though McKee was against it and Jiras had never made a film before.[51] He pieced together three stories, including "The River," and created a script that no one was interested in filming.[52]

In 1958, at Caroline Gordon's suggestion, Sue Jenkins Brown (see) indicated an interest in turning "The River" into a play. O'Connor stated the story was already being considered for a movie and added that if he (Jiras) came through with a script, she would want to be involved to keep him from sentimentalizing the story.[53]

He is best known for co-producing the landmark *Boys in the Band* (1970) and writing, producing, and directing *I am the Cheese* (1983). He taught at Dartmouth and Boston University.[54]

(Another film version of "The River," written and directed by Barbara Noble, was released in 1978.)

Carol Johnson
225 W. 80th St., #3W, NYC 24

Carol Johnson (1928–2015) is the rare example of a correspondent O'Connor approached first with a fan letter rather than the other way around. To read about her, see Chapter 7.

Jubilee
168 E. 91st St., NYC 28
377 Park Ave. S, NYC 16

   Jubilee: A Magazine of the Church and Her People was the Catholic answer to *Life* in its day. Published from 1953 to 1967, the magazine was founded by Ed Rice and co-edited by Robert Lax and Thomas Merton. It featured black-and-white photography, art, literature, journalism, and spiritual writing.[55]

   A review by Richard Gilman (see entry) of *A Good Man Is Hard to Find* appeared in the magazine. An interview with O'Connor by C. Ross Mullins was published in the magazine in 1963. After O'Connor's death, Merton wrote a tribute.

   Today, the location is part of St. John's University Manhattan Campus.

Mrs. Krystyn Jurasz-Damska, I.I.E. (*sic*)
667 Madison Ave.

   Author and translator Krystyna Jurasz-Dambska (1921–2000) was a Fullbright Exchange scholar who lived for several months in the United States.[56]

   Among those authors whose books Jurasz-Dambska translated are William Saroyen, Thomas Hardy, and Arthur Conan Doyle.[57]

   I.I.E. stands for the Institute of International Education, which was formed after World War I to promote peace.[58] O'Connor's address book includes her Warsaw address as well.

King Features Syndicate
235 E. 45th St., NYC 17

   Getting its start in 1915, King Features Syndicate changed the flavor of daily papers forever by distributing comics and editorial cartoons, puzzles and games, and columns to participating newspapers. It was founded by William Randolph Hurst, who, in searching for a distinctive name for the operation, found inspiration in the name of Moses Koenigsberg, the man he had sent on a four-year assessment tour of the nation's newspapers and the syndicate's first manager. ("Koenig" is the German word for "king.")[59]

   O'Connor lists King Features under her friend George Haslam's name (see entry).

Mrs. Colquitt Koepp
141–143 E. 37th St., NYC 16 / MU 4-8351

   This is the address of the Colquitt Girls' Club (see entry), which is listed under her entry.

Surprisingly, there is a Milledgeville connection here. Elizabeth Colquitt Newell Koepp (1887–1987) was a descendent of Isaac Newell, one of the first residents of the town that was then the capital of Georgia.[60] Her grandfather was General Alfred Colquitt, who served both as governor and state senator, and her father, Captain Tom Newell, was mayor of the town during the Reconstruction. The Newell-Watts House is included in the tour of historic Milledgeville homes and is right around the corner from the Cline mansion, where O'Connor spent her adolescence.

Koepp, a teacher, received her Bachelor's degree from the University of Missouri and her Master's degree from Wisconsin University, where she met her future husband. She married William P. Koepp in 1916.

Colquitt Koepp, like O'Connor, is buried in Memory Hill Cemetery in Milledgeville.

Erik Langkjaer
1 University Pl., NYC 3

Langkjaer (1926–2016), the son of a Danish father (a diplomat and attorney) and a Russian mother (a Vassar graduate who, as a child, had lived as an aristocrat in pre-revolution St. Petersburg), was born in Shanghai.[61] After several years in Copenhagen, his parents divorced, and his mother moved to New York. Erik occasionally saw her until World War II cut international travel, putting an ocean between them; he didn't see her for six years. In 1945, he moved to New York to be with his mother. After graduating from Princeton in 1948, he taught and studied at Fordham University before moving into the publishing trade.[62]

Langkjaer was a traveling textbook salesman for Harcourt, Brace (see entry) when he met O'Connor in 1953. Soon, he was driving out of his way to spend weekends in Milledgeville. Sensing O'Connor was in love with him, he recognized that he did not return the feeling. What's more, he understood O'Connor would be an invalid wife, and he was not up to the task. Finally, he was not interested in being considered merely the husband of a famous writer. He left for Denmark soon after; the following year, he wrote to say he was engaged.[63] He returned to the United States, wife in tow, a couple of years later, first moving to La Porte, Indiana, where he worked for Harcourt, Brace. By 1957, he had accepted a position with Scribner and thus moved to an apartment in Scarsdale, New York. In an interview, Langkjaer stated he and O'Connor lost touch after 1958.[64]

The University Place apartment listed as his mailing address was the home of his grandfather and his mother, Marguerite Langkjaer, who worked for the United Nations as a hostess for diplomats in the Delegates'

Lounge. In a 1984 interview published in *Vassar Quarterly*, she discussed her extraordinary life: escaping to Japan in 1918, working as a *Harper's Bazaar* fashion editor after her divorce, heading the diplomatic mail department during World War II, and living in a Franciscan monastery with the hope of becoming a nun.[65]

James Laughlin
333 Sixth Ave., NYC 14

Laughlin (1914–1997) started New Directions (see entry) publishing company with money from his father. Laughlin produced the books in his aunt's cottage in Norfolk and eventually moved to New York. He took chances on authors and was always on the lookout for the new and different and, as such, influenced not only literature but also American publishing.[66] As evidence of his influence, Laughlin published the works of Tennessee Williams, William Carlos Williams, Ezra Pound, Djuna Barnes, John Hawkes, and others. In addition, he was Vladimir Nabokov's first American Publisher and published F. Scott Fitzgerald's *The Crack-Up*.[67]

New Directions is mentioned under his listing.

Miss Maryat Lee / Maryat Foulkes-Taylor
192 Sixth Ave. / WO 6-1694

Mary Attaway Lee (1923–1989) was a Kentucky-born, New York playwright O'Connor met in Milledgeville. To read about Lee, see Chapter 7.

Though O'Connor does not mention it in her address books, Lee's stationery lists Apartment 3F as the location.

Frances Lewis
1234 Broadway
308 W. 82nd St / TRafalgar 7-0200

Frances Lewis was a friend from Milledgeville who visited O'Connor in 1952; at the time, O'Connor herself was a visitor, staying for a few weeks with Sally Fitzgerald (see entry: The Fitzgeralds) in Connecticut. In a letter to her mother, O'Connor stated that she needed to recuperate from the visit, as Lewis was "very strenuous."[68]

This is possibly Frances Way Lewis (1928–2003), who lived in Florida for a while (O'Connor's address books list a Tampa address). She, like O'Connor, is buried in Memory Hill Cemetery in Milledgeville.

The Broadway listing is the address of the Milner Hotel (see). The name of the building at West 82nd Street address is the Selkirk.

J. J. Lichtman (dentist)
2112 Broadway / EN 2-2583

Dr. Lichtman was a dentist who practiced in Manhattan. His office was located over Central Savings Bank. The building, built in 1928 in the Italian Renaissance Palazzo style, is now known as the Apple Bank Building.[69]

It is interesting to note that the building was only about twenty years old when O'Connor entered its doors. That is to say, she was older than the building.

Denver Lindley
1185 Park Ave., NYC 28

Denver Lindley (1906–1982) was an editor who had been assigned to O'Connor after Catharine Carver (see entry) resigned, only to leave for Viking Press (see) not long after.

Lindley was O'Connor's third editor at Harcourt, Brace (see) over a five-year period. While he was polite to her, he did not prove enthusiastic about her work. As Robert Giroux (see) pointed out to O'Connor, though he was sure Lindley would serve her well, the editor had never liked her work and had voted against publishing *Wise Blood*.[70]

While Lindley's leaving was a shock, it assured O'Connor that she was no longer obliged to remain with the publisher. She happily signed on with Farrar, Straus & Cudahy (see).

In addition to Harcourt, Brace, Lindley also worked at Collier's, Appleton-Century (see), Henry Holt (see), and then finally Viking Press. While working at Harcourt, Lindley translated Thomas Mann's final novel, *Confessions of Felix Krull, Confidence Man*, published by Alfred A. Knopf (see) in 1955.[71]

J. B. Lippincott Co.
521 Fifth Ave. 17

Now defunct, the publishing house was founded by Joshua Ballinger Lippincott in 1836.

Originally produced by the New American Library (see entry), the magazine *New World Writing* was published by Lippincott from 1960 to its final issue in 1964. O'Connor's "Everything That Rises Must Converge" appeared in Volume 19 in 1961; the story received the O'Henry Award in 1963.

O'Connor lists this publisher under her entry for Stewart Richardson (see), who edited Volume 19.

Mr. & Mrs. Robt. Lowell
29 W. 104th St. / UN 4-8602

O'Connor had been introduced to Robert Lowell in 1947 when he came to Iowa for a poetry reading, but he would not become her friend until the fall of 1948 when both were at Yaddo.

There has been much speculation about O'Connor's feelings for the handsome, charming, and intelligent poet whom she admitted, years down the line, to loving; the comments of Edward Maisel (see entry), Clifford Wright (see), and Alfred Kazin, all of whom witnessed her interactions with Lowell at Yaddo, support the notion that she was more than fond of him.[72] This speculation took artistic form in 2013 with Carlene Bauer's *Frances and Bernard*, a novel based very clearly on the real-life writers; in the book, the novelist and poet meet at a writer's colony and eventually reunite in New York, giving in to romantic feelings.

In real life, O'Connor and Lowell were fellow writers who became better acquainted during Yaddo's "small months," when few guests were on board. With only Lowell, O'Connor, and Wright staying on the grounds over the Christmas holidays, O'Connor had Lowell more or less to herself. That changed when poet Elizabeth Hardwick, who had been at Yaddo in September, returned at Lowell's request.[73] Lowell and Hardwick would marry in July 1949, between his stays at mental facilities.[74]

This address is of the apartment Hardwick moved into while her husband was still receiving care at Payne Whitney Clinic; in time, he joined her.

For more information on Lowell and Yaddo, see the Introduction; for more on Hardwick, see her entry (this chapter).

W. McNeil Lowry
477 Madison Ave., NYC 22

Wilson McNeil Lowry (1913–1993), known to most as "Mac," joined the Ford Foundation (see entry) in 1953; within four years, he had become the director of the arts and humanities programs. In 1964, he was vice president. With Lowry at the helm, the foundation began to make a name as a major supporter of the arts, particularly dance.

O'Connor lists his name under the Ford Foundation listing.

Robie Macauley (c/o Anne Draper)
123 Washington Pl. WAtkins 4-0538

Writer and editor Robie Macauley met O'Connor at the University of Iowa in 1947. He married fiancée Anne Draper (see entry) in June 1948.

While enrolled at Kenyon University, Macauley lived in a house with Robert Lowell (see), Peter Taylor, and Randall Jarrell. Upon graduating, as a special agent in the counterintelligence corps, Macauley helped to liberate several concentration camps; he was assigned the task of interviewing survivors.[75] In addition, he supervised the arrests of Nazis hiding in Japan, for which he was rewarded the Medal of Merit.[76]

He worked as a university professor and, as such, went on to edit *The Kenyon Review* from 1959 to 1966. From there, he went on to the job of fiction editor at *Playboy Magazine*, followed by work as executive editor at Houghton Mifflin.[77]

While four other stories by O'Connor had been published by *Kenyon Review* founding editor John Crowe Ransom, Macauley accepted "The Comforts of Home" in 1960. It proved to be the last piece O'Connor would submit to the journal, having taken offense at a cartoon image of a nude woman that appeared with her story.[78]

Macmillan Co.
60 Fifth Ave., NYC 11
The company that got its start in London in 1843 came to New York in 1869. Until 2019, most of Macmillan's publishers—such as Farrar, Straus & Giroux (see entry), and Henry Holt & Co. (see)—were located down the street in the iconic Flatiron Building.

Mlle
122 E. 42nd St.
In the brown book, the first address she listed (and then crossed out) under editor George Davis's (see entry) name was that of MLLE, the abbreviation for *Mademoiselle*.

The magazine published "The Capture" in its November 1948 issue. (Its original title is "The Turkey.") O'Connor submitted it in 1947, right after "The Train" was rejected with very thoughtful feedback.[79] In both cases, the correspondence "Mr." O'Connor received was not from Davis but rather from Margarita G. Smith, sister of Carson McCullers.[80]

In a letter to Betty Hester, O'Connor mentions she had once visited the magazine's office, and it was filled with bespectacled girls wearing peasant skirts and ballet flats.[81]

The Margaret Louisa
14 E. 16th St. / Algonquin 4-3340
In 1889, Margaret Louisa Vanderbilt Shepard (1845–1924) donated the funds necessary to build the Margaret Louisa Home for Protestant Women,

a homey YWCA residence set up as a response to the growing problem of lodging for the increasing numbers of women entering the workforce.

The Margaret Louisa was not run as a charity. Shepard allowed self-supporting Protestant women (those who met with her approval, that is) to stay four weeks, with an extra five days thrown in as a cushion. The hotel restaurant, however, was open to all women, regardless of religion.[82] By 1911, the four-week limit was disregarded, and in 1915, the Protestant requirement was lifted.[83]

Martha Washington Hotel
30 E. 30th St., NYC 16

Located in the neighborhood now known as NoMad (because it is north of Madison Square Park), the Martha Washington was the first New York City hotel to be established as a place of lodging exclusively for professional women. Construction on the Women's Hotel, as it was first known, was complete by 1903. In 1907, it was home to the Interurban Women's Suffrage Council.

It was known as the Martha Washington from 1920 to 1998. After a few name changes, it was renamed the Redbury New York Hotel in 2016.[84]

O'Connor's friend Charlye Wiggins (see entry) lived there for a time.

Miss Alice Ellen Mayhew
77 Charles St., NYC 14

In O'Connor's lifetime, Alice Mayhew (1932–2020) was a regular *Commonweal* contributor. O'Connor met Mayhew through her brother, Fr. Leonard F. X. Mayhew, another regular contributor to the magazine who was recognized for his translations of French sociologist Alain Touraine's writing. O'Connor mentions him a few times in *The Habit of Being*, particularly for his work with the Catholic *Georgia Bulletin*, which frequently published her book reviews.[85]

Both Mayhews were, as O'Connor noted, native New Yorkers.[86]

After O'Connor's lifetime, Alice became vice president and editorial director for Simon & Schuster. She was known for the authors she worked with (among them, historian Walter Isaacson, former president Jimmy Carter, and Supreme Court Justice Ruth Bader Ginsberg), but made her breakthrough as editor of the groundbreaking *All the President's Men*.[87]

Leonard, who wrote of O'Connor's death in *Commonweal*, was removed from ministry in 1966 and laicized in 1968. Six years after his 2012 death, his name was added to the Archdiocese's list of those publicly accused of child sexual abuse. Later, he was named in a report by the Prosecuting Attorneys' Council of Georgia.[88]

Murray McCain
311 E. 71st St., NYC 21
11 ½ W. 26th St.
257 Fourth Ave. NYC 10

Murray McCain was an editor and a writer. He is best known as the writer behind the children's picture books that explore the magic of words and reading: *Books!* (1962, and the *New York Times* Book of the Year) and *Writing!* (1964) were both illustrated by John Alcorn. *The Boy Who Walked Off the Page*, with Alvin Smith, came out in 1969.

O'Connor includes the address for Criterion Books (see entry) in one of the entries. McCain worked at the small publisher as a senior editor and was described by writer (and O'Connor correspondent) Richard Stern as "smart, energetic, gentle, and courteous."[89]

The Fourth Avenue address is the location of Criterion Books.

Vivian McCleod (*sic*)
22 E. 22nd St.

New York–born Vivienne C. Koch MacLeod Day (1912–1961) was a writer O'Connor met at Yaddo. To read more about her, see Chapter 7.

David McDowell
219 E. 61st St., NYC 21

McDowell (1918–1985) was an editor who, after working at New Directions (see entry) and Random House, started McDowell, Obolensky publishing firm (see) in 1957. He was both president and editor-in-chief. Although he did not publish O'Connor's work, he did correspond with her, sending books as requested.

McDowell was the editor of O'Connor's good friend Brainard Cheney. At one point, after McDowell resigned from the company he had started, Cheney and O'Connor exchanged a few letters in which Cheney indicated not only concern for what would become of his second novel (which he had given to McDowell to consider) but also worry about McDowell's future in the publishing industry, even going so far as to ask O'Connor to put in a good word with her editor, Robert Giroux (see).[90] Soon enough, McDowell became fiction editor at Curtis Publishing Co. and asked O'Connor to send short stories to be considered for the company's magazines.[91]

Those requests were not made personally to O'Connor but rather through Cheney. As O'Connor states (several times) in a letter to her friend, one in which she says she wrote to Giroux as requested, she never met McDowell.[92]

McDowell, Obolensky Inc.
219 E. 61st St., NYC 21

The publisher was established in 1957 by David McDowell (see entry) and Ivan Obolensky (who would continue the firm under his own name after his partner's departure three years later). While they didn't publish O'Connor's work, they did print the works of O'Connor's Iowa mentor Andrew Lytle and friends Robie Macauley (see) and Brainard Cheney.

McDowell, Obolensky produced William F. Buckley Jr.'s *Up from Liberalism*, his 1959 attack on American liberalism. Some thought that the decision to publish the conservative work was at least partially to blame for David McDowell's inability to find a job.[93]

O'Connor lists the firm under McDowell's listing.

McGraw Hill
330 W. 42nd St., NYC 36

McGraw Hill started in 1917 when James H. McGraw and John A. Hill merged their companies to form a publishing house. In 1930, the publishers entered the trade book field; today, the company is recognized as one of the top educational publishers.[94]

The McGraw Hill Building was completed in 1932, the same year as the Empire State Building, and featured that year in the Museum of Modern Art's *Modern Architecture: International Exhibition*. The publisher remained at 330 West 42nd Street until 1972. In 1989, the distinctive art deco building was declared a national historic landmark.[95]

M. McIntosh
30 E. 60th St. / PLaza 9-2225

Mavis McIntosh Riordan (1903–1986) was an agent who represented John Steinbeck, Hiram Haydn (see entry), Edna O'Brien, John Gardner, and Robert Coover. Because she worked with O'Connor's agent, Elizabeth McKee (see), McIntosh also occasionally worked with O'Connor, who once described her as an old lady who sat at her desk, wearing her hat.[96]

Because Robert Giroux (see) knew McIntosh, he would contact her over matters regarding O'Connor for the first six years of his professional relationship with the young writer.[97] O'Connor's only recorded mention of McIntosh in the address books, however, is one which includes McKee.

Both McIntosh and her husband, a mathematician, followed the teachings of Georges Ivanovich Gurdjieff (1866–1949), a philosopher, mystic, and composer from the Caucasus who founded the Fourth Way movement.[98]

Elizabeth McKee
30 E. 60th St. / PLaza 9-2225
45 Christopher St. / CHelsea 2-3015

O'Connor first wrote to Elizabeth McKee Purdy (1911–1997) in 1948, saying she had been recommended by mutual acquaintance Paul Moor.[99] McKee became O'Connor's first and only literary agent and a good friend.

McKee was formerly an editor at *Atlantic Monthly*. As an agent, she represented a list of writers that included William Styron, John Irving, and Charles Webb (it was McKee who sold *The Graduate* to Hollywood).[100] After O'Connor died, McKee continued to represent the writer until her own death thirty-three years later.

Arthur Axelman, whom McKee also represented, described her as a "no-nonsense, principled and hard-working woman who . . . was, if nothing else, candid."[101]

O'Connor lists McKee in four of the five address books. In the small black, however, she does not list contact information but, at the very, very top of a page dedicated to *M* entries, notes that McKee is her agent and that her married name is Mrs. Ted Purdy (see entry). As the last name gets lost in the design of the page, she repeats *Purdy* in large, round letters.

The Christopher Street address was McKee's home address at the time of O'Connor coming to Manhattan in 1949.

McKee & Batchelder
624 Madison Ave., NYC 22

When O'Connor wrote to Elizabeth McKee (see entry) to ask if she would represent her, she sent her letter to the office of McKee & Batchelder. Soon, McKee joined Mavis McIntosh (see) and Elizabeth Otis at McIntosh & Otis at their office on East 60th.[102] The firm later became McIntosh, McKee & Dodds and was acquired by Harold Matson Company in 1965.[103]

Mrs. Neil McKenzie
18 W. 8th St., NYC 11

Miriam Tanzer McKenzie (1923–2015?) and O'Connor were published in *New World Writing* in 1961. Their stories, "Déjà vu" and "Everything That Rises Must Converge," respectively, would be featured in the 1962 *Best American Short Stories*. McKenzie's was named a finalist in the 1962 O. Henry competition. O'Connor's won first place the following year.

"Déjà vu" was McKenzie's first published story.[104]

Evidently, O'Connor reached out to Miriam (a name she mentions at the very end of the listing) with a kind word about her story. In 1963, McKenzie sent O'Connor a "much delayed thank you for your very nice note."[105]

McKenzie was married to playwright Neil McKenzie (1916–2004).

Ed Meisel (sic)
301 E. 38th St.

O'Connor met writer Edward Maisel (1917–2008) at Yaddo. For more, see Chapter 7.

Miss Phyllis Meras
425 Riverside Dr.

Phyllis Meras (b.1931) is a writer who is likely the last to interview O'Connor. To read about her, see Chapter 7.

Milner Hotel
1234 Broadway (c - 38th)

Though O'Connor indicates that this building is at the corner of 38th, it is actually located at the corner of 31st.

The hotel, built in 1868, was originally known as the Grand Hotel and was meant to accommodate families who, with no kitchens in the suites, would eat in the dining room. By 1948, the hotel (and the area itself) had a bit of a fleabag reputation, charging one dollar or so for a night's stay.[106]

O'Conner mentions the hotel as part of friend Frances Lewis's listing.

Edgar Moran
230 E. 50th St.

Musician Charles Edgar Moran (1892–1972), like O'Connor, was from Milledgeville. To read about him, see Chapter 7.

Miss Alice S. Morris
572 Madison Ave., NYC 22

Alice S. Morris (1903–1993) was the *Harper's Bazaar* (see entry) fiction editor from 1951–1968 and, as such, accepted O'Connor's "A Late Encounter with the Enemy," "Good Country People," and "The Enduring Chill" for publication. O'Connor asked that an advance copy of *A Good Man Is Hard to Find* be sent to Morris.[107]

O'Connor notes that this is the address of *Harper's Bazaar*, and also mentions Harvey Breit (1909–1968), as he was Morris's ex-husband. A poet and a reviewer for the *New York Times Book Review*, he featured O'Connor on the first episode of his new NBC show *Galley Proof* in 1955. This was O'Connor's only television appearance.

Miss Anne Brooks Murray
135 W. 13th St., NYC 11

Anne Brooks Murray was Robert Giroux's (see entry) administrative assistant at Farrar, Straus & Cudahy (see) and, as such, corresponded with O'Connor on occasion. It was Murray, who, in 1958, met O'Connor and her mother at Idlewild airport in a limousine to drive them back to the hotel when they arrived in New York for a brief stay.[108]

She once added a personal touch in her correspondence with O'Connor by including a packet of mint seeds.[109]

Nation
333 Sixth Ave., NYC 14

The magazine was founded by abolitionists in 1865 and has long championed independent journalism. In 1953, *The Nation* moved to this address, a building known as The Little Flatiron for its resemblance to the landmark structure.

O'Connor includes the name of film critic Robert Hatch (see entry) here (see Figure 9).

New American Library
501 Madison Ave., NYC 22

Under the guidance of editor Arabel Porter (see entry), New American Library's Mentor Books imprint published the biannual anthology *New World Writing* from 1952 to 1959. O'Connor's "Enoch and the Gorilla" (rewritten as Chapter 11 of *Wise Blood*) appeared in the debut edition; "You Can't Be Any Poorer Than Dead" (rewritten as Chapter 1 of *The Violent Bear It Away*) was published in Volume 8 in 1955.

New American, under its Signet imprint, published second editions of O'Connor's books. In addition, it published the first edition of *Three by Flannery O'Connor*.

New American Library was founded in 1948.

"Aarabel" Porter's name is added at the end.

New Directions Publishing Co.
333 Sixth Ave., NYC 14

While still a student at Harvard, James Laughlin (see entry) founded New Directions publishing company in 1936 after spending several months studying with Ezra Pound.[110] Known at first for its early series of anthologies, New Directions published books that have become classics, such as Henry Miller's *The Air-Conditioned Nightmare* (1945), Herman Hesse's *Siddhartha* (1951), Lawrence Ferlinghetti's *A Coney Island of the Mind* (1958), and Ezra Pound's *The Cantos* (1970).

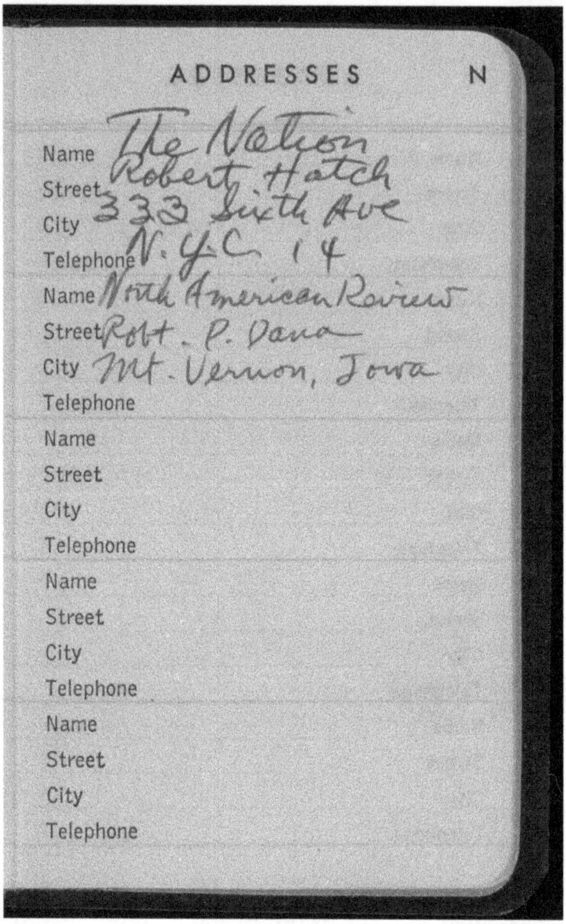

FIGURE 9: From the small black address book. (Used with permission from Flannery O'Connor Papers, Stuart A. Rose Manuscript, Archives, and Rare Book Library, Emory University.)

Like *The Nation* (see), New Directions' office was located in a building called The Little Flatiron (for its resemblance to the iconic building).

The company is listed under Laughlin's entry.

New Weston Hotel
49th & Madison

In 1955, O'Connor traveled to New York to promote the release of her second book.

Originally booked to stay in the Woodstock (see entry), O'Connor asked her editor, Catharine Carver (see), if she could stay closer to Grand Central Station, explaining that her physician thought long walks, the kind Manhattan is known for, would be detrimental. She had just weaned herself from the cane (this was before she had to rely on crutches). Carver responded by booking a room at the New Weston, a place she felt would be nicer, not to mention quieter. It also boasted a couple of lobbies that would come in handy when O'Connor wanted to meet with people.[111]

New York Hospital
525 E. 68th St., NYC 21

The site is now the location of New York–Presbyterian/Weill Cornell Medical Center. O'Connor includes the hospital as the residence in Lyman Fulton's listing (see entry).

9 / Three Correspondents

Any public figure will attract letters from unknown others who want to share praise, give criticism, or even reach out because of a particular attachment they may feel. O'Connor was no stranger to such attention and was known, on occasion, to welcome further, and sometimes regular, contact.

Among such correspondents, three with Manhattan addresses stand out: Crandell Price, Beverly Brunson, and Fred Darsey. That they are all writers is a trait they share, but what is more striking is that all three are, as the saying goes, square pegs in a round-hole world.

One could say the same was true of the writer they admired.

What follows is an explanation of who these interested and interesting individuals were and an exploration of their known correspondence with O'Connor.

Crandell Price

The son of the town's fire chief, Crandell Price (1909–1969) was born Richard Joseph Price in Flint, Michigan. Early on, his life was marked by dramatic occurrences that possibly influenced his literary tastes and perhaps led him to write. In 1912, his mother, Donna Crandell Price, died when her son was three years old. She succumbed to Pott's Disease, a tuberculosis of the spine, from which she had suffered for eight years (a period that included both pregnancy and the act of giving birth).[1]

A couple of years later, his father, Edward Henry Price, was at lunch when a fire erupted. George D. Hanna, the city's first electrical inspector and a part-time firefighter, filled in. Upon arriving at the fire, Hanna's legs became tangled in the hose, and he was accidentally run over by the fire truck. His chest was crushed, and he died from his injuries an hour later.[2]

In 1918, Chief Price married widow Nellie Hanna. Her son and daughter joined Richard in the new blended family.[3] That new stepsister, Wave, recalled many years later how Price "loved to write poems and make up fancy names for himself."[4]

It was an indication of what was to come.

Price grew up and, in 1932, was listed in the Flint telephone directory as a clerk. Two years later, his position was that of timekeeper, an old-fashioned job for which there are a couple of different possible definitions. Regardless, he resided still in his family's large wooden house. But then, in 1936, Chief Price died at the age of sixty-nine, and Price moved to New York. The new location might not have been all that arbitrary; Chief Price, the son of Irish immigrants, had been born there.[5]

A NEW LIFE IN NEW YORK

In 1940, Richard Price lived in Greenwich Village and described himself as an author on the federal census.[6] Later that year, he registered for the draft under the name Richard du Calm Price.[7] As Richard Price in the 1950 census, he defined his occupation as a secretary for a writer's estate, which perhaps could have been a vague way of saying he was a writer. He stated he was otherwise not employed but was looking.[8]

In later years, Price legally changed his first name from Richard to Crandell, his mother's surname.[9]

THE CORRESPONDENCE

There are two letters in the Emory archive from Price, but there were likely others written. The letters are undated, unless one counts "St. Cecilia's Day" (November 22) as a date. However, there are some clues, perhaps, as to the year they were written. In the first letter, he asked when the novel *You Can't Be Any Poorer Than Dead* (actually, *The Violent Bear It Away*) was to be published and mentioned having enjoyed the excerpt that appeared in *New World Writing*, which came out in October 1955. Also, he refers to the review in *The Commonweal* that stated (erroneously) that O'Connor, despite having two Irish names, was a convert to Catholicism.[10]

His letters are chatty and intelligent. He tells O'Connor that he picked up *Wise Blood* because Caroline Gordon, O'Connor's friend and mentor, had recommended it. *Wise Blood* was, he said, the best book he'd read since *Nightwood* by Djuna Barnes. (This comment is all the more interesting because O'Connor had recently, in a letter to Betty Hester about the writers whose work she had read, categorized Barnes as a nut.)[11] Price also deemed *Wise Blood* the best book to have come out of the South since Frances Newman's 1926 *Hard-Boiled Virgin*.[12] Not surprisingly, upon learning that O'Connor had not read the book, Price indicated (in the second letter) that he would send her a pristine copy he had recently stumbled upon.[13]

Perhaps O'Connor had meant that she had not read *HBV* (as he referred to it) all the way through. In January 1956, she told Betty Hester that she had read fifty pages of the copy *she* had sent her.[14]

O'Connor listed one address for Price in the black Elite that is repeated in the red book. In the red, she scratched out that address in favor of another one and then, in the same blue ballpoint ink, added "NY State Dept. of Law / 80 Centre / NYC 13." (See Figure 10.)

One might assume that that address was a work address. However, as distant relative Susan Bridges points out, as Price had legally changed his name, he might have been sharing information about how and where he achieved this.[15]

Price told O'Connor, jokingly, that he had severed "till purgatory" family ties by becoming both Catholic and a Democrat.[16] Still, the "severance" did not keep him from coming home one last time. After Price died in 1960, Sunset Hills Cemetery in Flint was notified that his body was coming its way. Price's nephew, George D. Hanna III of Lansing, Michigan, followed his uncle's coffin from the train station to the cemetery. Price was laid to rest in an unmarked grave next to his father.[17]

Beverly Brunson

Beverly Elizabeth Brunson (1928–2000) hailed from Joplin, Missouri—a fact she disclosed to O'Connor in what she called her first fan letter. She had just finished reading "A Good Man Is Hard to Find" in *The Avon Book of Modern Writing*, and with her bosses at the American Culinary Federation involved in a conference, she said she could pretty much do as she pleased.

She had so much she wanted to say. For example, John Wesley reminded her of John Henry from Carson McCullers' *A Member of the Wedding*. And The Misfit reminded her of one of her own characters from a book she was writing, based on her hometown. And was the crime described in O'Connor's story based on the real-life Billy Cook crimes that took place just down the street from where Brunson herself grew up?

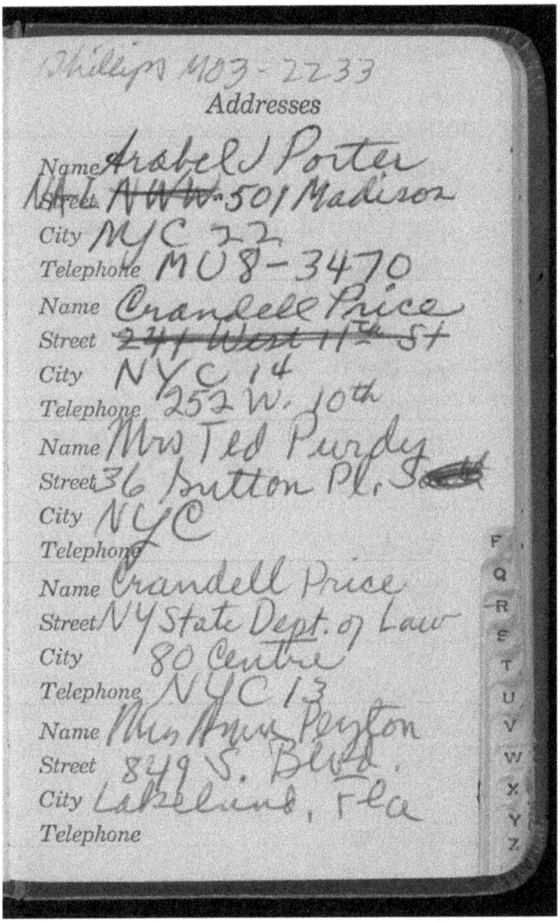

FIGURE 10: From the red address book. (Used with permission from Flannery O'Connor Papers, Stuart A. Rose Manuscript, Archives, and Rare Book Library, Emory University.)

She had bought a copy of *Wise Blood*, she continued, but had given it away before she read it. But now, of course, having read O'Connor's story, she was going to ask for the book back. And, by the way, O'Connor's work really had much in common with the novel she wanted to write.[18]

O'Connor replied cordially (no, there was no connection between John Wesley and John Henry and, no, she had never heard of Billy Cook but she hoped he was as polite as The Misfit), and a correspondence was born.[19] In a letter to Sally and Robert Fitzgerald early in 1954, she indicated that

Brunson, whom she referred to simply as the Secretary of *The Culinary Review,* had in a four-month period sent her five letters and a sonnet.[20]

O'CONNOR AND BRUNSON

Though the two letters Sally Fitzgerald chose to present in *Collected Works* (there are none in *Habit of Being*) might suggest O'Connor was dismissive of Brunson's thoughts, reading all of O'Connor's letters to her suggests otherwise. A couple of months into their correspondence, she told Brunson that she enjoyed her letters.[21] She sent off for the issue of *Epoch* featuring Brunson's poetry.[22] When Brunson complained that she believed O'Connor treated her as a mere reader (even though Brunson herself included voluntary commentary on O'Connor's writing and went so far as to read *Wise Blood* a second time[23]), O'Connor apologized and enclosed a peacock feather.[24] Though (repeatedly) stating she was not a good judge of poems and therefore would not comment on their worth, O'Connor acknowledged their receipt.[25] When she promised to send an advance copy of *A Good Man Is Hard to Find,* she asked that Brunson let her know if her address were to change.[26]

When taken as a whole, the letters from both Brunson and O'Connor feel less like a conversation than a series of questions and comments from one followed by responses from the other. By 1955, O'Connor was not always kind. In one letter, she said that, compared to her troubled protagonist Hazel Motes, Brunson was not nearly as enlightened.[27] By March, she said that as much as Brunson spoke of rebelling, she could not fathom what Brunson was rebelling against and doubted that Brunson herself knew.[28] In the same letter, O'Connor questioned her understanding of Kierkegaard and stated that Brunson's perception of God seemed to be of the Midwestern Protestant variety, "which of course is enough to make everybody vomit but them and Roy Roger's horse."[29]

THE GOOD WRITER WAS HARD TO FIND

Initially, there had been some talk of meeting during O'Connor's upcoming June 1955 trip to New York, staying at the Woodstock for a couple of days to publicize *A Good Man Is Hard to Find.* Such a gathering never occurred, however, and Brunson's letter to O'Connor after the fact makes it evident that O'Connor did not update Brunson when her itinerary changed. In mid-June, Brunson wrote pointedly to say that she was unsure whether the writer was still in New York (she wasn't; she had been home for about two weeks).[30] Brunson said she had called the Woodstock several times to the point of feeling she was harassing the switchboard operator (O'Connor's editor had changed the reservation to the New Weston days before the trip).[31] Because O'Connor had not shared the date and time of her televised appearance, Brunson missed seeing *Galley Proof*, this despite, as she said, it was as though all of New York had been celebrating Flannery O'Connor Week, and she had been prepared for the writer to walk through the door of her workplace at any time.[32]

The rest of the letter reads like an apology and, ultimately, a farewell:

WHAT I have learned from you will never know. From your stories I mean.

Aw, Flannery, Haw Haw.

Beverly[33]

Even though they did not get together in New York, or maybe because they did not, O'Connor wrote to her agent Elizabeth McKee later that year to say she had recommended her services to Brunson, a writer she admitted to never having met.[34] Perhaps McKee, or O'Connor herself, was instrumental in Brunson's work appearing in *New World Writing* the following year. Whatever the case, the correspondence between O'Connor and Brunson continued through at least 1956, with the New Yorker sending clippings from gossip columns about Gene Kelly's upcoming appearance in Schlitz Playhouse's televised presentation of "The Life You Save May Be Your Own."[35]

It is interesting to consider that O'Connor's responses to Brunson's letters on the topic of same-sex love perhaps foretell an attitude that would become clear in the near future, specifically when she became close friends with two lesbians: Betty Hester, who first wrote to O'Connor in July 1955, and Maryat Lee, whom O'Connor met in December 1956. The topic was introduced when Brunson suggested there were Sapphic undertones in "A Temple of the Holy Ghost." O'Connor, who dismissed the interpretation as well off the mark, stated she considered lesbianism much as she considered other acts of (and here she reaches for a biblical term) uncleanness.[36] Later, when O'Connor somewhat apologizes for her attitude in the previous letter, she stated she was not casting judgment on Brunson and felt she didn't have the right to.[37]

THE KENNEDY ASSASSINATION CONSPIRACY

In time, Brunson would move back to Baxter Springs, Kansas, where her father, LeRoy Brunson, had become mayor in 1954.[38]

In the 1960s, the details of President John F. Kennedy's assassination drew her attention. Brunson pored over the twenty-six volumes of the Warren Commission report and noticed many inconsistencies between film footage, photographs, and eyewitness accounts of the horrific event.[39] Her research spanned from 1966 to 1968.[40]

Her noticing of discrepancies was itself noticed. In 1967, Brunson drove to nearby Joplin to discuss the subject with a woman she had not yet met, presumably to discuss assassination details. The evening ended with Brunson coming out of a blackout in her car, five police officers telling her she was drunk and had caused an accident. When examined by a physician, it was determined she was not drunk and thus was not charged.[41] She saw the incident as a warning, and her intensive research soon came to a halt. Decades later, her work would be lauded by assassination conspiracy theorists.[42]

Brunson spent the rest of her life quietly with her parents and her companion, Mary Gibson.[43] Outliving them all, Brunson died in 2000.

Fred Darsey

Frederick Freeman Darsey (1922–1980), otherwise known as Fred, was a Sunny Side, Georgia, native who first wrote to O'Connor in 1955. He was already a World War II veteran when he graduated with a degree in journalism from the University of Georgia.[44] He published the *Spalding County Times* from 1950 to 1952.[45]

Darsey first wrote to O'Connor in January 1955, admitting that he was currently a resident of Central State Hospital (CSH), the infamous mental institution on the outskirts of Milledgeville. O'Connor responded to his mail, telling him that reading his letter gave her both "pleasure and pain."[46] She spoke about writing, asked which fiction writers he liked to read, and a correspondence was born. Their letters discussed his writing (usually her giving him advice), her writing (her announcing a publication), and birds, a shared passion.

He told her that he could identify a killdeer by sound alone.[47]

Their correspondence was briefly interrupted when Darsey eloped—a term used to indicate that a patient had escaped the facility. Soon enough, though, he wrote to her from New York City. He was thrilled to know that O'Connor would soon be in town.[48]

With the help of her editor, Catharine Carver, O'Connor arranged to meet with him during her 1955 visit to promote her book.[49] (To read about O'Connor's and Darsey's meeting, see Chapter 3.) It is interesting that, although O'Connor tended to mention every person she saw or spoke to in the letters written to her mother during the trip, she did not allude to her time with Darsey, spent sitting on a park bench in the summer sun. Even more secretive, she does not include his first name in her address book, only his first initial.

Perhaps coincidentally, it was not long after starting the correspondence that she wrote "Good Country People," which indicated her recognition that any hope for romance with Erik Langkjaer was fruitless.

There were a few letters between them that summer, and at Christmas, O'Connor thanked him for the gift of a small box intended for her pills and vitamins.[50] As time passed, there were fewer letters. O'Connor would write to recommend or send a book about the craft of fiction. She would offer advice on his writing or give tips on how to mail his short stories to editors (for example, putting cardboard in the envelope to prevent dog-earing).[51] But the rush that had accompanied the first letters had passed.

AN UNEASY LIFE

Though O'Connor did advise him as a fiction writer, he established himself professionally in New York after his time (or, one might say, despite his time) in CSH. In 1956, he worked for a New York public relations agency.[52] In 1958, he was in charge of non-fashion publicity for Lane Bryant and, as such, was associated with the local chapter of the Chubby Club. A press release issued that summer, which promoted a Department of Parks story hour, noted that his services (as a reader) had been arranged by a baroness associated with the Danish American Women's Association and that he was not only a newspaper writer but also a former church camp advisor.[53]

His letters to O'Connor fell from 1958 until the summer of the following year, but there was more to his disappearance than work obligations or a lack of interest. Darsey admitted, in his unpublished article about O'Connor's letters to him, to depression caused by "the terrifying experience of what had happened to (him) in Georgia."[54] In 1959, he wrote to tell her he had started seeing an analyst.[55]

O'Connor's response to his 1955 admission of being at CSH had been warm and supportive. Her response to this disclosure was brief, and tellingly so, offering only a few sentences rather than a few paragraphs.[56] (Also of interest is that, when she states that she had been wondering about him, she uses the Regina-inclusive "we." As Sally Fitzgerald points out in her essay about O'Connor's relationships, she conducted the same kind of distancing shift with Langkjaer after learning of his engagement.)[57] O'Connor responded that an analyst must be expensive. Rather than offering more on the subject, she mentioned her thirty peafowl, her finished novel, and the fact that New York was too far away to visit.[58]

When Darsey sent her clippings the following year, her response was more relaxed, taking on the chatty tone of earlier letters.[59] But another stretch of silence followed, ending in 1962 when Darsey wrote of his recent marriage. Beyond her brief, handwritten congratulatory note, there were no more letters from O'Connor to Darsey after that.[60] She did not include him in her final address book.

AFTER O'CONNOR

In an unpublished article comprising her letters to him, he noted that his son was born in 1963, and with O'Connor dying in 1964, he wished he had kept up both their correspondence and his own writing.[61]

Though there was interest from Gordon Lish of *Esquire*, the article remained unpublished because Darsey could not secure permission to use O'Connor's letters.[62] In another bit of bad luck, he did not have copies of his own letters to add to the article. While O'Connor had agreed to keep copies of his correspondence, her mother was unable to find any when Darsey asked her to look. He also asked Sally Fitzgerald and the curator of the Flannery O'Connor Collection at Georgia College. No one could find anything.

Furthermore, he had learned that the copies of O'Connor's letters that he had sent to Farrar, Straus had been mislaid. Fitzgerald said she regretted this misplacement upon reading the letters for the first time soon after the publication of *The Habit of Being*.[63]

This turn of events (or perhaps we should call it a non-turn) seemed just one more disappointment in a life fraught with disappointments and, at times, bad decisions. Some of these decisions led to newspaper coverage. For example, in 1966, when he threw a going-out-of-business sale for the Manhattan gift shop he owned with his wife, the event hit the papers because he did not have a permit for such a sale.[64] Actually, the problem went a little deeper than that. To go out of business, Darsey was required to apply for a license to do so.[65]

The shop, Terra Cotta, was not an ordinary one. In 1964, Darsey had quit his position at an advertising firm to devote time to the East Village pottery and china shop that not only featured handcrafted pieces but also sponsored local artisans. The shop's 1966 closure had been brought about by the effects of a transit strike on sales for two months running. To go out of business, however, Darsey was required to pay a twenty-five-dollar fee and file daily inventories.[66]

When Darsey was served a warrant for not having a permit, he placed a large photocopy of the summons in the store window, which led to a second summons. When asked why he didn't simply pay the fine, he responded that he didn't have the money because he was going out of business.[67] He was placed in the infamous Tombs; when the story of his arrest hit the evening news, a neighbor paid the jail fines and bought him a drink.[68]

That arrest was not the first of Darsey's legal troubles and far from the worst of them. After his divorce trial, Darsey kidnapped his son in the middle of the night, an event that captured local front-page headlines.[69] There was a nationwide alert, and once the child was found (a relative reported his whereabouts), Darsey was not only charged with kidnapping and breaking and entering but also was arrested by the FBI and charged with making harassing phone calls from New York to the judge who had handled the divorce proceedings in another state. The Bureau stated it was likely the first charge of its kind, coming after the recent passage of the Omnibus Crime Control and Safe Streets Act, signed by President Lyndon B. Johnson in 1968.[70] Darsey was convicted of the federal charge and three misdemeanors.[71]

Years later, when Darsey reached out to Fitzgerald, his tone was one of resignation. He told her he knew she must be happy to be working on their mutual friend's biography, but that his own life had gotten in the way of completing either of the two books he had been working on over the years.[72] She promised to include information about his and O'Connor's friendship, as well as parts of O'Connor's letters to him, in that biography.[73]

Fitzgerald died in 2000, before she was able to complete the book. Still, she did mention Darsey, albeit briefly, in a 1998 article about O'Connor's relationships. Fitzgerald wrote of Darsey in a sentence that appeared toward the end of the article, in a section that was not about him but about Maryat Lee, and in a sentence that was as much about Paul Curry Steele as it was about Darsey.

Fitzgerald described him (well, each man) as an erratic individual who had enjoyed O'Connor's support.[74] She mentioned nothing of Darsey's death, but perhaps she didn't know that, in 1980, he had died, the coroner listing the cause as shotgun wounds to the heart and lungs.[75]

Smith Oliver
25 Claremont Ave., Apt. 6-A, NYC 27
    Smith Oliver (1921–1992) was a writer of poetry, short fiction, and drama. To read about him, see Chapter 7.

Irene Orgle (*sic*)
545 West End Ave. / EN 2-6956
    Irene Orgel (1922–2016?) was a writer O'Connor met at Yaddo. To read about her, see Chapter 7.

Ann Orr
151 E. 36ᵗʰ St. / MU 3-9420
    Ann Orr Morris (1924–1987) was a distant relative.[1] A goldsmith, silversmith, and enamelist, she studied her craft both in New York under Adda Husted-Anderson (see entry) and in Europe.
    In 1957, Orr took part in a writing workshop led by O'Connor at the University of Georgia.[2]
    Though Orr was admired for her work, she is remembered by many for an unsettling reason. She, along with her sister and her niece, was murdered in 1987 by a teenager who had killed an elderly couple months before.[3] The murderer, Clinton Bankston, Jr., was sixteen at the time of the murder and pled insanity during his trial. He was sentenced to five consecutive life terms, "his trial and verdict punctuated by his own unsettling laughter."[4] In 2020, the Georgia Supreme Court upheld both the guilty pleas and the sentences.[5]

This was the address of Roberts House, which O'Connor mentions in the entry. It was one of six women's residences founded by the Ladies Christian Union. It closed in 2000.[6]

Paperbook Gallery
90 W. 3rd St., NYC 12

The address would eventually change, but this is the address O'Connor recorded in the black Elite book. O'Connor said she always got prompt service from the shop, noting that when they didn't have a book in stock, they sent her a note to let her know it would arrive later.[7]

Partisan Review
45 Astor Pl.
22 E. 17th St., NYC 3
513 Sixth Ave., NYC 11
30 W. 12th St., NYC 11

Partisan Review was founded in 1934 by William Phillips and Philip Rahv (whom O'Connor lists with the magazine; see entry). It got its start in the New York chapter of the John Reed Club, an American federation of social organizations for Marxist intellectuals, writers, and artists. But by the end of the 1930s, there had been a bit of a political climate change in this country, and the magazine found its true voice. By then, to identify with *Partisan Review* was to "oppose the defenders of the Moscow trials and to deplore Stalin's cynical pact with Hitler," not to mention denounce the corruption of art in the name of propaganda.[8]

The last issue was published in 2003.

Partisan Review first published O'Connor's work in 1949 with "The Peeler" and "The Heart of the Park," both chapters of the upcoming *Wise Blood*. O'Connor, excited to learn of the acceptance, explained to her mother that this was "really something. They publish the best that is published."[9] "A View from the Woods" appeared in the magazine in 1957.

Editor Catharine Carver (see) is listed under the 12th Street address entry.

Pricilla (*sic*) Poor
145 E. 49th St., Apt. 4D

Priscilla Ann Merrill Poor (1915–1979) was known, but not known. She was part of the Social Register but later "lived a little below the radar,"[10] so much so that her name is missing from both 1940 and 1950 censuses. (In fact, other women are recorded as living in the apartment listed here, which she lived in from 1944 to 1957).[11] It's not known how she knew

O'Connor, though it is for certain that she made her acquaintance at some point in the late 1940s or thereabouts. Poor's name appears in the earliest of O'Connor's address books.

Priscilla was the daughter of Ruth O. Ashmore and Henry Varnum Poor. While the births of her three siblings (two older and one younger) are registered, hers is not. Though some records (including her tombstone) show her as being born in August 1915, with one travel record noting her birth place as Syosset, Long Island (where her family lived for a while[12]), her birth was officially recorded as taking place in Manhattan one year later. No first name is listed; she is recorded, simply, as "female."[13]

Poor was far from poor, coming from a family that had made both name and fortune through the railroad industry and other endeavors. Though they lost much in the Bank Panic of 1907 (her grandfather not only lost his house in Gramercy Park, but his financial losses made the front page of the *New York Times*), they recovered.[14] Her father, an attorney employed by a Wall Street legal firm, purchased a five-story townhouse in the Lenox Hill neighborhood in 1928.[15] The house, with its eighteen rooms, six bathrooms, and elevator, was purchased for $127,500.[16] Two years later, the federal census would list four servants as part of this household.[17]

In 1929, Henry was spending much time in Europe for business reasons. His family followed him to the Continent that summer, returning to the States mere weeks before the stock market crashed.[18] To say that the severe recession affected the family would be an understatement; two years later, almost to the day of the Black Friday anniversary, Henry took his life at the family home in Maine. The family's tragedy was, unfortunately, not uncommon in 1931. The U.S. experienced its highest suicide rate ever from 1929 to 1932 as a result of the Crash and the Great Depression.[19]

Poor was only fifteen when her family's circumstances changed. Mere weeks after Henry's death, the house was sold in an all-cash deal.[20] After that point, her mother, who still occupied the home at the time of the sale, began taking boarders.[21] Still, the family was able to maintain certain aspects of their pre-Crash lifestyle. For Poor, this included parties that she attended as a debutante, all of which were reported in the newspapers. She was presented to society in September 1933.[22] At the end of the year, she was named in the *Washington Evening Star* as a guest at a dance hosted by First Lady Eleanor Roosevelt.[23]

Poor kept busy. In addition to school, there was volunteer work as a member of the Junior Committee of the Travelers Aid Society.[24] She continued to travel, sailing to the Mediterranean in 1934[25] and to Bermuda in 1936 and 1937.[26] And there were the family weddings in which she stood, her gowns putting her in the sartorial spotlight. As the "only attendant, and a very chic one," she wore delphinium blue chiffon in 1935.[27] She donned lavender chiffon as maid of honor in her sister's 1936 wedding—a quiet affair as the family was mourning the death of their mother.[28] Later that year, she carried gilded wheat and roses while wearing a Medieval-style red velvet gown and Juliet cap.[29]

Poor's name grows scarce in society columns after this point, but that isn't to say her life lacked luster. In fact, her nephew David Poor suggests that, as the social obligations thinned, she was able to enjoy "a pretty high-powered life flirting with the stage and literary worlds, living a very different kind of life than her older siblings."[30] While nothing is known of her literary endeavors, references to her Thespian activities surface here and there. In 1940, a review deemed her performance "effective" in a Lake Placid production.[31] Two years later, the "young Broadway actress" was playing the lead in a New Rochelle theater. (In the supporting cast? Shelley Winter, as she was known then.[32])

In 1943, the "actress and diseuse" provided entertainment at a tea party, where she illustrated her talk on the necessary versatility of an actress with scenes from *Pygmalion* and *Our Town*.[33] And with that, Poor, who proved to be quite versatile herself, disappears from the papers save for a description of what she wore in her brother Daniel's wedding (emerald green crepe and a gold feather headband).[34] She worked as a secretary, taking mostly temp work, and died of cancer in 1979, with no obituary to mark her passing.[35]

Hermine Isaacs Popper
1 W. 64th St., NYC 23 / TR 7-6967

Popper (1915–1968) was a fiction writer, film critic, and freelance editor who edited Martin Luther King's *Stride Toward Freedom* and his later books.[36] (In 2009, a rocking chair Popper had given to the civil rights leader to be used as he wrote at her White Plains cabin was auctioned.[37]) She also edited and combined three separate drafts that would become Constantin Stanislavski's (posthumous) *Creating a Role*.[38]

Popper is first listed in O'Connor's brown book, indicating an early acquaintance.

Arabel J. Porter
501 Madison Ave. / MU 8-3470

Porter (1911–1983) was the executive director of *New World Writing*, which (at first) was distributed by New American Library's (see entry) Mentor Books. Porter was described by her boss as "a bohemian Quakeress with inspired eyes and ears" when it came to the "literary, dramatic, and graphic arts."[39]

She published O'Connor's "Enoch and the Gorilla" in the first edition of *New World Writing* in 1952. In 1955, when discussing an upcoming trip to New York, editor Catharine Carver (see) stated that her friend Porter very much wanted to meet the writer. O'Connor responded she had long wanted to meet Porter herself.[40]

Porter is included in three address books. In the final one, O'Connor scratches through *NWW* (*New World Writing*) and adds *NAL* (New American Library).

Crandell Price
252 W. 10th St.
241 W. 11th St., NYC 14
NY state dept of law—80 Centre, NYC 13

Crandell Price (1909–1969) corresponded briefly with O'Connor. To read more about him, see Chapter 9.

Mrs. Ted Purdy
36 Sutton Place

To proper society, perhaps, she was the wife of Theodore Purdy (see entry), but professionally she was known as Elizabeth McKee (see), literary agent. McKee first met and signed O'Connor in 1948; she continued to represent O'Connor's work until her own death in 1997.

Theodore M. Purdy
210 Madison Ave., NYC 16

Theodore Martindale Purdy (1903–1979) was known as "Ted" to O'Connor, who also knew him as the husband of her agent, Elizabeth McKee (see entry). At the time of his meeting O'Connor, he was the editor-in-chief of Appleton-Century-Crofts (see); by the time of his retirement, he had also held leading positions at G. P. Putnam's Sons, Coward McCann, Inc. (see), Purdy-Carlisle-Dodds, Inc., and Meredith Press.[41]

This was the address of Coward-McCann, Inc., which is listed under his name.

Mr. Philip Rahv
45 Astor Pl.

Born in Russia, Philip Rahv (originally Greenberg, 1908–1973) was an editor, critic, and college professor. Known as a left-wing theorist and apologist, he cofounded *Partisan Review* (see entry) in 1934; he was listed as an editor until 1969. He anthologized novels of Henry James and Tolstoy and, at his death, was working on a critical study of Dostoyevsky.[42]

As a writer, he published various articles and reviews in various magazines, and his critical essays were gathered into the collections *Image and Idea* (1949), *The Myth and the Powerhouse* (1965), and *Literature and the Sixth Sense* (1969).

In addition to the O'Connor stories that he chose for *Partisan Review*, he also included "A Good Man Is Hard to Find" in *The Avon Book of Modern Writing* (1953). The anthology featured contemporary poetry and prose from both the United States and Europe that included, among other pieces, a long selection from Collette's autobiography and a short story by O'Connor's friend Robie Macauley (see).

This was the address of the *Partisan Review*.

Stewart Richardson
521 Fifth Ave., NYC 17

Stewart Richardson (1926–2004) was lauded as an editor of many respected writers, and at the height of his career he was a top editor at Doubleday. As such, he negotiated an agreement with the (former) Soviet Union in which the country recognized, for the first time, the copyright of an American publishing house.[43]

When J. B. Lippincott, Co. (see entry) took over the publication of *New World Writing*, Richardson took the reins as editor with Volume 16.

Rinehart & Company
232 Madison Ave., NYC 16

The sons of mystery writer Mary Roberts Rinehart, Stanley and Frederick Rinehart started this company with John Farrar in 1927. When Farrar left in 1946, Rinehart & Company was born. In 1960, the company merged with Henry Holt & Company (see entry) and the John C. Winston Company, forming Holt, Rinehart and Winston. CBS acquired it in 1986.[44]

O'Connor was awarded the Rinehart-Iowa Fiction award in 1947. She was assigned John Selby (see) as editor.

The company is listed under John Selby's name.

Lettie Rogers
Hotel Dover, Apt. 2G, 687 Lexington Ave., NYC 22

Lettie Logan Hamlett Rogers (1917–1957) was a novelist O'Connor met during a visit to the Women's College of the University of North Carolina, where Rogers taught. To read about her, see Chapter 7.

W. G. Rogers
50 Rockefeller Plaza, NYC 20

William Garland Rogers (1896–1978) was the literary, music, and art editor of Associated Press when he retired in 1961.[45] He interviewed O'Connor Wednesday, June 1, 1955, when she was in Manhattan to promote *A Good Man Is Hard to Find*.[46] A review of O'Connor's book (with no mention made of the interview) appeared two days later in Rogers' syndicated column, *Literary Guidepost*. In it, he called O'Connor both "canny and uncanny" and added that "no American of her years can match" the short stories appearing in the book.[47] In some papers, the photo that had appeared on the back of *Wise Blood* accompanied the story.[48] The 1952 photo is from a period when O'Connor was clearly suffering ill health—her hair thin from having lost so much of it during high fevers and her face still swollen from cortisone.

O'Connor wrote a thank you note upon returning home, telling Rogers that he had made the interview process as enjoyable as possible (she didn't like to be interviewed) and adding that, thanks to him, Harcourt, Brace had arranged for a photo session while she was in New York. Saying that she hoped he would remember her, O'Connor enclosed a photo of her self-portrait with a pheasant.[49]

This is the address for the Associate Press, which is mentioned under his name in the listing.

For more information on her interview with Rogers, see Chapter 3.

Miss Mildred Salivar
383 Madison Ave.

In 1952, Mildred Salivar was listed as the Publicity and Advertising manager for Harcourt, Brace (see entry). In 1955, as publicity director, she wrote to thank O'Connor for granting interviews (with W. G. Rogers and Rochelle Girson; see) and posing for publicity photos shot by Erich Hartmann while in New York. She signed the letter "Sallie."[50]

This was the address of Harcourt, Brace (see), which O'Connor notes by adding *HB* to the entry.

The Eugene F. Saxton Memorial Trust
49 E. 33rd St., NYC 16

In 1943, Harper & Brothers (later Harper & Row; see entries) established the Eugene F. Saxton Memorial Trust. The fellowships were awarded to young writers with the intention of helping them finish their books of fiction or non-fiction. The application process included submitting ten thousand words of the unfinished manuscript.[51]

It appears that O'Connor herself did not apply for the grant, though she did make note of the address in the brown book. In a February 1959 letter to writer Cecil Dawkins, O'Connor mentions the grant and adds that she wasn't very familiar with the application process.[52] In October, she consoled Dawkins that it was just as well she didn't get the grant and goes on to tell her about a bad experience of her own with a fellowship.[53]

Evalyn (*sic*) Seide
156 E. 85th St., NYC 28 / RE 7-5760

Not to be confused with the Evelyn D. Seide who was Helen Keller's secretary (and later, companion), this Evelyn Seide was a painter that O'Connor met at Yaddo. Married to artist and illustrator (and Yaddo alum) Charles Seide, she taught at the Brooklyn Museum of Art and was recognized with a few prizes, including a fellowship from Pepsi Cola in 1948.

In a letter written in the summer of 1948, O'Connor mentions to her mother that she and Seide went to an antique shop together.[54] In another letter, she mentions Elizabeth Fenwick (see entry) taking her and Margaret Sutton (see) to visit Seide after dinner.[55]

John Selby, Editor
232 Madison Ave., NYC 16

Though John Selby (1897–1980) was a well-regarded novelist, he goes down in the O'Connor story as one who brought the writer much grief as a Rinehart & Company (see entry) editor.

While a student in the Iowa Writers' Workshop, O'Connor was chosen to receive the first Rinehart Fellowship, thus making the writer a standout among her workshop colleagues.[56] O'Connor was clearly thrilled to have been chosen for the honor, which gave her ample reason to tend to the writing of *Wise Blood* rather than seek employment. The problems began with what O'Connor perceived as Selby's less-than-enthusiastic reception of her work and a lack of respect for her writing process. Still, author Paul Elie states that O'Connor perhaps was already looking for a way out of her ties to Rinehart after talking to other writers at Yaddo, some of whom had ideas of their own about who should publish her work.[57]

The author of ten novels, including best sellers *Sam* and *Starbuck*, Selby started out as a reporter in Kansas. Ill health forced him to quit after eleven years; he spent the next three years with his wife in France, recovering. Returning to the States, he taught courses in short story writing at Columbia University before becoming editor-in-chief at Rinehart. In 1965, he moved to Sicily. He is buried there.[58]

Rinehart & Company is listed under his name.

Sheed & Ward
64 University Pl., NYC 3

The husband-wife team of Fred Sheed (1897–1981) and Maisie Ward (1889–1975) made for an unforgettable pair: He was an Australian who, despite his background in law, became a street-corner evangelist, and she was a six-footer from an English family with strong Catholic roots.[59] In 1926, the two activists started their own publishing house in London to help other Catholic writers to publish. Some of these writers included Evelyn Waugh, Clare Luce, and Dorothy Day. The main office moved to New York in 1933; today it is a Rowman & Littlefield imprint.[60]

O'Connor frequently reviewed books for two Catholic diocesan newspapers in her home state. As such, she reviewed a good many Sheed & Ward titles. But before she was known to them as a reviewer, she was a Catholic novelist who made sure to send them a complimentary copy of *Wise Blood*.[61] She no doubt knew Sheed & Ward through her friend Robert Lowell (see entry), who had worked there as an editor until he declared himself a conscientious objector during World War II. He was put in federal prison.[62]

Catharine R. Hughes (see) is listed as the contact.

Mr. J. Harold Smith
620 W. 116th St., NYC 27

J. Harold Smith was a broker for Hirsch & Co. O'Connor, in a letter to Maryat Lee (see entry), said she had received an advertisement from a New York broker. O'Connor asked if Smith was Lee's broker; if not, she joked, perhaps brokers had become aware that she was awarded $8,000 from the Ford Foundation (see).[63]

An article on (then) recent rentals mentions Smith leasing this apartment in 1943.[64] He was there as late as 1960.

Helen Stone
MUrray Hill 2-1234

There is no address listed for Helen Stone (1895–1955) in O'Connor's address book, only a Murray Hill phone number and the mention of the *Daily News*, where Stone worked.

Stone reported to the 1940 Federal Census that she was a stenographer/accountant for the newspaper. At the time of her death fifteen years later, she was listed as an auditor and still sharing a home with her mother, Grace Stone, in Montclair, New Jersey.[65] O'Connor was a guest in their home in the summer of 1943. For more about that visit, see Chapter 1.

Roger W. Straus
19 Union Sq. W, NYC 3

Roger W. Straus, Jr. (1917–2004) came to publishing with a background that included well-known family members—the Strauses and the Guggenheims. His father, Roger W. Straus, Sr., was president of American Mining and Smelting Company. One grandfather, Oscar S. Straus, had served as Secretary of Commerce in President Theodore Roosevelt's cabinet, and his maternal grandfather, philanthropist David Guggenheim, owned a copper mine.[66]

When Straus married the well-heeled Dorothea Liebmann, the young couple could live on their combined trusts, which allowed Straus the opportunity to explore journalism and book publishing. Realizing he preferred the latter, he decided to open a publishing company of his own. Upon meeting Farrar, a company was born; Straus used $30,000 of his inheritance and $120,000 from other people that he knew to this end.[67]

Straus was known for being outspoken about two subjects: new books and the effect of big chain bookstores in the industry. He was especially critical of conglomerates taking over the publishing business, though, in 1993, that is what happened to what was by then called Farrar, Straus & Giroux. Still, as part of the deal, the firm was able to maintain its independent status.[68]

O'Connor met Straus (and Sheila Cudahy) during a brief trip to New York on her way to Lourdes.

His name is included under O'Connor's Farrar, Straus & Cudahy (see entry) listing.

Studio Club
210 E. 77th St. / RH 4-2174

Studio Club was a YWCA residence hall located in Lenox Hill.[69]

O'Connor never lived here, and is it not known if she knew any of the residents. However, it may have been a place of residence she was considering in 1949.

Margaret Sutton
604 W. 112th St. / MO 2-6395
210 W. 14th St. / CH 2-5281

Margaret Sutton (1905–1990) was a surrealist painter. To read about her, see Chapter 7.

The address on W. 14th, known as the Pompeo Coppini Studio, dates back to 1848. In 1923, the sculptor Coppini and his wife purchased and renovated the building so that the top floor housed art studios. Many assume that the carved tympanum over the main entrance—its image, that of an artist at work—was the creation of Coppini.[70]

O'Connor mentions Sutton's hometown of Bluefield, Virginia, in one entry.

Tatum (*sic*) House
138 E. 38th St. / MUrray Hill 5-5142

The twelve-story Tatham House was named after Cora Tatham, who had served on the YWCA's Metropolitan Board.[71] Opening its doors to young women making moderate salaries in 1918, Tatham House boasted of 250 rooms with running water. In addition, the rooms were bright, thanks to access to natural light guaranteed by a plot of land owned on Lexington. In addition, it offered club accommodations, a restaurant, and a rooftop solarium. Built in 1910, the residence had been known previously as the second Allerton House, an apartment building with a "home influence" for men. The first Allerton was located in Chelsea.[72]

In 1974, the YWCA announced its plan to sell all of its remaining residences, including the building on Lexington and 38th. Tatham House was sold for $900,000 to a developer who transformed the single dorm rooms into studio and one-bedroom apartments.[73]

O'Connor took a room at Tatham House, located between Lexington and Third Avenue, after staying with Elizabeth Hardwick (see entry) for a few days in winter of 1949. For more about O'Connor's time there, see Chapter 2.

That O'Connor listed it in the brown book is natural, but it is a little surprising that she recorded it in the next address book as well (with name still misspelled).

The Third Hour Inc.
319 E. 91st St.

The Third Hour was both a journal and an ecumenical movement started by Russian émigré Helene Iswolsky (see entry).

The title is a reference to the time associated with the crucifixion of Jesus Christ.

J & D Thompson
214 Riverside Dr. / AC 2-9234
1125 Fifth Ave., NYC 28

In 1948, O'Connor was invited to a church wedding followed by a gathering at the John Thompsons; she did not know the Thompsons, and she attended neither. But in 1949, she would get to know the couple, Jack and Dilly, and spend pleasant evenings with them. She mentions in a letter to her mother that she planned on dropping in on them one evening.[74] In another letter, she says she attended the ballet with them (her first).[75]

John Anderson Thompson, Jr. (1918–2002) met O'Connor's friends Robert Lowell and Robie Macauley (see entries) while attending Kenyon University. By the late 1940s, the war veteran was a graduate student at Columbia. He had yet to make his name as a scholar and poet.[76]

Helen Louise Keeler (1918–2004), known to all as Dilly, would go on to establish the Helen Keeler Burke Charitable Foundation.

Transatlantic Review
156 E. 52nd St., NYC 22

This quarterly literary journal was based in London from 1959 to 1977. It published a variety of short fiction and poetry from many well-known writers and also featured drawings and interviews. In all, sixty issues were produced.[77]

Ellis Amburn (see entry) is listed under this entry.

Miss Pauline Turkel
333 W. 57th St. / CIrcle 6-5975

O'Connor wrote to her mother that, following her time in New York to promote A Good Man Is Hard to Find, she would take the train with "Miss Turkel" and head out to Caroline Gordon's for the weekend.[78] That weekend, a party was given in O'Connor's honor at the Tory Valley home of Susan Jenkins Brown (see entry), a place known among writers as Robber Rocks.[79]

Pauline Turkel (1899–1987) was not just Brown's neighbor; she was also a political activist who had worked on the staff of the Provincetown Players (an experimental theater that launched the careers of Eugene O'Neill and Susan Glaspell)[80] and as a secretary to anarchist Emma Goldman at the progressive magazine Mother Jones.

Viking Press
625 Madison Ave., NYC 22 / PL 5-4330

In 1925, Harold K. Guinzburg, of Simon & Schuster, and George S. Oppenheim, of Alfred A. Knopf (see entry), founded Viking with the goal of publishing fiction and nonfiction that had more lasting power than what appealed to popular tastes. The name "Viking" and its logo—a Viking ship drawn by the distinctive pen of Rockwell Kent—were chosen to suggest adventure and exploration. Before even the first book was published, Guinzburg and Oppenheim acquired the firm of B. W. Huebsch and thus had an instant backlist of titles, including books by Sherwood Anderson, James Joyce, and D. H. Lawrence.[81]

In November 1941, nine months after the death of her father, a sixteen-year-old O'Connor submitted books (she does not state how many) to the press, then located at 18 East 48th Street. In her cover letter, she says they are not intended as children's books, adding that if the (nameless) editor didn't think they would sell, they could be sent back, collect. She remarked that she had seen worse books make it to print.[82]

Mrs. D. J. Way
430 Hudson St. / CH 2-4720
517 E. 77th St.

O'Connor often listed married women in the proper manner of the day, and that is to say, as "Mrs. John Doe" rather than as Jane.

Mrs. D. J. Way was Mrs. David Jacques Way, otherwise known as writer Elizabeth Fenwick. Way (1919–1994) and Fenwick were married in 1950. They divorced in 1970.

In the brown book, O'Connor scribbled directions to this address (see Figure 11).

To read about Fenwick, see Chapters 2 and 7.

Dr. John P. West
215 E. 72nd St. / Office: RH 4-0084
Home: RE 7-1347

O'Connor's friends, Ted and Ann Amussen (see entry) recommended Dr. West to O'Connor in 1949. She mentions in a letter to her mother that the doctor, whom she was seeing about a pain in her side, told her she could call him at any time and gave her his home number.[83] In a later letter, she says West was treating her for trench mouth and charged her ten dollars for two visits.[84]

While it is not unusual that he is listed in the brown address book (since that is the one she used in 1949), it is worth noting that she repeated the listing, minus the home phone number, in the black Elite. Perhaps she thought his number could come in handy on the rare occasions she came to New York.

He is possibly the same John P. West (1905–1978) who was on the attending staff at St. Luke's Hospital (now Mount Sinai St. Luke's) in Morningside Heights and was president of the New York Surgical Society 1961–1963.[85]

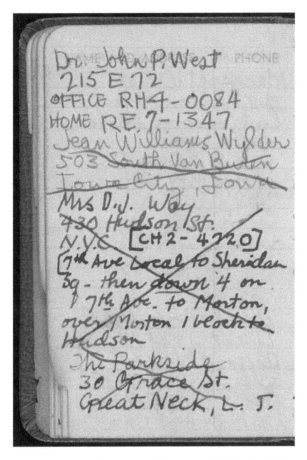

FIGURE 11: From the brown address book. Mrs. D. J. Way
was the married name of O'Connor's good friend, writer
Elizabeth Fenwick. Fenwick had helped O'Connor find a
furnished room to stay in 1949—a place that was not far
from her own home in Morningside Heights. But when
Fenwick married in early 1950, she moved. Here, O'Connor
records directions to Fenwick's new home in the West
Village. (Used with permission from Flannery O'Connor
Papers, Stuart A. Rose Manuscript, Archives, and Rare Book
Library, Emory University.)

The Westbury
Madison at 69th

Built in 1927, the Westbury Hotel transformed its 238 rooms into 47 luxury condominiums in the late 1990s, taking care not to change the pre-war exterior.[86]

That O'Connor lists a location rather than an address suggests she visited a friend there or considered staying there herself.

Wiggins
Martha Washington Hotel, 30 E. 30th St., NYC 16, Rm. 239
17 W. 63rd St., NYC 23
31 W. 63rd St., Apt. S-D, NYC 23

Barbara Charlene "Charlye" Wiggins Prescott (1935–2006) was a young poet at Wesleyan when she wrote to Maryat Lee (see entry) late in 1956. Knowing that Lee was spending time in Milledgeville, Wiggins wrote to the playwright about O'Connor and, it seems, to O'Connor about Lee. As a result, the two met a few days after Christmas; their friendship would last until O'Connor's death.[87]

For more information about the Martha Washington Hotel, see entry.

Elsie Mae Williams
135 W. 136th St., NYC 30
Work: 1349 Lexington Ave / ENright 9-5638

O'Connor lists her name in the brown and black Elite books, making note in the earlier one that Williams worked in the home of Mrs. S. S. Blackman (actually, Mrs. Samuel W. Blackman). At the time of the 1950 census, Blackman, thirty-six, was a research chemist; his wife, Claire, twenty-eight, perhaps tended to their children.[88]

Unfortunately, there is no Elsie Mae Williams listed at this Harlem address in the 1950 census. That O'Connor lists her work phone number seems to indicate that Williams did not have a telephone (back then, not everyone did). In 1959, however, Elsie M. Williams is listed in the city directory at this address, and with a phone number.

Williams is a Manhattan mystery in O'Connor's address books: twice listed, and one is left to ponder the connection.

John Woodburn
257 Fourth Ave.

John Woodburn (1901–1952) made his name as an editor, starting first with his high school literary magazine and then *The Princeton Tiger,* the second oldest college humor magazine in the country. Professionally, he worked as an editor for the *New Yorker*; Doubleday; Harcourt, Brace (see entry); Henry Holt (see); and the New York office of Little, Brown & Co.[89] He contributed to *Saturday Review of Literature,* the *New Republic*, and the *New York Times*.[90]

At Doubleday, he was Eudora Welty's first editor. At Henry Holt, he replaced Allen Tate as *Belles Lettres* editor.[91] At Little, Brown, Woodburn encountered difficulties with J. D. Salinger as he prepared *Catcher in the Rye* for publication.[92]

He wrote to "Mr." O'Connor in February 1948, to let the author know how much he had enjoyed "The Geranium," both in *Accent* and again in *Coraddi*. He offered to discuss writing plans with her and consider any work she'd want to show him.[93]

The address would soon be changed in 1959 after the New York City Council changed the name of Fourth Avenue, running from 17th Street to 32nd Street, to Park Avenue South.[94] Noting which addresses are listed as Fourth and which as Park offers an interesting way of dating entries.

Woodstock Hotel
W. 43rd St

O'Connor stayed at the Woodstock when she first met with agent Elizabeth McKee (see entry) in 1948. She had planned to stay there again in 1955 but stayed at the New Weston because of mobility difficulties. To read about these trips, see Chapters 2 and 3.

In 1979, Project Find purchased the Woodstock, a hotel off Times Square whose prestige had long plummeted. Though still serving as a single-room occupancy hotel, more than half the rooms are reserved for referrals from the NYC Department of Homeless Services. All residents must be at least fifty-five years old and earn less than sixty percent of the local median income.[95]

Clifford Wright
352 E. 51st St.
223 Mott St., Apt. 1

Clifford Wright (1919–1989) was an American abstract artist and illustrator who met O'Connor at Yaddo. To read about him, see Chapter 7.

Miss Ruth York
244 Riverside Dr.

In 1960, Ruth York wrote a brief letter to O'Connor, addressing her by her first name and congratulating her on her most recent book. She goes on to mention the time when the female dean visited Currier Graduate House, where York and O'Connor lived while attending the University of Iowa. The dean had, York recalled, announced her amazement over how much talent lived under that roof. York noted how, in the case of one particular resident, that comment had "proved prophetic."[96]

Indeed, it had.

Acknowledgments

I am grateful for the support I received in the form of grants and sabbatical leave during the research and writing of this book. These include the Emory University Rose Library Short-Term Fellowship; the *Flannery O'Connor Review* Senior Fellowship; two XULA CAT+FD Scholarly Travel Mini-Grants, funded by the Andrew W. Mellon Foundation; and sabbatical leave provided by Xavier University of Louisiana.

I am thankful to the following collections for allowing me access to letters, images, documents, and more:

> Dudley Huppler Papers, Archives of American Art, Smithsonian Institution
>
> Flannery O'Connor Papers, Stuart A. Rose Manuscript, Archives, and Rare Book Library, Emory University
>
> Flannery O'Connor Collection, Stuart A. Rose Manuscript, Archives, and Rare Book Library, Emory University
>
> Flannery O'Connor Collection, Ina Dillard Russell Library Special Collections, Georgia College and State University
>
> Sally Fitzgerald Papers, Stuart A. Rose Manuscript, Archives, and Rare Book Library, Emory University
>
> Flannery O'Connor, Yale Collection of American Literature Manuscript Miscellany, Beinecke Rare Book and Manuscript Library, Yale University

Finally, I wish to thank the following people:

Mr. Gerald "Jay" Naquin, for introducing me to O'Connor's work in my freshman year at Grace King High School. What for you was an in-class reading assignment was, for me, a waking up and a realization.

The following librarians for their assistance: Hannah White, (then) librarian at Xavier; Kate Feighery, archivist at the New York Archdiocese; Emily Walhout of Houghton Library, Harvard University; Gregory Waksmulski of Providence Public Library; Lindsey G. Bright of the Smithsonian Institution's Archives of American Art; and Mary Ellen Budney of Beinecke Library, Yale University;

it is with particular appreciation (and fondness) that I thank Kathy Shoemaker of the Stuart A. Rose Manuscript, Archives, & Rare Book Library at Emory University and Nancy Bray of the Ina Dillard Library Special Collections at Georgia College and State University;

those I met through their association with Andalusia Farm or Milledgeville over the years: Craig Amason, Meghan Anderson, Irene Burgess, Tammie Burke, Matt Davis, Susan Smith Fenwick, April Moon, Revel Wylly Pogue, Daniel Wilkinson, and Elizabeth Wylie;

Marshall Bruce Gentry, editor of *Flannery O'Connor Review*, for his wit, wisdom, and belief in this project;

the late Louise Florencourt for her time, commentary, and the gift that was being able to spend two afternoons sipping tea in the magnificent house on Greene Street;

authors and scholars Benjamin B. Alexander, Trudie Harris, Robin Hemley, Lorraine V. Murray, Marjorie Och, Fr. Pat Samway, Mab Segrest, Robin G. Vander, and Jerry Ward for your information and insight;

Frances Florencourt for entertaining my eleventh-hour questions;

Lois Benjamin, Susan Bridges, Claude Oliver, David Poor, Denley Poor-Reynolds, Addy Sage, Constance M. Taylor, Deborah Way, and Jessica Way for their information and insight;

K. Jacob Ruppert, for guidance;

Kemala Karmen and Beth Herstein (thank you for not making me take the subway);

Carol Kilgore, who was willing to go to Emory for me when the Pandemic closed everything down;

Emily Banks, who allowed me to continue my research during the Pandemic (and made doing so seem an adventure);

English Department colleagues who listened as I read what would become the preface at a department colloquium and made valuable suggestions; in particular, Thomas Bonner, Jr., whose ear I bent more than a few times;

Silent G for our talks on all things O'Connor;

Elizabeth Yost Hammer for her support;

Margaret Earley Whitt and Mark Bosco for their feedback;

Michael Garanzini and Farrell O'Gorman for their timely assistance;

Pepper Caruso for her feedback and red pen on the second and third versions;

Fred Nachbaur and Angela Alaimo O'Donnell for their patience and kindness over the years;

and to the one who recognized that what I had initially conceived to be a very long essay would be far better realized as a book: you were right, and thank you.

APPENDIX. PARTS OF TOWN: RESIDENTS AND BUSINESSES

What follows is a listing of the parts of town that make up Flannery O'Connor's Manhattan. The categories are based on contemporary Manhattan zip code "neighborhoods."

Central Harlem

Smith Oliver; J. Harold Smith; Elsie Mae Williams.

Clinton, Chelsea

Appleton-Century-Crofts; Associated Press; Brentano's; Beverly Brunson; Catholic Unity League; Lillian Chiriaka; Robert Fitzgerald; Rochelle Girson; Harvard Club; Hotel Marlton; *Hudson Review*; Frances Lewis; Macmillan Co.; McGraw Hill; Mrs. Neil (Miriam) McKenzie; Milner Hotel; Anne Brooks Murray; *Partisan Review*; W. G. Rogers; Margaret Sutton; Pauline Turkel; Cyrilly (Abels) Weinstein; Woodstock Hotel.

Gramercy Park, Murray Hill

Alfred A. Knopf Inc.; Ellis Amburn; Adda H. Andersen; Ted Amussen; Atheneum Books; Beverly Brunson; Daniel Callahan; Colquitt Girls' Club; Columbia Gas System; *Commonweal*; Coward–McCann, Inc., Fred Darsey; George Davis; Candida Donadio; *Esquire*; the Ford Foundation; Richard Gilman; Robert Giroux; John Simon Guggenheim Memorial Foundation; Harcourt, Brace; Harper & Brothers; *Harper's Bazaar*; George

Haslam; Hiram Haydn; Health Foods Distributors; Patricia Highsmith; Rust Hills; Franz J. Horch, Associates; Hotel Dover; Edith Ivey; Robert Jiras; *Jubilee*; King Features Syndicate; Mrs. Colquitt Koepp; J. B. Lippincott Co.; W. McNeil Lowry; *Mademoiselle*; Ed Maisel; Martha Washington Hotel; Murray McCain; Vivienne Koch MacLeod; Mavis McIntosh Riordan; Elizabeth McKee; McKee & Batchelder; Edgar Moran; Alice S. Morris; the New American Library; New Weston Hotel; Ann Orr; Priscilla Poor; Arabel J. Porter; Mrs. Ted Purdy (Elizabeth McKee); Theodore M. Purdy; Stewart Richardson; Rinehart & Co.; Lettie Rogers; Mildred Salivar; Eugene F. Saxton Memorial Trust; John Selby; Helen Stone; Tatham House; *Transatlantic Review*; Viking Press; Charlye (Barbara) Wiggins; Clifford Wright.

Greenwich Village, SoHo

James Agee; Beverly Brunson; Sue Jenkins Brown; Anne Draper; Elaine Gottlieb; Robert Hatch; *Hudson Review*; James Laughlin; Maryat Lee; Robie Macauley; Alice Ellen Mayhew; Elizabeth McKee; *The Nation*; New Directions Publishing Co.; Paperbook Gallery; Crandell Price; Mrs. D. J. Way (Elizabeth Fenwick); Clifford Wright.

Lower East Side

Gino Ardito; Criterion Books, Inc.; Fred Darsey; Farrar, Straus & Cudahy; Robert Giroux; Elizabeth Hardwick; H. Stanley Hillyer; Holt & Co.; Catharine R. Hughes; Dudley Huppler; Edith Ivey; Robert Jiras; Erik Langkjaer; The Margaret Louisa; Murray McCain; *Partisan Review*; Philip Rahv; Sheed & Ward; Roger W. Straus; John Woodburn.

Lower Manhattan

Desclee Co., Inc.

Upper East Side

Drs. Richard & Mortimer Bader; Catharine Carver; Fred Darsey; the Fitzgeralds (Robert and Sally); Dr. Lyman A. Fulton; Robert Giroux; Helene Iswolsky; *Jubilee*; Krystyn Jurasz-Damska; Denver Lindley; Murray McCain; David McDowell; McDowell, Obolensky Inc.; New York Hospital; Evelyn Seide; Studio Club; The Third Hour Inc.; John & Dilly Thompson; Mrs. D. J. Way (Elizabeth Fenwick); Dr. John P. West; the Westbury.

Upper West Side

The Beiswangers (George and Barbara); Martha Bell; Beverly Brunson; Fr. Daniel M. Dougherty; Mary B. Duncan; Elizabeth Fenwick; Robert Jiras; Carol Johnson; Frances Lewis; Dr. J. J. Lichtman; Mr. & Mrs. (Elizabeth Hardwick) Robert Lowell; Phyllis Meras; Irene Orgel; Hermine I. Popper; Margaret Sutton; John & Dilly Thompson; Charlye (Barbara) Wiggins; Ruth York.

Abbreviations

The following abbreviations are used in the endnotes.

DHAAA   Dudley Huppler Papers, Archives of American Art, Smithsonian Institution

FOCPEU   Flannery O'Connor Papers, Stuart A. Rose Manuscript, Archives, and Rare Book Library, Emory University

FOCCEU   Flannery O'Connor Collection, Stuart A. Rose Manuscript, Archives, and Rare Book Library, Emory University

FOCCGC   Flannery O'Connor Collection, Ina Dillard Russell Library Special Collections at Georgia College and State University

SFPEU   Sally Fitzgerald Papers, Stuart A. Rose Manuscript, Archives, and Rare Book Library, Emory University

YCAL   Flannery O'Connor, Yale Collection of American Literature Manuscript Miscellany, Beinecke Rare Book and Manuscript Library, Yale University

NOTES

Preface

1. See *Dear Regina: Flannery O'Connor's Letters from Iowa*, ed. Monica Carol Miller (Athens: University of Georgia Press, 2022).

2. Flannery O'Connor Papers, Stuart A. Rose Manuscript, Archives, and Rare Book Library, Emory University (FOCPEU).

3. To learn about O'Connor's relationships with those mentioned here, see Jean Cash, *Flannery O'Connor: A Life* (Knoxville: University of Tennessee Press, 2002); and Brad Gooch, *Flannery: A Life of Flannery O'Connor* (New York: Back Bay Books, 2009).

4. Gooch, *Flannery*, 143.

5. Qtd. in Jean Wylder, "Flannery O'Connor: A Reminiscence and Some Letters," *North American Review* 255, no. 1 (Spring, 1970), 63.

6. Clyde McLeod to FOC, n.d. (1948), FOCPEU.

7. FOC to Regina Cline O'Connor, postmarked July 19, 1948, FOCPEU

8. FOC to Regina Cline O'Connor, July 14, 1948, and undated (likely September 1948), FOCPEU.

9. Clyde McLeod to FOC, n.d. (1948), FOCPEU.

Introduction: The Tour Begins

1. Brad Gooch, *Flannery: A Life of Flannery O'Connor* (New York: Back Bay Books, 2009), 279.

2. FOC to Erik Langkjaer, August 12, 1956, in "Letters to Erik Langkjaer," *Asymptote*, April 2015, https://www.asymptotejournal.com/nonfiction/flannery-oconnor-letters-to-erik-langkjaer/.

3. See Gooch, *Flannery*, Chapter 4.

4. Carla Blumenkranz, "'Deeply and Mysteriously Implicated': Communist Sympathies, FBI Informants, and Robert Lowell at Yaddo," Poetry Foundation, December 18, 2006, https://www.poetryfoundation.org/articles/68753/deeply-and-mysteriously-implicated.

5. Gooch, *Flannery*, 168.

6. FOC to Elizabeth McKee, February 24, 1949, in *The Habit of Being: Letters of Flannery O'Connor*, ed. Sally Fitzgerald (New York: Farrar, Straus & Giroux, 1979), 1.

7. Gooch, *Flannery*, 170.

8. This and the following biographical details of Lowell's life, unless otherwise noted, come from *Lost Puritan* by Paul Mariani (W. W. Norton, 1994) and Ian Hamilton's *Robert Lowell: A Biography* (Faber & Faber, 1982).

9. Hamilton, *Robert Lowell*, 162; 166.

10. FOC to Robert and Sally Fitzgerald, January 4, 1954, *Habit*, 6.

11. Fitzgerald, *Habit*, 64.

12. FOC to "A" [Betty Hester], April 20, 1957, *Habit*, 217.

13. FOC to Robert Lowell, December 25, 1958, *Habit*, 311.

14. FOC to Cecil Dawkins, January 26, 1962, *Habit*, 464.

15. Robert Drake, "The Writer as Observer, the Writer as Outsider," 1997, republished in *For the Record: A Robert Drake Reader*, ed. Randy Hendricks and James A. Perkins (Macon, GA: Mercer University Press, 2001), 295.

16. FOC to Rainulf Stelzman, April 4, 1963, in Stelzman's "Two Unpublished Letters by Flannery O'Connor," *Xavier Review* 5, Nos. 1–2 (1985): 50.

1 / The Education of Mary Flannery O'Connor

1. FOC to Katie Semmes, postmarked July 29, 1943, Flannery O'Connor Papers, Stuart A. Rose Manuscript, Archives, and Rare Book Library, Emory University (FOCPEU).

2. FOC to Regina Cline O'Connor, postmarked August 3, 1943, FOCPEU.

3. Brad Gooch, *Flannery: A Life of Flannery O'Connor* (New York: Back Bay Books, 2009), 83.

4. Gooch, *Flannery*, 55.

5. FOC to Regina Cline O'Connor, postmarked May 21, 1943, FOCPEU.

6. FOC to Regina Cline O'Connor, postmarked August 3, 1943, FOCPEU.

7. FOC to Regina Cline O'Connor, postmarked May 29, 1943, FOCPEU.

8. "Lydia A. Bancroft," *GSCW Catalog 1942–1943*, Georgia State College for Women, 12.

9. FOC to Regina Cline O'Connor, postmarked August 7, 1943, FOCPEU.

10. FOC to Katie Semmes, postmarked July 29, 1943, FOCPEU.

11. FOC to Regina Cline O'Connor, postmarked August 12, 1943, FOCPEU.

12. FOC to Regina Cline O'Connor, postmarked July 20, 1943, FOCPEU.

13. FOC to Regina Cline O'Connor, postmarked July 29, 1943, FOCPEU.

14. FOC to Katie Semmes, postmarked July 29, 1943, FOCPEU.

15. FOC to Regina Cline O'Connor, postmarked July 29, 1943, FOCPEU.

16. FOC to Regina Cline O'Connor, postcard, postmarked July 26, 1943, FOCPEU.

17. "Flannery O'Connor Buried," *New York Times*, August 5, 1964, 33.

18. FOC to Regina Cline O'Connor, postmarked July 22, 1943, FOCPEU.

19. FOC to Regina Cline O'Connor, postmarked July 29, 1943, FOCPEU.

20. FOC to Regina Cline O'Connor, postcard, postmarked July 26, 1943, FOCPEU.

21. FOC to Regina Cline O'Connor, postmarked July 29, 1943, FOCPEU.

22. Sylvia Lovegren, *Fashionable Food: Seven Decades of Food Fads* (New York: Macmillan, 1995), 95.

23. FOC to Regina Cline O'Connor, postcard, postmarked July 26, 1943, FOCPEU.

24. FOC to Regina Cline O'Connor, postcard, postmarked July 26, 1943, FOCPEU.

25. FOC to Regina Cline O'Connor, postmarked July 29, 1943, FOCPEU.

26. FOC to Regina Cline O'Connor, postmarked July 22, 1943, FOCPEU.

27. FOC to Regina Cline O'Connor, n.d. (July 1943), FOCPEU.

28. FOC to Regina Cline O'Connor, Sunday, n.d. (July 1943), FOCPEU.

29. FOC to Regina Cline O'Connor, postcard, postmarked August 21, 1943, FOCPEU.

30. FOC to Regina Cline O'Connor, postmarked October 27, 1945, FOCPEU.

31. FOC to Regina Cline O'Connor, postmarked November 2, 1945, FOCPEU.

2 / City Life

1. Brad Gooch, *Flannery: A Life of Flannery O'Connor* (New York: Back Bay Books, 2009), 135.

2. FOC to Regina Cline O'Connor, postmarked July 7, 1948, Flannery O'Connor Papers, Stuart A. Rose Manuscript, Archives, and Rare Book Library, Emory University (FOCPEU).

3. Patrick Samway, SJ, *Flannery O'Connor and Robert Giroux: A Publishing Partnership* (Notre Dame, IN: University of Notre Dame Press, 2018), 33.

4. FOC to Regina Cline O'Connor, postmarked September 14, 1948, FOCPEU.

5. FOC to Regina Cline O'Connor, postmarked September 14, 1948, FOCPEU.

6. FOC to Regina Cline O'Connor, postmarked September 14, 1948, FOCPEU.

7. Stephen G. Driggers, Robert J. Dunn, and Sarah Gordon, *The Manuscripts of Flannery O'Connor at Georgia College* (Athens: University of Georgia Press, 1989), xii.

8. Driggers, Dunn, and Gordon, xii.

9. Paul Elie, *The Life You Save May Be Your Own: An American Pilgrimage* (New York: Farrar, Straus & Giroux, 2003), 173.

10. FOC to Elizabeth McKee, December 15, 1948, in *The Habit of Being: Letters of Flannery O'Connor*, ed. Sally Fitzgerald (New York: Farrar, Straus & Giroux, 1979), 8.

11. Sally Fitzgerald, "Flannery O'Connor: Patterns of Friendship, Patterns of Love," *Georgia Review* 52, no. 3 (Fall 1998): 415.

12. Paul Mariani, *Lost Puritan* (New York: W. W. Norton, 1994), 179.

13. Elie, *Life You Save*, 172.

14. FOC to Elizabeth McKee, February 24, 1949, in *The Habit of Being: Letters of Flannery O'Connor*, ed. Sally Fitzgerald (New York: Farrar, Straus & Giroux, 1979), 11.

15. Gooch, *Flannery*, 170.

16. Gooch, 170.

17. FOC to "A" [Betty Hester], September 8, 1962, *Habit*, 491.

18. Jean Cash, *Flannery O'Connor: A Life* (Knoxville: University of Tennessee Press, 2002), 99.

19. FOC to Regina Cline O'Connor, Wednesday, n.d. (March 1949), FOCPEU.

20. FOC to Regina Cline O'Connor, Wednesday, n.d. (March 1949), FOCPEU.

21. FOC to Regina Cline O'Connor, Monday, n.d. (March 1949), FOCPEU.

22. FOC to Regina Cline O'Connor, Wednesday, n.d. (March 1949), FOCPEU.

23. FOC to "A" [Betty Hester], December 16, 1955, *Habit*, 124–25.

24. FOC to Robert Giroux, n.d. (1952), Flannery O'Connor Collection, Ina Dillard Russell Library Special Collections at Georgia College and State University (FOCCGC).

25. Cash, *A Life*, 123.

26. FOC to Regina Cline O'Connor, Wednesday, n.d. (March 1949), FOCPEU.

27. Mariani, *Lost Puritan*, 178.

28. Kay Redfield Jamison, *Robert Lowell: Setting the River on Fire* (New York: Alfred A. Knopf, 2017), 99.

29. Jamison, *Robert Lowell,* 100–01.

30. FOC to Regina Cline O'Connor, Wednesday, n.d. (March 1949), FOCPEU.

31. FOC to Regina Cline O'Connor, Wednesday, n.d. (March 1949), FOCPEU.

32. FOC to Regina Cline O'Connor, Wednesday, n.d. (March 1949), FOCPEU.

33. Per author's conversations with Margaret Florencourt Mann's sisters: Louise Florencourt (in Milledgeville, June 1, 2017) and Frances Florencourt (by email, August 20, 2022).

34. 1940 U.S. census, New York County, New York, population schedule, Manhattan, p. 1002 (stamped), enumeration district (ED) 31-874, sheet 13A, A.H. Levitt; https://catalog.archives.gov.

35. Eric Pace, "Alfred Levitt, Prolific Painter and Photographer, Dies at 105," *New York Times,* May 29, 2000, 7.

36. U.S., Departing Passenger and Crew Lists, 1914–1966, database entry for Alfred Levitt, 54, and Gertruce [Gertrude] Levitt, 49, departed April 13, 1949 on the RMS *Queen Elizabeth.*

37. FOC to Paul Engle, April 7, 1949, *Habit,* 13.

38. FOC to Regina Cline O'Connor, postmarked June 24, 1948, FOCPEU.

39. Pace, "Alfred Levitt," 7.

40. Flannery O'Connor, *Flannery O'Connor: The Collected* Works, ed. Sally Fitzgerald (New York: Library of America, 1988), 1244.

41. *Habit,* 66.

42. FOC to "A" [Betty Hester], March 19, 1960, *Habit,* 384.

43. FOC to Elizabeth McKee, February 13, 1950, *Collected Works,* 887.

44. 1950 U.S. census, New York County, New York, population schedule, Manhattan, n.p., enumeration district (ED) 31-1078, sheets 7–8, dwelling 51, Mary B. Duncan; https:// 1950census.archives.gov.

45. "Furnished Rooms–West Side," *New York Times,* April 18, 1950, 50.

46. "Furnished Rooms–West Side," *New York Times,* November 6, 1951, 53.

47. "Record 'Phone Book Out; New Manhattan Directory has 23,000 More Listings," *New York Times,* June 12, 1949, 57.

48. Information that follows comes from FOC's letters to Janet McKane, *Habit,* June 5 and June 19, 1963, 522–26.

49. FOC to Janet McKane, June 5, 1963, *Habit,* 523.

50. FOC to Regina Cline O'Connor, Friday, n.d. (1949), FOCPEU.

51. FOC to Regina Cline O'Connor, Sunday, n.d. (1949), FOCPEU.

52. FOC to Regina Cline O'Connor, postmarked June 17, 1949, FOCPEU.

53. Louise Florencourt and Robert Donahoo, "Wondering and Wandering: An Interview with Louise Florencourt on Her Life and Her Family," *Flannery O'Connor Review* 20 (2022): 92.

54. FOC to Mary Virginia Harrison, March 12, 1950, FOCCGC.

55. FOC to Regina Cline O'Connor, Thursday, n.d. (1949), FOCPEU.

56. FOC to Regina Cline O'Connor, postmarked May 24, 1949, FOCPEU.

57. FOC to Regina Cline O'Connor, Friday, n.d. (1949), FOCPEU.

58. FOC to Janet McKane, June 5, 1963, *Habit,* 523.

59. FOC to Regina Cline O'Connor, Thursday, n.d. (1949), FOCPEU.

60. Robert Lowell to Peter Taylor, August 6, [1949], in *The Letters of Robert Lowell*, ed. Saskia Hamilton (New York: Farrar, Straus & Giroux, 2005), 143.

61. FOC to Mavis McIntosh, October 31, 1949, *Habit*, 18. (The next letter in the book, written to Betty Boyd Love and postmarked November 5, confirms that FOC had just returned from a two-day trip to New York.)

62. FOC to Robert Fitzgerald, n.d., December 1949, in *The Letters of Robert Lowell*, ed. Saskia Hamilton (New York: Farrar, Straus & Giroux, 2005), 150–51.

63. FOC to Robert Lowell and Elizabeth Hardwick, n.d. (early 1950), *Habit*, 20.

64. Lyman Fulton in "Flannery O'Connor on the West Side: Dr. Lyman Fulton's Recollections of a Short Acquaintance, an Interview with Virginia Wray," by Virginia Wray, *English Language Notes* 39, no. 1 (2001): 76.

65. FOC to Mary Virginia Harrison, March 12, 1950, FOCCGC.

66. Gooch, Flannery, 185.

67. *Habit*, 22

68. *Habit*, 22

69. Gooch, *Flannery*, 216.

70. Gooch, 215.

71. FOC to Regina Cline O'Connor, n.d. (June 1952), FOCPEU.

72. FOC to Sally Fitzgerald, n.d. (July 1952), *Habit*, 38.

73. FOC to Robert and Sally Fitzgerald, n.d. (August 1953), *Habit*, 62.

74. Samway, Publishing Partnership, 132.

3 / *A Good Man Is Hard to Find*

1. Catharine Carver to FOC, May 16, 1955, Flannery O'Connor Collection, Ina Dillard Russell Library Special Collections at Georgia College and State University (FOCCGC).

2. Catharine Carver to FOC, May 16, 1955, FOCCGC.

3. FOC to Catharine Carver, May 18, 1955, FOCCGC.

4. Catharine Carver to FOC, May 20, 1955, FOCCGC.

5. FOC to Catharine Carver, May 24, 1955, in *The Habit of Being: Letters of Flannery O'Connor*, ed. Sally Fitzgerald (New York: Farrar, Straus & Giroux, 1979), 82–3.

6. Catharine Carver to FOC, telegram, May 27, 1955, FOCCGC.

7. Catharine Carver to FOC, May 27, 1955, FOCCGC.

8. FOC to Regina Cline O'Connor, postmarked May 31, 1955, Flannery O'Connor Papers, Stuart A. Rose Manuscript, Archives, and Rare Book Library, Emory University (FOCPEU).

9. FOC to Regina Cline O'Connor, postmarked May 31, 1955, FOCPEU.

10. FOC to Regina Cline O'Connor, postmarked May 31, 1955, FOCPEU.

11. Patrick Samway, SJ, *Flannery O'Connor and Robert Giroux: A Publishing Partnership* (Notre Dame, IN: University of Notre Dame Press, 2018), 158.

12. FOC to Regina Cline O'Connor, postmarked June 2, 1955, FOCPEU.

13. Jean Cash, *Flannery O'Connor: A Life* (Knoxville: University of Tennessee Press, 2002), 237.

14. FOC to Elizabeth McKee, June 29, 1955, *Habit*, 88.

15. FOC to Regina Cline O'Connor, postmarked June 2, 1955, FOCPEU.

16. FOC to Regina Cline O'Connor, postmarked June 2, 1955, FOCPEU.

17. Mildred Salivar to FOC, June 17, 1955, FOCPEU.

18. FOC to W.G. Rogers, June 9, 1955, Yale Collection of American Literature Manuscript Miscellany, Beinecke Rare Book and Manuscript Library, Yale University (YCAL).

19. Doug Monroe, "Asylum: Inside Central State Hospital, Once the World's Largest Mental Institution," *Atlanta Magazine,* February 18, 2015, https://www .atlantamagazine.com/great-reads/ asylum-inside-central-state-hospital-worlds-largest-mental-institution.

20. Fred Freeman [Fred Darsey], "Letters from Flannery," Sally Fitzgerald Papers, Stuart A. Rose Manuscript, Archives, and Rare Book Library, Emory University (SFPEU), 2.

21. Fred Darsey to FOC, May 23, 1955, SFPEU.

22. Fred Darsey to FOC, May 23, 1955, SFPEU.

23. Fred Darsey to FOC, May 23, 1955, SFPEU.

24. FOC to Fred Darsey, May 25, 1955, SFPEU.

25. Catharine Carver to FOC, May 27, 1955, FOCCGC.

26. Fred Freeman [Fred Darsey], "Letters from Flannery," SFPEU, 9.

27. FOC to Robert and Sally Fitzgerald, September 30, 1955, *Habit,* 108.

28. FOC to Robert and Sally Fitzgerald, June 10, 1955, *Habit,* 85.

29. Brad Gooch, *Flannery: A Life of Flannery O'Connor* (New York: Back Bay Books, 2009), 264.

30. Flannery O'Connor and Caroline Gordon, *The Letters of Flannery O'Connor and Caroline Gordon,* ed. Christine Flanagan (Athens: University of Georgia Press, 2018), 118–19.

31. FOC to Regina Cline O'Connor, postmarked May 31, 1955, FOCPEU.

32. FOC to Fred Darsey, June 8, 1955, SFPEU.

33. FOC to W.G. Rogers, June 9, 1955, YCAL.

34. W.G. Rogers to FOC, June 15, 1955, FOCPEU.

35. FOC to Regina Cline O'Connor, postmarked June 2, 1955, FOCPEU.

36. FOC to Fred Darsey, June 8, 1955, SFPEU.

37. FOC to Fred Darsey, June 8, 1955, SFPEU.

38. FOC to Denver Lindley, April 6, 1957, FOCCGC.

39. Denver Lindley to FOC, April 12, 1957, FOCCGC.

40. FOC to Denver Lindley, April 19, 1957, FOCCGC.

4 / Lourdes Bound

1. Brad Gooch, *Flannery: A Life of Flannery O'Connor* (New York: Back Bay Books, 2009), 297.

2. FOC to "A" [Betty Hester], December 14, 1957, in *The Habit of Being,* ed. Sally Fitzgerald (New York: Farrar, Straus & Giroux, 1979), 258.

3. FOC to Robert and Sally Fitzgerald, February 11, 1958, *Habit,* 266.

4. Gooch, *Flannery,* 298.

5. Unless otherwise noted, information about this trip to New York comes from the typed copy of Regina Cline O'Connor's 1958 travel diary, in Flannery O'Connor Papers, Stuart A. Rose Manuscript, Archives, and Rare Book Library, Emory University. Flannery O'Connor herself typed the document from the original handwritten document, also at MARBL.

6. Gooch, *Flannery,* 299.

7. George L. White to FOC, April 14, 1958, Flannery O'Connor Collection, Ina Dillard Russell Library Special Collections at Georgia College and State University (FOCCGC).

8. Patrick Samway, SJ, *Flannery O'Connor and Robert Giroux: A Publishing Partnership* (Notre Dame, IN: University of Notre Dame Press, 2018), 185–87.

9. Angela Alaimo O'Donnell, *Flannery O'Connor: Fiction Fired by Faith* (Collegeville, MN: Liturgical Press, 2015), 97–8.

10. FOC to John McCallum, May 17, 1958, FOCCGC.

11. George L. White, handwritten note on letter from FOC to John McCallum, May 17, 1958, FOCCGC.

5 / New York, O'Connor, and Lee

1. Brad Gooch, *Flannery: A Life of Flannery O'Connor* (New York: Back Bay Books, 2009), 313, 315.

2. Flannery O'Connor, *Flannery O'Connor: The Collected* Works, ed. Sally Fitzgerald (New York: Library of America, 1988), 1253–54.

3. Gooch, *Flannery*, 346–47.

4. Fitzgerald, *Collected Works*, 1254.

5. Fitzgerald, *Collected Works*, 1255.

6. FOC to Maryat Lee (unedited), March 26, 1961, Flannery O'Connor Collection, Ina Dillard Russell Library Special Collections at Georgia College and State University (FOCCGC).

7. Connie Ann Kirk, *Critical Companion to Flannery O'Connor* (New York: Facts on File, 2008), 382.

8. FOC to Richard Stern, June 2, 1960, in *The Books in Fred Hampton's Apartment* by Richard Stern (New York: E. P. Dutton, 1973), 213.

9. FOC to Janet McKane, July 25, 1963, in *The Habit of Being: Letters of Flannery O'Connor*, ed. Sally Fitzgerald (New York: Farrar, Straus & Giroux, 1979), 531.

10. "EcoTheater's Humanities Foundation Summer Guests," *Hinton News,* July 5, 1983, 3.

11. Maryat Lee to FOC, March 7, 1957, FOCCGC.

12. *Australian Dictionary of Biography*, "Taylor, David Phillips Foulkes (1929–1966)," by Dorothy Erickson, accessed May 16, 2023, https://adb.anu.edu.au/biography /taylor-david-phillips-foulkes-11824.

13. FOC to Maryat Lee, March 10, 1957, *Habit*, 209.

14. FOC to Maryat Lee, March 15, 1957, *Habit*, 209.

15. FOC to Maryat Lee, March 15, 1957.

16. FOC to Maryat Lee, April 4, 1957, FOCCGC.

17. Maryat Lee to FOC, March, 1958, FOCCGC.

18. FOC to Maryat Lee (unedited), April 15, 1958, FOCCGC.

19. Maryat Lee TO FOC, April, 1958, FOCCGC.

20. FOC to Maryat Lee, May 11, 1958, FOCCGC.

21. FOC to Maryat Lee, May 20, 1958, *Habit*, 284.

22. Maryat Lee to FOC, n.d. (April or May 1959), FOCCGC.

23. Maryat Lee to FOC, n.d. (August or September 1959), FOCCGC.

24. FOC to Maryat Lee, September 6, 1959, *Habit*, 348.

25. FOC to Maryat Lee, July 21, 1961, FOCCGC.

26. FOC to Maryat Lee, n.d. (August 1961), *Habit*, 447.

27. Maryat Lee to FOC, June 17, 1961, FOCCGC.
28. FOC to Maryat Lee, August 12, 1961, FOCCGC.
29. FOC to Maryat Lee, August 16, 1962, FOCCGC.
30. FOC to Maryat Lee, June 6, 1963, FOCCGC.

6 / A through G

1. "Cyrilly Abel, Authors' Agent," *New York Times*, November 19, 1975, 71.
2. FOC to Cecil Dawkins, October 9, 1958, in *The Habit of Being: Letters of Flannery O'Connor*, ed. Sally Fitzgerald (New York: Farrar, Straus & Giroux, 1979), 297.
3. FOC to Robert Giroux, April 26, 1955, Flannery O'Connor Collection, Ina Dillard Russell Library Special Collections at Georgia College and State University (FOCCGC).
4. Will Blythe, "Agee, Unfettered," *New York Times*, June 15, 2008, https://www.nytimes.com/2008/06/15/books/review/Blythe-t.html.
5. Poetry Foundation, s.v. "James Agee," accessed July 25, 2019, https://www.poetryfoundation.org/poets/james-agee.
6. FOC to Janet McKane, December 13, 1963, *Habit*, 553.
7. "Obituary Note: Ellis Amburn," *Shelf Awareness,* August 21, 2018, https://www.shelf-awareness.com/issue.html?issue=3317#m41524.
8. "Theodore S. Amussen, Book Editor, Dies at 73," *New York Times*, December 26, 1988, 64.
9. FOC to Elizabeth McKee, February 3, 1949, *Habit*, 9.
10. FOC to Regina Cline O'Connor, postmarked May 24, 1949, Flannery O'Connor Papers, Stuart A. Rose Manuscript, Archives, and Rare Book Library, Emory University (FOCPEU).
11. *Online Encyclopedia of Silver Marks, Hallmarks & Makers' Marks*, s.v. "Adda Husted-Andersen," accessed August 19, 2021, https://www.925-1000.com/M_HustedA.html.
12. FOC to Regina Cline O'Connor, September 1948, FOCPEU.
13. "Appleton-Century Mss., 1846–1962," Archives Online at Indiana University, Lilly Library, Bloomington, Indiana, accessed August 19, 2021, https://webapp1.dlib.indiana.edu/findingaids/view?doc.view=entire_text&docId=InU-Li-VAA1233.
14. *Catalog of Copyright Entries*, 3rd series, July-Dec. 1964, s.v. "The Life You Save May Be Your Own," 86.
15. Gino Ardito to FOC, August 10, 1963, FOCPEU.
16. David Farmer, *Flannery O'Connor: A Descriptive Bibliography* (New York: Garland Publishing, 1981), 117.
17. FOC to Gino Ardito, September 25, 1963, FOCPEU.
18. Carol Loeb Shloss, "O'Connor's Real Estate: Farming Intellectual Property," in *Reconsidering Flannery O'Connor*, ed. Alison Arant and Jordon Cofer (Jackson: University Press of Mississippi, 2020), 247.
19. "Miss Oppenheimer Wed to a Physician," *New York Times*, March 31, 1955, 34; "Elisa Loti is Married to Dr. Mortimer Bader," *New York Times*, June 9, 1960, 36.
20. "Pauline Gilbert is Married to Dr. Mortimer E. Bader," *New York Times*, August 1, 1982, 47.
21. Maryat Lee to FOC, n.d. (1961), FOCCGC.
22. Brad Gooch, *Flannery: A Life of Flannery O'Connor* (New York: Back Bay Books, 2009), 112.

23. Gooch, *Flannery*, 115.

24. Jack Anderson, "George W. Beiswanger, 91, Dies; Dance Critic and Esthetician," *New York Times,* October 11, 1993, 8.

25. "Mrs. Barbara P. Beiswanger," *Atlanta Constitution,* January 5, 1996, 106.

26. "Brentano's," Biblio, accessed July 19, 2019, https://www.biblio.com/publisher /brentanos.

27. "Brentano's."

28. FOC to Maryat Lee, March 3, 1959, FOCCGC.

29. FOC to Robert and Sally Fitzgerald, June 10, 1955, *Habit,* 85.

30. FOC to Maryat Lee, March 29, 1959, FOCCGC.

31. Sue Jenkins Brown to FOC, June 30, 1959, in "An Unwritten Drama: Sue Jenkins Brown and Flannery O'Connor" by Ashley Brown," *Southern Review* 22 (Autumn 1986): 735.

32. Sue Jenkins Brown to FOC, July 14, 1959, in Brown, "An Unwritten Drama," 736.

33. Nancylee Novell Jonza, *The Underground Stream: The Life and Art of Caroline Gordon* (Athens: University of Georgia Press, 1995), 262.

34. Jonza, *Underground Stream,* 264.

35. Jonza, 277.

36. FOC to Beverly Brunson, March 4, 1955, Sally Fitzgerald Papers, Stuart A. Rose Manuscript, Archives, and Rare Book Library, Emory University (SFPEU).

37. Emily Langer, "Daniel Callahan, Preeminent and Probing Bioethicist, Dies at 88," *Washington Post,* July 23, 2019, https://www.washingtonpost.com/local/obituaries /daniel-callahan-preeminent-and-probing-bioethicist-dies-at-88/2019/07/23/.

38. Patrick Samway, SJ, *Flannery O'Connor and Robert Giroux: A Publishing Partnership* (Notre Dame, IN: University of Notre Dame Press, 2018), 147.

39. Lawrence, Van Gelder, "Catharine Carver, 76, an Editor of a Luminous List of Writers," *New York Times*, November 16, 1997, 50.

40. FOC to Regina Cline O'Connor, n.d. (1955), FOCPEU.

41. Samway, *Publishing Partnership*, 193.

42. Patrick J. Hayes, "The Catholic Unity League," *Ecclesiastical Review* LXIX, no. 3 (September 1923): 297.

43. FOC to Lillian Chiriaka, May 5, 1952, FOCPEU.

44. FOC to Lillian Chiriaka, May 6, 1952, FOCPEU.

45. FOC to "A" [Betty Hester], August 11, 1956, *Habit,* 169.

46. *Futures for College Women in New York* (United States: Alumnae Advisory Center, 1960), 11.

47. "A Brief History of *Commonweal*," *Commonweal Magazine,* accessed August 7, 2019, https://www.commonwealmagazine.org/history.

48. FOC to "A" [Betty Hester], May 19, 1956, *Habit,* 158.

49. "Criterion Books, Inc.," FOB (Firms Out of Business), Harry Ransom Center, University of Texas at Austin, accessed August 6, 2019, https://norman.hrc.utexas. edu/Watch/fob_search_results_next.cfm.

50. "Publisher: Thomas Y. Crowell & Co., New York, 1876–1979," Lucile Project, accessed 8/6, 2019, http://sdrc.lib.uiowa.edu/lucile/publishers/crowell/cr_intro.htm.

51. Matt Falber, January 16, 2014, updated Dec 06, 2017, answer to "Why is There No 4th Ave. in Manhattan?" The Blog, HuffPost, https://www.huffpost.com/entry/why -is-there-no-4th-ave-i_b_4611034#:~:text.

52. Gooch, *Flannery*, 155.

53. FOC to Regina Cline O'Connor, n.d. (September 1948), FOCPEU; FOC to Regina Cline O'Connor, n.d. (March 1949), FOCPEU.

54. Rachel Shteir, "Everybody Slept Here," *New York Times,* November 10, 1996, 71.

55. Paulina Bren, *The Barbizon: The Hotel That Set Women Free* (New York: Simon & Schuster, 2021), 98.

56. Bren, *Barbizon*, 101–5.

57. Bren, 107–108.

58. "A Creative Commune in 1940s Brooklyn Heights," *Ephemeral New York* (blog), WordPress, July 28, 2011, https://ephemeralnewyork.wordpress.com/tag/george-davis-harpers-bazaar/.

59. Bren, *Barbizon*, 100.

60. Encyclopedia.com, s.v. "Lenya, Lotte (1898–1981)," accessed April 29, 2023, https://www.encyclopedia.com/women/encyclopedias-almanacs-transcripts-and-maps/lenya-lotte-1898–1981.

61. Arthur Vermeersch, "Catholic Encyclopedia (1913), s.v. Henri and Jules Desclee," accessed July 24, 2019, https://en.wikisource.org/wiki/Catholic_Encyclopedia_(1913)/Henri_and_Jules_Desclee (site discontinued).

62. Lawrence Van Gelder, "Candida Donadio, 71, Agent Who Handled 'Catch-22,' Dies," *New York Times,* January 25, 2001, 9.

63. "Msgr. Daniel M. Dougherty Dies," *New York Times,* December 8, 1978, 6.

64. FOC to Regina Cline O'Connor, postmarked July 15, 1948, FOCPEU.

65. Sally Fitzgerald, "Flannery O'Connor: Patterns of Friendship, Patterns of Love," *Georgia Review* 52, no. 3 (Fall 1998): 413.

66. FOC to Regina Cline O'Connor, September 1948, FOCPEU.

67. *Encyclopaedia Brittanica*, s.v. "Esquire American Magazine," last modified August 17, 2017, https://www.britannica.com/topic/Esquire-American-magazine.

68. Laura Miller, "Death of the Red-Hot Center," *Salon*, August 11, 2000, https://www.salon.com/2000/08/11/guide_intro/.

69. FOC to Maryat Lee, June 6, 1963, FOCCGC.

70. "Farrar, Straus and Giroux Inc. History," Funding Universe, http://www.fundinguniverse.com/company-histories/farrar-straus-and-giroux-inc-history.

71. "Farrar, Straus and Giroux Inc. History."

72. Christopher Lehmann-Haupt, "Roger W. Straus Jr., Book Publisher from the Age of the Independents, Dies at 87," *New York Times,* May 27, 2004, 10.

73. Gooch, *Flannery*, 181.

74. Gooch, 184.

75. Fitzgerald, "Patterns of Friendship," 415–16.

76. Fitzgerald, 416.

77. FOC to Thomas Stritch, March 28, 1959, in *Flannery O'Connor: The Collected Works*, ed. Sally Fitzgerald (New York: Library of America, 1988), 1090–91.

78. FOC to Mary Virginia Harrison, March 12, 1950, FOCCGC.

79. Lyman Fulton, in "Flannery O'Connor on the West Side: Dr. Lyman Fulton's Recollections of a Short Acquaintance" by Virginia Wray, *English Language Notes* 39, no. 1 (2001): 77.

80. Fulton, "Recollections," 76.

81. Richard Gilman, "On Flannery O'Connor," *New York Review of Books*, August 21, 1969, https://www.nybooks.com/articles/1969/08/21/on-flannery-oconnor/.

82. Samway, *Flannery O'Connor*, 19.

NOTES TO PAGES 67-72 / 157

83. Christopher Lehmann-Haupt, "Robert Giroux, Editor, Publisher and Nurturer of Literary Giants, is Dead at 94," *New York Times*, September 6, 2008, 6.

84. Gooch, *Flannery*, 162.

85. Gooch, 272.

7 / Writers and Other Artists

1. Curtis Evans, "Hello, Miss Fenwick: Getting Reacquainted with a Crime Fiction Great," in *The Make-Believe Man/A Friend of Mary Rose* by Elizabeth Fenwick (Eureka, CA: Stark House Press, 2022), 8.

2. Jessica Way (daughter of David Way), email to author, August 25, 2018.

3. Evans, "Hello, Miss Fenwick," 8.

4. Jessica Way, email.

5. Evans, "Hello, Miss Fenwick," 10.

6. Deborah Way (daughter of Elizabeth Fenwick and David Way), email to author, August 26, 2019.

7. Deborah Way, email.

8. Evans, "Hello, Miss Fenwick," 10.

9. Evans, 13.

10. Jessica Way, email to author, May 12, 2023.

11. Deborah Way, email to author, August 26, 2019.

12. Evans, "Hello, Miss Fenwick," 16.

13. Jessica Way, email to author, May 12, 2023.

14. Evans, 19-20.

15. FOC to "A" [Betty Hester], March 16, 1960, in *Habit of Being*, ed. Sally Fitzgerald (New York: Farrar, Straus, Giroux, 1979), 383.

16. FOC to Robert Giroux, April 26, 1955, Flannery O'Connor Collection, Ina Dillard Russell Library Special Collections at Georgia College and State University (FOCCGC).

17. Evans, "Hello, Miss Fenwick," 18.

18. Evans, 20.

19. "Rochelle Girson," *Gale Literature: Contemporary Authors*, Gale, 2002. *Gale Literature Resource Center*, document number GALEIH1000036945, link.gale.com /apps/doc/H1000036945/LitRC?

20. Tony Burton, "Novelist Elaine Gottlieb (1916–2004) Wrote a Short Story Based in 1940s Ajijic," Lake Chapala Artists, February 22, 2016. http://lakechapalaartists .com/?p=3116.

21. Robin Hemley, *Nola: A Memoir of Faith, Art, and Madness* (St. Paul, MN: Graywolf Press, 1998), 72–73.

22. Burton, "Novelist Elaine Gottlieb (1916–2004)."

23. Valerie Miner, "A Writer Looks Back at His Sister, His Family, and Himself," *Chicago Tribune*, September 20, 1998, https://www.chicagotribune.com/news/ct -xpm-1998-09-20-9809200250-story.html.

24. Mark Krupnick, "Elizabeth Hardwick: U.S. Writer and Wife of Poet Robert Lowell, She Co-founded the New York Review of Books," *The Guardian*, December 6, 2007, https://www.theguardian.com/news/2007/dec/06/guardian obituaries.usa.

25. Brad Gooch, *Flannery: A Life of Flannery O'Connor* (New York: Back Bay Books, 2009), 170.

26. Godfrey Hodgson, "Obituary: Patricia Highsmith," *The Independent*, February 6, 1995, https://www.independent.co.uk/news/people/obituary-patricia-highsmith-1571740.html.

27. Patricia Highsmith, *Patricia Highsmith: Her Diaries and Notebooks*, ed. Anna Von Planta (New York: Liveright Publishing, 2021), 428.

28. FOC to Regina Cline O'Connor, postmarked June 24, 1948, Flannery O'Connor Papers, Stuart A. Rose Manuscript, Archives, and Rare Book Library, Emory University (FOCPEU).

29. Joan Schenkar, *The Talented Miss Highsmith: The Secret Life and Serious Art of Patricia Highsmith* (New York: Picador, 2009), 256–57.

30. FOC to Regina Cline O'Connor, postmarked July 13, 1948, FOCPEU.

31. Patricia Highsmith to FOC, July 12, 1948, FOCPEU.

32. Andrew Wilson, *Beautiful Shadow: A Life of Patricia Highsmith* (London: Bloomsbury, 2003), 137.

33. Paul Masterson, "Remembering Wisconsin's Forgotten Gay Artist, Dudley Huppler," Shepherd Express, July 3, 2017, shepherdexpress.com/lgbtq/my-lgbtq-pov/remembering-wisconsin-s-forgotten-gay-artist-dudley-huppler.

34. Addy Sage, email to author, May 10, 2023.

35. Sage, email to author, May 13, 2023.

36. Robert Cozzolino, "Dudley Huppler: A Chronology," in *Dudley Huppler: Drawings*, ed. Robert Cozzolino, (Madison, WI: Elvehjem Museum of Art, University of Wisconsin-Madison, 2002), 94, https://digital.library.wisc.edu/1711.dl/KZ7QLX3S54ZDT85.

37. "About," Dudley Huppler, https://www.dudleyhuppler.com.

38. Addy Sage, email to author, May 13, 2023.

39. FOC to Dudley Huppler, August 13, 1961, Dudley Huppler Papers, Archives of American Art, Smithsonian Institution (DHAAA).

40. Edward Field, "Clifford Wright, Painting Yaddo Red," *Gay & Lesbian Review Worldwide* 11, no.4 (July–August 2004), https://go.gale.com.

41. Dudley Huppler, unpublished and undated book manuscript, courtesy of Addy Sage. Shared in email to author, May 10, 2023.

42. FOC to Robert Lowell, December 25, 1958, *Habit,* 311.

43. Addy Sage, email to author, May 13, 2023

44. Sage, email to author.

45. William Alfred Sessions, "*Shenandoah* and the Advent of Flannery O'Connor," *Shenandoah* 60, nos. 1–2 (March 2010), https://www.thefreelibrary.com/Shenandoah+and+the+Advent+of+Flannery+O%27Connor.-a0233492505.

46. FOC to Catharine Carver, June 27, 1955, *Habit*, 88.

47. "Carol Virginia Johnson (09/07/1928–06/10/2015)," *Victoria Times Columnist,* June 17–June 20, 2015, https://www.legacy.com/obituaries/timescolumnist.

48. "September 18, 1989: Playwright Maryat Lee Dies in Lewisburg," West Virginia Public Broadcasting, September 18, 2018, https://www.wvpublic.org/post/september-18-1989-playwright-maryat-lee-dies-lewisburg (site discontinued).

49. FOC to Regina Cline O'Connor, postmarked July 12, 1948, FOCPEU.

50. Jean Cash, *Flannery O'Connor: A Life* (Knoxville, TN: University of Tennessee Press, 2002), 119.

51. "Maisel, Edward," paid notice-Deaths, *New York Times,* March 30, 2008. https://legacy.com/us/obituaries/nytimes/name/edward-maisel-obituary?id=29192783.

52. "Vivienne Koch, 47, an Author, Critic," *New York Times,* November 30, 1961, 37.

53. "Vivienne Koch, 47."

54. "Mrs. Macleod Wed to John F. Day Jr," *New York Times*, May 16, 1955, 21.

55. Bill Eville, "For Phyllis Meras, Ink in the Veins Keeps the Spirit Young," *Vineyard Gazette*, May 13, 2021, https://vineyardgazette.com/news/2021/05/13/phyllis -meras-ink-veins-keeps-spirit-young.

56. Phyllis Meras, email to author, June 10, 2022.

57. Phyllis Meras, "Talking to Writers," in *Pages: The World of Books, Writers, and Writing*, ed. Matthew J. Bruccoli (Detroit: Gale Research Company, 1976), 168.

58. Phyllis Meras, "A Southerner and Her Stories," *Providence Sunday Journal*, May 31, 1964, W-20.

59. FOC to Robert Giroux, May 28, 1964, *Habit*, 581.

60. Phyllis Meras, phone conversation with author, May 2022.

61. Phyllis Meras, email to author, June 10, 2022.

62. 1900 U.S. census, Baldwin County, Georgia, population schedule, Gumm, p. 203A (stamped), enumeration district (ED) 1, sheet 3, dwelling 49, family 49, Edgar Moran; www.ancestry.com.

63. 1910 U.S. census, Baldwin County, Georgia, population schedule, Milledgeville, p. 164 (stamped), enumeration district (ED) 5, sheet 13A, dwelling 71, family 79, Edgar Moran; www.ancestry.com.

64. "Students of Miss Treanor Performed a Musical in the College Chapel," *Union-Recorder* (Milledgeville, GA), May 26, 1908, 2.

65. "Personal Mention," *Union-Recorder* (Milledgeville, GA), August 31, 1909, 9.

66. "Personal Mention," *Union-Recorder* (Milledgeville, GA), October 19, 1909, 14; "Personal Mention," *Union-Recorder* (Milledgeville, GA), January 4, 1910, 10.

67. "U.S., World War I Draft Registration Cards, 1917–1918," digital image s.v. "Edgar Moran," www.ancestry.com.

68. "U.S., World War I Draft Registration Cards, 1917–1918," digital image s.v. "Charles Edgar Moran," www.ancestry.com.

69. "United States Department of Veterans Affairs BIRLS Death File, 1850–2010," s.v. "Charles Edgar Moran" (1892–1972), www.ancestry.com.

70. "Service Flag at the Baptist Church," *Union-Recorder* (Milledgeville, GA), April 24, 1918, 1.

71. "U.S., World War II Draft Registration Cards, 1942," digital image s.v. "Charles Edgar Moran," www.ancestry.com.

72. 1950 U.S. census, New York County, New York, population schedule, Manhattan, n.p., enumeration district (ED) 31-1247, sheet 7, dwelling 177, Charles Edgar Moran; https://1950census.archives.gov.

73. Harold Phillips, "Smart, Gay, and Every Inch a Pip," *The Washington Times*, September 19, 1927, 9.

74. 1930 U.S. census, New York County, New York, population schedule, Manhattan, p. 37 (stamped), enumeration district (ED) 31-515, sheet 19A, dwelling 19, family 424, Edgar Moran; NARA microfilm publication T626, roll 1560.

75. 1940 U.S. census, New York County, New York, population schedule, Manhattan, n.p. enumeration district (ED) 31-860, sheet 7B, household 75, Edgar Moran; https://catalog.archives.gov.

76. 1950 U.S. census, New York County, New York, population schedule, Manhattan, n.p., enumeration district (ED) 31-1247, sheet 7, dwelling 177, Charles Edgar Moran; https://1950census.archives.gov.

77. "United States Social Security Death Index, 1935–2014," s.v. "Ida M. Boozer" (1883–1966), *Ancestry.com.*

78. Find-a-Grave, memorial page for Charles Edgar Moran (April 13, 1892–August 3, 1972), memorial ID 17255691, added January 2, 2007, created by Jack Johnson, maintained by David Hutchins Israel, https://www.findagrave.com/memorial/17255691 /charles-edgar-moran.

79. Unless otherwise noted, information about Smith Oliver comes from author's telephone interviews with Lois Benjamin (Oliver's niece) and Claude Oliver (nephew), April 2022.

80. David Leeming, *James Baldwin: A Biography* (New York: Arcade Publishing, 1984), 44.

81. Leeming, 82.

82. Information about marriage comes from Jennings' niece, Constance M. Taylor, in an email to the author, May 16, 2022.

83. People, *Jet,* February 9, 1967, 41.

84. Irene Orgel, *The Odd Tales of Irene Orgel* (New York: Eakins Press, 1967), dust jacket.

85. Irene Orgel, biographical note in *American Scholar* 15, no. 2 (Spring 1946), 146.

86. Wilson, *Beautiful Shadow,* 141.

87. Phillip Ramey, *Irving Fine: An American Composer in His Time* (Hillsdale, NY: Pendragon Press, 2005), 190–91.

88. FOC to Regina Cline O'Connor, n.d. (June 1948), FOCPEU.

89. "Lettie Rogers, 39, author, teacher," *New York Times,* May 15, 1957, 35.

90. Lettie Rogers to FOC, January 26, 1957, FOCPEU.

91. Lettie Rogers to FOC, January 26, 1957, FOCPEU.

92. "'U.S. Post Office' is Sign Over Fire Station," Bluefield Virginia News, *Bluefield (WV) Daily Telegraph,* April 7, 1938, 12.

93. "To Tour Europe," Virginia Sidelights, Bluefield Virginia News, *Bluefield (WV) Daily Telegraph,* June 26, 1932, 8.

94. "Home Town is Proud of Dr. Margaret Sutton," Bluefield Virginia News, *Bluefield (WV) Daily Telegraph,* June 11, 1926, 5.

95. Graham Personals, Bluefield Virginia News, *Bluefield (WV) Daily Telegraph,* June 13, 1923, 5; "Where Boys and Girls Are Going to College," Bluefield Virginia News, *Bluefield (WV) Daily Telegraph,* September 21, 1924, 10.

96. Virginia Sidelights, Bluefield Virginia News, *Bluefield (WV) Daily Telegraph,* April 11, 1928, 3; "Leaves for Georgia," Virginia Sidelights, Bluefield Virginia News, *Bluefield (WV) Daily Telegraph,* September 7, 1930, 7.

97. "Thirteen New Members Added to Faculty," *Colonnade,* October 4, 1930, 1.

98. Virginia Side Personals, Bluefield Virginia News, *Bluefield (WV) Daily Telegraph,* June 14, 1932, 5; "Miss Margaret Sutton Returns to New York," Bluefield Virginia News, *Bluefield (WV) Daily Telegraph,* July 27, 1939, 12.

99. Virginia Side Personals, Bluefield Virginia News, *Bluefield (WV) Daily Telegraph,* August 16, 1931, 4.

100. "To Tour Europe," Virginia Sidelights, 8.

101. Virginia Side Personals, Bluefield Virginia News, *Bluefield (WV) Daily Telegraph* July 17, 1934, 10.

102. UMW Galleries, "In 1936–37, Margaret Sutton studied with Hans Hofmann," Facebook, March 28, 2018, https://m.facebook.com/umwgalleries/photos

/in-1936-37-margaret-sutton-studied-with-hans-hofmann-hofmann-taught-at-the
-art-s/.

103. "Local Artist Paints Picture at Coal Mine," Bluefield Virginia News, *Bluefield
(WV) Daily Telegraph,* August 19, 1937, 12.

104. "Faculty Adds Thirteen New Members," *Colonnade,* September 30, 1939, 1.

105. "Miss Margaret Sutton Returns to New York," Bluefield Virginia News, 12.

106. Marjorie Och, "Margaret Sutton," Margaret Sutton, accessed July 19, 2019,
https://margaretsutton.maoch.org.

107. Marjorie Och, email to author, June 9, 2021.

108. Marjorie Och, email to author, January 19, 2020.

109. "Levitt, Alfred H. (Alfred Hofmann), 1894–2000 Photographer, Painter,"
Archives of American Art, Smithsonian Institution, accessed August 29, 2022,
https://www.aaa.si.edu/collections/alfred-levitt-papers-9028.

110. Marjorie Och, ". . . what the mind and senses conceive . . . Margaret Sutton,"
Margaret Sutton, accessed July 20, 2019, https://margaretsutton.maoch.org/what
-the-mind-and-senses-conceive-margaret-sutton/.

111. Och, ". . . what the mind and senses conceive."

112. Marjorie Och, email to author, August 20, 2022.

113. 1940 U.S. census, New York County, New York, population schedule,
Manhattan, p.1002 (stamped), enumeration district (ED) 31-874, sheet 13A, A.H.
Levitt; https://catalog.archives.gov.

114. 1950 U.S. census, New York County, New York, population schedule,
Manhattan, n.p., enumeration district (ED) 31–90, sheet 4, dwelling 69, George
Levitt; https://1950census.archives.gov.

115. Gooch, *Flannery,* 162–63.

116. "Four letters to artist Clifford Wright, comprising three Typed Letters Signed
('Flannery') and one Autograph Letter Signed ('Flannery')," Antiquarian Booksellers'
Association of America, inventory #310753, accessed August 1, 2018, https://www.abaa
.org/book/1083402714 (page discontinued).

117. Kirsten Gress, "Clifford Wright (1919–1999)," Clifford Wright, ARS Longa.dk
v/Kirsten Gress, http://arslonga.dk/Clifford_Wright.htm#English.

118. "Villa Gress," AIR database, Transartists, accessed August 1, 2018, https://
www.transartists.org/air/villa-gress/.

119. Gress, "Clifford Wright (1919–1999)."

120. Gress.

121. Edward Field, "Clifford Wright, Painting Yaddo Red," Gay & Lesbian Review
Worldwide 11, no. 4 (July–August 2004), *Gale Literature Resource Center,* link.gale
.com/apps/doc/A119024537/LitRC?u=lln_xavieru&sid=googleScholar&xid=03e
3edaf.

122. Gress, "Clifford Wright (1919–1999)."

123. Clifford Wright to FOC, July 31, 1948, FOCPEU.

124. FOC to Clifford Wright, February 20, 1954, FOCPEU.

8 / H through N

1. *Encyclopedia.com,* s.v. "Harcourt Brace Jovanovich, Inc.," accessed August 12,
2019, https://www.encyclopedia.com/books/politics-and-business-magazines/har
court-brace-jovanovich-inc.

2. *Encyclopedia.com,* s.v. "Harcourt Brace Jovanovich, Inc."

3. Patrick Samway, SJ, *Flannery O'Connor and Robert Giroux: A Publishing Partnership* (Notre Dame, IN: University of Notre Dame Press, 2018), 90–93.

4. Samway, *Publishing Partnership*, 186.

5. "Clubhouse History," Harvard Club of New York City, accessed July 19, 2019, https://www.hcny.com/about-the-club/public-history/public-clubhouse-history /#:~:text.

6. Kelly Gerald, "The Habit of Art," Afterword in *Flannery O'Connor: The Cartoons*, ed. Kelly Gerald (Seattle: Fantagraphics Books, 2012), 105.

7. Derrick Henry, "George Haslam, 89, Teacher, Journalist, Art Subject," *Atlanta Journal-Constitution,* December 5, 2001, B8.

8. George Haslam to FOC, June 12, 1955, Flannery O'Connor Papers, Stuart A. Rose Manuscript, Archives, and Rare Book Library, Emory University (FOCPEU).

9. "19th & 20th Century Literature: Sale 2355—Lot 192," *Swann Galleries Catalogue,* June 19, 2014 sale, https://catalogue.swanngalleries.com/Lots/auction-lot /OCONNOR-FLANNERY-A-Good-Man-is-Hard-to-Find?saleno=2355&lotNo =192&refNo=684022.

10. "Robert Hatch, 83, Critic and Editor," *New York Times,* June 3, 1994, https:// www.nytimes.com/1994/06/03/obituaries/robert-hatch-83-critic-and-editor.html.

11. FOC to Cecil Dawkins, March 23, 1960, in *The Habit of Being: Letters of Flannery O'Connor*, ed. Sally Fitzgerald (New York: Farrar, Straus & Giroux, 1979), 384.

12. FOC to Maryat Lee, October 9, 1962, *Habit*, 495.

13. FOC to Hiram Haydn, May 18, 1963, FOCPEU.

14. "All Health Foods Distributors Inc.," *New York Age Defender*, June 12, 1954, 6.

15. Sally Fitzgerald in *The Habit of Being: Letters of Flannery O'Connor*, ed. Sally Fitzgerald (New York: Farrar, Straus & Giroux, 1979), 22.

16. FOC to Mary Cline, n.d. (July 1943), FOCPEU.

17. FOC to Regina Cline O'Connor, postmarked June 24, 1948, FOCPEU.

18. FOC to Regina Cline O'Connor, postmarked May 31, 1955, and June 1, 1955, FOCPEU.

19. FOC to Cecil Dawkins, May 23, 1960, *Habit*, 397.

20. FOC to Maryat Lee, May 31, 1960, *Habit*, 399.

21. Laura Miller, "Death of the Red-Hot Center," *Salon*, August 11, 2000, https:// www.salon.com/2000/08/11/guide_intro/.

22. Rust Hills to FOC, October 31, 1963, FOCPEU.

23. FOC to Rust Hills, November 6, 1963, FOCPEU.

24. "H. Stanley Hillyer, 67, Williams '08, Succumbs," *North Adams, Massachusetts Transcript,* January 3, 1955, 11.

25. *Catalog of Copyright Entries*, 3rd series, vol. 6., s.v. "1952, Published Music: Hillyer, H. Stanley, 1887," 99.

26. Matt Falber, January 16, 2014, updated December 06, 2017, answer to "Why Is There No 4th Ave. in Manhattan?" The Blog, HuffPost, https://www.huffpost.com /entry/why-is-there-no-4th-ave-i_b_4611034#:~:text.

27. John Maher, "Obituary: Roslyn Targ, Longtime Agent, Dies at 92," *Publishers Weekly,* November 3, 2017, https://www.publishersweekly.com/pw/by -topic/industry-news/Obituary/article/75278-obituary-roslyn-targ-longtime -agent-dies-at-92.html."

28. "Franz Horch Dies; A Literary Agent," *New York Times,* December 16, 1951, 91.

29. Terry Trucco, "The Fitzpatrick Manhattan Hotel," Overnight New York, accessed July 31, 2019, https://overnightnewyork.com/portfolio-item/fitzpatrick -manhattan-hotel.

30. Lois Weiss, "Literary Hotel to Return," *New York Post,* September 9, 2011, nypost.com/2011/09/09/literary-hotel-to-return.

31. FOC to Robert Giroux, April 16, 1952, *Habit,* 34.

32. FOC to Elizabeth McKee, November 26, 1952, *Habit,* 48.

33. Mary Rourke, "Frederick Morgan, 81; Founder, Editor of Hudson Review Literary Magazine," *Los Angeles Times,* February 25, 2004, https://www.latimes.com /archives/la-xpm-2004-feb-25-me-morgan25-story.html.

34. Catharine Hughes, "Ionesco's 'Approaches to Truth,'" review, *The Antioch Review* 21, no. 1 (Spring 1961), 105.

35. "Catharine R. Hughes Service," *New York Times,* August 4, 1987, B-4.

36. FOC to "A" [Betty Hester], August 28, 1955, *Habit,* 97.

37. "Administrative/Biographical History," Helene Iswolsky Collection, McHugh Special Collections, University of Scranton, https://digitalservices.scranton.edu/digital /collection/iswolsky/custom/iswolsky-collectionguide#acquisition.

38. Dorothy Day, "Catholic Worker Movement," *Catholic Worker,* January 1976, republished in CatholicWorker.org, February 5, 2022, https://catholicworker. org/566-html.

39. Paul Elie, *The Life You Save May Be Your Own: An American Pilgrimage* (New York: Farrar, Straus & Giroux, 2003), 221.

40. 1940 U.S. census, New York County, New York, population schedule, Manhattan, p. 10339 (stamped), enumeration district (ED) 31-900, sheet 8A, Edith Ivey; https://catalog.archives.gov.

41. 1950 U.S. census, Fulton County, Georgia, population schedule, Atlanta, n.p., enumeration district (ED) 160–432, sheet 3, Edith Ivey; https://catalog.archives.gov.

42. Henry Hart, *James Dickey: The World as a Lie* (New York: Picador, 2001), 221.

43. FOC to Edith Ivey, December 25, 1962, Flannery O'Connor Collection, Stuart A. Rose Manuscript, Archives, and Rare Book Library, Emory University (FOCCEU).

44. Edith Ivey to FOC, March 2, 1963, FOCCEU.

45. "Miss Edith Ivey," *Macon Telegraph,* September 21, 1970, 14.

46. Find-a-Grave, memorial page for Edith Ivey (April 8, 1911–September 20, 1970), memorial ID 16198927, October 15, 2006, created by Jack Johnson, maintained by David Hutchins Israel, https://www.findagrave.com/memorial/16198927/edith -ivey.

47. "Herb Jaffe Biography (c. 1921–1991)," Film Reference, accessed July 19, 2021, www.filmreference.com/film/52/Herb-Jaffe.html.

48. Chris Chase, "At the Movies," *New York Times,* November 18, 1983, 66.

49. Michael Konsmo, "Robert Jiras," *Variety,* February 24, 2000, https://variety .com/2000/scene/people-news/robert-jiras-1117883538.

50. FOC to "A" [Betty Hester], August 24, 1956, *Habit,* 171.

51. FOC to "A" [Betty Hester], September 8, 1956, *Habit,* 174.

52. Chase, "At the Movies," 66.

53. Sue Jenkins Brown to FOC, January 17, 1958, in "An Unwritten Drama: Sue Jenkins Brown and Flannery O'Connor" by Ashley Brown, *Southern Review,* 22 (Autumn 1986): 733.

54. Konsmo, "Robert Jiras."

55. Claire Kelley, "Remembering *Jubilee* Magazine," *Moby Lives* (blog) Melville House Publishing, February 13, 2013, https://www.mhpbooks.com/remembering -jubilee-magazine/.

56. Estolv Ethan Ward, "Organizing and Reporting on Labor in the East Bay, California and the West, 1925–1987," oral history conducted in 1987 by Lisa Rubens, Regional Oral History Office, Bancroft Library, University of California, Berkeley, 1989.

57. "Jurasz-Dambska, Krystyna (1921–2000)," WorldCat Identities, WorldCat.org., http://worldcat.org/identities/viaf-101798931.

58. "Through the Decades," IIE (The Power of International Education), accessed July 19, 2019, https://www.iie.org/en/Why-IIE/History.

59. "King Features History," King Features website, accessed July 31, 2019, http://kingfeatures.com/about-us/king-features-history.

60. Information for this entry comes from Anna Maria Green Cook's *History of Baldwin County, Georgia* (Anderson, SC: Keys-Hearn Print Co., 1925), 418–23.

61. Robert Maas, "My Changeable Life: The Story of Marguerite Baralevsky Langkjaer '24, from Czarist Palaces to Vassar, and Beyond," *Vassar Quarterly* 50, no.4 (June 1, 1984): 27.

62. Brad Gooch, *Flannery: A Life of Flannery O'Connor* (New York: Back Bay Books, 2009), 230.

63. Sally Fitzgerald, "Flannery O'Connor: Patterns of Friendship, Patterns of Love," *Georgia Review* 52, no. 3 (Fall 1998): 420.

64. Klaus Rothstein, "Kiss of Death" *Asymptote*, October 2014, https://www .asymptotejournal.com/nonfiction/klaus-rothstein-flannery-oconnors-kiss-of -death/#:~:text.

65. Maas, "My Changeable Life," 27.

66. Mel Gussow, "James Laughlin, Publisher with Bold Taste, Dies at 83," *New York Times*, November 14, 1997, D-19.

67. Gussow, "James Laughlin."

68. FOC to Regina Cline O'Connor, postmarked June 27, 1952, FOCPEU.

69. "Building: Central Savings Bank, Now Apple Bank," Streeteasy, accessed July 16, 2019, https://streeteasy.com/building/central-savings-bank-now-apple-ban.

70. Samway, *Publishing Partnership*, 172.

71. "Denver Lindley, Editor, Dies; Translator of Mann, Maurois," *New York Times*, February 15, 1982, D-7.

72. Gooch, *Flannery*, 160; 165.

73. Gooch, 159.

74. Robert Lowell to Peter Taylor, August 6, [1949], in *The Letters of Robert Lowell*, ed. Saskia Hamilton (New York: Farrar, Straus & Giroux, 2005), 143.

75. Robie Macauley, "Who Should Mourn?" Letters to the Editor, *New York Times*, Aug. 8, 1976, 169.

76. "26 Germans in Spy Ring Seized," *New York Times*, October 30, 1945, 2.

77. Eric Pace, "Robie Macauley, 76, Editor, Educator and Fiction Writer," *New York Times*, November 23, 1995, D-21.

78. Margaret Whitt, "Stopped by a Naked Woman: O'Connor's Departure from the Kenyon Review," *Flannery O'Connor Bulletin*, 26–27 (1998–2000): 173.

79. Margarita G. Smith to FOC, June 19, 1947, FOCPEU.

80. Margarita G. Smith to FOC, September 11, 1947, FOCPEU.

81. FOC to "A" [Betty Hester], May 5, 1956, *Habit*, 156.

82. Tom Miller, "The 1891 Margaret Louisa Home—No. 14 East 16th Street," *Daytonian in Manhattan* (blog), March 8, 2011, http://daytonianinmanhattan .blogspot.com/2011/03/1891-margaret-louisa-home-no-14-east.html.

83. Daphne Spain, *How Women Saved the City* (Minneapolis: University of Minnesota Press, 2001), 146.

84. Lisa M. Santoro, "How the Martha Washington Went from Women-Only Lodging to Hip Hotel," Curbed Classics, *Curbed New York*, September 21, 2016, https://ny.curbed.com/2016/9/21/13005332/nyc-hotels-martha-washington-history.

85. FOC to "A" [Betty Hester], January 19, 1963, *Habit*, 505–506.

86. FOC to Janet McKane, May 17, 1963, *Habit*, 520.

87. Anita Gates, "Alice Mayhew, Who Edited a Who's Who of Writers, Dies at 87," *New York Times*, February 4, 2020, https://www.nytimes.com/2020/02/04/books/alice -mayhew-dead.html.

88. Tyler Arnold, "Report Finds 28 Credible Child Sex Abuse Claims of Georgia Priests in Last 70 Years," *Catholic News Agency*, March 29, 2023, https://www .catholicnewsagency.com/news/253972/report-finds-28-credible-child-sex-abuse -claims-of-georgia-priests-in-last-70-years.

89. Richard Stern, "On Reprinting 'Golk,'" *Agni* 26 (1988): 32.

90. Brainard Cheney to FOC, September 25, 1963, in *Correspondence of Flannery O'Connor and the Brainard Cheneys*, ed. C. Ralph Stephens (Jackson: University Press of Mississippi, 1986), 74.

91. Cheney to FOC, October 12, 1963, *Correspondence*, 177.

92. Cheney to FOC, September 27, 1963, *Correspondence*, 175.

93. Cheney to FOC, September 25, 1963, *Correspondence*, 173.

94. "Company History," McGraw-Hill, https://www.mheducation.com/about.html.

95. Mark Maurer, "The McGraw-Hill Building's Top Half to Receive Resi Conversion," *The Real Deal*, June 27, 2018, https://therealdeal.com/2018/06/27/the -mcgraw-hill-buildings-top-half-to-receive-resi-conversion.

96. FOC to Maryat Lee, February 24, 1957, *Habit*, 203.

97. Samway, *Publishing Partnership*, 31.

98. "Mavis McIntosh Riordan, 83; Represented Noted Writers," *New York Times*, August 6, 1986, https://www.nytimes.com/1986/08/06/obituaries/mavis-mcintosh -riordan-83-represented-noted-writers.html.

99. FOC to Elizabeth McKee, June 19, 1948, *Habit*, 4.

100. William Hjortsberg, *Jubilee Hitchhiker: The Life and Times of Richard Brautigan*, (Berkeley: Counterpoint; Reprint edition, 2013), 243.

101. Arthur Axelman, "'Son of the Morning Star'—the Battle of Three Networks," *The Wrap*, November 10, 2011, https://www.thewrap.com/son-morning-star-battle-3 -networks-32681.

102. Samway, *Publishing Partnership*, 31.

103. Hjortsberg, *Jubilee Hitchhiker*, 243.

104. "Notes on Current Books," *Virginia Quarterly Review* 39, no. 1 (Winter 1963): xv.

105. Miriam McKenzie to FOC, postcard, postmarked 1963, FOCPEU.

106. Tom Miller, "The 1868 Grand Hotel—Broadway and 31st Street," *Daytonian in Manhattan* (blog), July 3, 2010, http://daytoninmanhattan.blogspot.com/2010/07 /1868-grand-hotel-broadway-and-31st.html/.

107. FOC to Robert Giroux, April 26, 1955, Flannery O'Connor Collection, Ina Dillard Russell Library Special Collections at Georgia College and State University (FOCCGC).

108. Samway, *Publishing Partnership*, 187.

109. "New York Public Library. Collection: Farrar, Straus & Giroux, Inc. Records 1899–1992," Postmarked Milledgeville, last modified September 2022, https://www .postmarkedmilledgeville.com/new-york-public-library.

110. "About," New Directions, accessed July 19, 2022, https://www.ndbooks.com /about/.

111. Correspondence between FOC and Catharine Carver, May 24 and May 27, 1955, FOCCGC.

9 / Three Correspondents

1. "Michigan, U.S., Death Records, 1867–1952," digital image s.v. "Donna Crandall [*sic*] Price," (1878–1912), www.ancestry.com.

2. Susan Bridges (Price's relative), email to author, September 19, 2021.

3. Bridges, email, September 19, 2021.

4. Qtd in Bridges, email to author, September 20, 2022.

5. "Michigan, U.S., Death Records, 1867–1952," digital image s.v. for "Edward H. Price," (1866–1936), www.ancestry.com.

6. 1940 U.S. Federal Census. New York County, New York, population schedule, Manhattan, n.p., enumeration district (ED) 31-878B, sheet 4B, household 213, Richard Price; https://catalog.archives.gov.

7. "U.S., World War II Draft Cards Young Men, 1940–1947," digital image s.v. "Richard Du Calm Price," www.ancestry.com.

8. 1950 U.S. Federal Census. New York County, New York, population schedule, Manhattan, n.p., enumeration district (ED) 31–96, sheet 80, dwelling 225, Richard J. Price; https://1950census.archives.gov.

9. Susan Bridges, email to author, August 3, 2019.

10. James Greene, "The Comic and the Sad," *Commonweal,* July 22, 1955, 404.

11. FOC to "A" [Betty Hester], August 28, 1955, in *Habit of Being*, ed. Sally Fitzgerald (New York: Farrar, Straus, Giroux, 1979), 98.

12. Crandell Price to FOC, n.d. (November 1955), Flannery O'Connor Papers, Stuart A. Rose Manuscript, Archives, and Rare Book Library, Emory University (FOCPEU).

13. Crandell Price to FOC, n.d. (1955 or 1956), FOCPEU.

14. FOC to "A" [Betty Hester], January 13, 1956, *Habit*, 128.

15. Susan Bridges, email to author, August 9, 2019.

16. Crandell Price to FOC, n.d. (1955 or 1956), FOCPEU.

17. Susan Bridges, email to author, September 19, 2021.

18. Beverly Brunson to FOC, n.d. (1953), Sally Fitzgerald Papers, Stuart A. Rose Manuscript, Archives, and Rare Book Library, Emory University (SFPEU).

19. FOC to Beverly Brunson November 16, 1953, SFPEU.

20. FOC to Robert and Sally Fitzgerald, January 4, (1954), *Habit*, 916.

21. FOC to Beverly Brunson, December 31, 1953, SFPEU.

22. FOC to Beverly Brunson, February 17, 1954, SFPEU.

23. Beverly Brunson to FOC, January 11, 1954, SFPEU.

24. FOC to Beverly Brunson, January 22, 1954, SFPEU.

25. FOC to Beverly Brunson, November 26, 1953, SFPEU; FOC to Beverly Brunson, February 17, 1954, SFPEU; FOC to Beverly Brunson, March 4, 1955, SFPEU.

26. FOC to Beverly Brunson, March 4, 1955, SFPEU.

27. FOC to Beverly Brunson, January 1, 1955, in *Flannery O'Connor: The Collected Works*, ed. Sally Fitzgerald (New York: Library of America, 1988), 928.

28. FOC to Beverly Brunson, March 4, 1955, SFPEU.

29. FOC to Beverly Brunson, March 4, 1955, SFPEU.

30. Beverly Brunson to FOC, June 21, 1955, SFPEU

31. Beverly Brunson to FOC, June 21, 1955, SFPEU.

32. Beverly Brunson to FOC, June 21, 1955, SFPEU.

33. Beverly Brunson to FOC, June 21, 1955, SFPEU.

34. FOC to Elizabeth McKee, December 2, 1955, FOCPEU.

35. FOC to "A" [Betty Hester], December 28, 1956, *Collected Works*, 1016.

36. FOC to Beverly Brunson, September 13, 1954, *Collected Works*, 925.

37. FOC to Beverly Brunson, January 1, 1955. *Collected Works*, 928.

38. Beverly Brunson to FOC, December 27, 1954, SFPEU.

39. Larry Rivera, *The JFK Horsemen: Framing Lee, Altering the Altgen6, and Resolving Other Mysteries* (Crestview, FL: Moon Rock Books, 2018), 430.

40. Rivera, *JFK Horsemen*, 429.

41. Rivera, *JFK Horsemen*, 482.

42. Project JFK, "The New JFK Show: #237 Beverly Brunson the Great," YouTube video, May 22, 2019. 56:59, https://www.youtube.com/watch?v=f_AlqKsfN5w

43. Rivera, *JFK Horsemen*, 429.

44. "U.S., School Yearbooks, 1900–2016 for Fred F. Darsey," database with images, *Ancestry* (https://www.ancestry.com: accessed July 30, 2019) > Georgia > Athens > University of Georgia > 1947, image 90.

45. "About the Spalding County Times (Griffin, Spalding County, Ga.) 1950–1952," *Chronicling America*, Library of Congress, https://chroniclingamerica.loc.gov/lccn /sn89053343.

46. FOC to Fred Darsey, January 22, 1955, SFPEU.

47. FOC to Fred Darsey, March 6, 1955, SFPEU. (Because most of Darsey's letters to O'Connor are unavailable, much is inferred from reading O'Connor's responses.)

48. Fred Darsey to FOC, May 23, 1955, SFPEU.

49. Brad Gooch, *Flannery: A Life of Flannery O'Connor* (New York: Back Bay Books, 2009), 263.

50. FOC to Fred Darsey, December 28, 1955, SFPEU.

51. FOC to Fred Darsey, July 29, 1956, SFPEU.

52. "News of Advertising and Marketing," *New York Times,* November 22, 1956, 68.

53. "Saturday, June 21, 1958," Department of Parks press release, accessed July 29, 2019, https://www.nyc.gov/html/records/pdf/govpub/42451958_press_releases_part1. pdf.

54. Fred Freeman [Fred Darsey], "Letters from Flannery," 21. SFPEU.

55. Freeman, 21.

56. FOC to Fred Darsey, July 13, 1959, SFPEU.

57. Sally Fitzgerald, "Flannery O'Connor: Patterns of Friendship, Patterns of Love," *Georgia Review* 52, no. 3 (Fall 1998), 421.

58. FOC to Fred Darsey, July 13, 1959, SFPEU.

59. FOC to Fred Darsey, May 25, 1960, SFPEU.

60. Gooch, *Flannery*, 263.

61. Fred Freeman [Fred Darsey], "Letters from Flannery," SFPEU, 30.

62. Regina Cline O'Connor to Fred Darsey, May 29, 1973, SFPEU.

63. Sally Fitzgerald to Fred Darsey, June 1, 1979, SFPEU.

64. "Signs Proclaiming 'Closing Out Sale' Send Owner to Jail," *New York* Times, March 2, 1966, 43.

65. Sandra Adickes, "Terra Cottta Terrorized," *East Village Other*, March 15, 1966, 11.

66. Adickes, 11.

67. "Signs Proclaiming," 43.

68. Adickes, "Terra Cottta Terrorized," 11.

69. Ed Bewley, "Statewide Alert Out for Kidnap Suspect," *Herald-Tribune* (Sarasota), August 8, 1968, 1.

70. "Father Arrested in Son's Seizure," *Herald-Tribune* (Sarasota), August 9, 1968, 1.

71. "United States v. Frederick Freeman Darsey, 431 F.2d 963 (5th Cir. 1970)," Court Listener, https://www.courtlistener.com/opinion/292179/united-states-v-frederick -freeman-darsey/.

72. Fred Darsey to Sally Fitzgerald, July 9, 1979, SFPEU.

73. Sally Fitzgerald to Fred Darsey, June 1, 1979, SFPEU.

74. Fitzgerald, "Patterns of Friendship," 423.

75. "Massachusetts, Town and Vital Records, 1620–1988," s.v. "Frederick Freeman Darsey," (died Feb. 7, 1980), www.ancestry.com.

10 / O through Z

1. Louise Florencourt, conversation with author, August 10, 2018, Milledgeville, Georgia.

2. R. Neil Scott, ed., *Flannery O'Connor: An Annotated Reference Guide to Criticism* (Milledgeville, GA: Timberlane Books, 2002), 77.

3. Tiffany Stevens and Maura Friedman, "Still Silent: After 24 Years, a Family's Yellow House Sits Quietly," *Red and Black*, October 6, 2011, last modified September 28, 2022, https://www.redandblack.com/magazine/35-years-later-remembering-the-athens -murders-of-1987/article_cff0871c-3f6d-11ed-a736-9f2c4f83d2e9.html.

4. Stevens and Friedman, "Still Silent."

5. Wayne Ford, "High Court Upholds Life Terms for Athens Killer," *Athens Banner-Herald*, Onlineathens.com., January 30, 2020, https://www.onlineathens. com/story/news/crime/2020/01/30/high-court-upholds-life-terms-for-athens -killer/1795772007/.

6. Monte Williams, "Instant Nostalgia as Two Havens for Young Women Close," *New York Times,* June 28, 2000, B-1.

7. FOC to "A" [Betty Hester], August 5, 1961, in *Habit of Being*, ed. Sally Fitzgerald (New York: Farrar, Straus & Giroux, 1979), 446.

8. Sam Tanenhaus, "Hello to All That: The Irony behind the Demise of the *Partisan Review*," *Slate,* April 16, 2003, https://slate.com/culture/2003/04/the-demise -of-the-partisan-review.html.

9. FOC to Regina Cline O'Connor, August 2, 1948, Flannery O'Connor Papers, Stuart A. Rose Manuscript, Archives, and Rare Book Library, Emory University (FOCPEU).

10. David Poor (Priscilla Poor's nephew), interview with author, April 12, 2023.

11. 1950 U.S. census, New York County, New York, population schedule, Manhattan, n.p., enumeration district (ED) 31-1410, sheet 73, dwelling 165, Lyn Masters; https://1950census.archives.gov.

12. "The Winter Social Season Awakens," *New York Times,* November 5, 1916, 3.

13. "New York, New York, U.S., Birth Index, 1910–1965," database with images. *Ancestry* (https:www.ancestry.com: accessed August 5, 2022) >1916> Manhattan, certificate 43[?]3[?]11, Female Poor, born September 9; citing New York Department of Health, www.vitalsearch-worldwide.com.

14. "Henry W. Poor Fails: Loss Over a Million," *New York Times,* December 27, 1908, 1.

15. "Henry V. Poor Buys Hoagland Residence on East Sixty-Sixth Street," *New York Times,* March 3, 1928, 32.

16. "Lenox Hill Home Sold to Operator," *New York Times*, December 3, 1931, 51.

17. 1930 U.S. census, New York County, New York, population schedule, Manhattan, p. 212 (stamped), enumeration district (ED) 31-562, sheet 8A, dwelling 71, family 152, Priscilla Poor; NARA microfilm publication T626, roll 1567.

18. New York, U.S., Arriving Passenger and Crew Lists (including Castle Garden and Ellis Island), 1820–1957, database entry for Priscella (*sic*) Poor, 14, arrived September 25, 1929 on the S.S. *Homeric.*

19. Feijun Luo, Curtis S. Florence, Miriam Quispe-Agnoli, Lijing Ouyang, and Alexander E. Crosby, "Impact of Business Cycles on U.S. suicide rates, 1928–2007, *American Journal of Public Health*, 101, no. 6 (2011): 1141, https://doi.org/10.2105/AJPH .2010.300010.

20. "Lenox Hill Home Sold to Operator," 51.

21. David Poor, interview, 2023.

22. "Priscilla Poor's Debut," *New York Times*, September 9, 1933, 10-L.

23. "Younger Social Set Entertained at Dance at the White House," *Washington Evening Star*, December 31, 1933, 21.

24. "Travelers Aid Society Benefit Committees for Garden Party on Friday," *Brooklyn Daily Eagle,* June 3, 1934, 4 B-C.

25. New York, U.S., Arriving Passenger and Crew Lists (including Castle Garden and Ellis Island), 1820–1957, database entry for Priscilla Poore (*sic*), 18, arrived January 31, 1934, on the SS *Aquitania.*

26. New York, U.S., Arriving Passenger and Crew Lists (including Castle Garden and Ellis Island), 1820–1957, database for Priscilla Poor, 20, departed April 25, 1936, on the SS *Queen of Bermuda*; New York, U.S., Arriving Passenger and Crew Lists (including Castle Garden and Ellis Island), 1820–1957, database entry for Priscilla Poor, 22, departed September 5, 1937, on the SS *Monarch of Bermuda.*

27. "Two More Debutantes Trip up to Altar," *Daily News* (New York), September 21, 1935, 8.

28. "Ruth Poor Wears Veil Used by Four Others," *Daily News* (New York), June 25, 1936, 55.

29. "Heirlooms Add Bit of Sentiment to Four Weddings," *Chicago Tribune,* November 15, 1936, 18.

30. Denley Poor-Reynolds (Priscilla Poor's niece) quotes brother David Poor in email to author, November 18, 2022.

31. "Cast of Stock Players Do Well with Mystery," *Lake Placid News,* August 16, 1940, 9.

32. Shelley Winters, *Shelley: Also Known as Shirley* (New York: William Morrow and Co., 1980), 53.

33. "College Club Names Officers for Year," *Citizen and Chronicle* (Cranford, NJ), March 11, 1943, 1.

34. Corbin Old, "Miss Walker is Married to Lt. Poor," *Richmond Times-Dispatch*, October 21, 1944, 7.

35. Denley Poor-Reynolds (Priscilla Poor's niece), telephone conversation with author, August 27, 2022.

36. *King Encyclopedia*, s.v. "Popper, Hermine Rich Isaacs," accessed July 19, 2019, The Martin Luther King, Jr. Research and Education Institute Stanford University, https://kinginstitute.stanford.edu/encyclopedia/popper-hermine-rich-isaacs.

37. "Ruby Hat goes for 53k in Auction," ABC 13, Houston, November 8, 2009, https://abc13.com/archive.

38. Elizabeth Reynolds Hapgood, "Foreword to the Second Edition," in *Stanislavski's Legacy, A Collection of Comments on a Variety of Aspects of an Actor's Art and Life* by Constantin Stanivslavski, ed. and trans. Elizabeth Reynolds Hapgood (New York: Routledge, 1968), v.

39. Emily Witt, "How Catch-18 Became Catch-14 and Finally Catch-22," *Observer*, July 20, 2011, http://observer.com/2011/07/how-catch-18-became-catch-14-and-finally -catch-22/.

40. Correspondence between FOC and Catharine Carver, May 16, 1955 and May 18, 1955, Flannery O'Connor Collection, Ina Dillard Russell Library Special Collections at Georgia College and State University (FOCCGC).

41. "Theodore M. Purdy, 75; Book-Publishing Leader," *New York Times*, July 15, 1979, 34.

42. "Philip Rahv, Critic, Dead at 64; English Professor at Brandeis," *New York Times*, December 24, 1973, 16.

43. Ben Sisario, "Stewart Richardson, 78, Editor with a Roster of Noted Writers." *New York Times,* July 8, 2004, C-12.

44. "Frederick Rinehart, 78, Led Publishing Houses," *New York Times,* June 17, 1981, B-5.

45. "William G. Rogers Dies; Arts Editor for the A.P.," *New York Times*, March 2, 1978, B-22.

46. FOC to Regina Cline O'Connor, postmarked June 2, 1955, FOCPEU.

47. W.G. Rogers, Associated Press, Literary Guidepost, Associated Press. *Corsicana Daily Sun* (Texas), June 3, 1955, 8.

48. See, for example, *The Daily Advertiser* (Lafayette, LA), June 5, 1955, 27.

49. FOC to W.G. Rogers, June 9, 1955, Yale Collection of American Literature Manuscript Miscellany, Beinecke Rare Book and Manuscript Library, Yale University.

50. Mildred Salivar to FOC, June 17, 1955, FOCPEU.

51. "Archives: Books and Authors," *New York Times,* September 25, 1964, https://www.nytimes.com/1964/09/25/archives/books-and-authors.html.

52. FOC to Cecil Dawkins, February 22, 1959, *Habit*, 320.

53. FOC to Cecil Dawkins, October 31, 1959, *Habit*, 356.

54. FOC to Regina Cline O'Connor, July 21, 1948, FOCPEU.

55. FOC to Regina Cline O'Connor, September, 1948, FOCPEU.

56. David O. Dowling, *A Delicate Aggression: Savagery and Survival in the Iowa Writers' Workshop*, New Haven, CT: Yale University Press, 2019, 43.

57. Paul Elie, *The Life You Save May Be Your Own: An American Pilgrimage* (New York: Farrar, Straus & Giroux, 2003), 173.

58. "Novelist of Note: John Selby," Davies County Historical Society, March 2, 2004, http://daviesscountyhistoricalsociety.com/2004/03/02/novelist-of-note-john -selby.

59. Christopher Lehmann-Haupt, "Wilfrid Sheed, Writer of Gentle Wit, Dies at 80," *New York Times,* January 19, 2011, https://www.nytimes.com/2011/01/20 /books/20sheed.html.

60. "Sheed & Ward," Biblio, accessed May 6, 2023, https://www.biblio.com /publisher/sheed-ward.

61. FOC to Robert Giroux, n.d. (1952), FOCCGC.

62. Wilfrid Sheed, "Frank Sheed and Maisie Ward: Writers, Publishers, and Parents," The Good Word, *The New York Times Book Review*, April 2, 1972, 24.

63. FOC to Maryat Lee (unedited), March 29, 1959, FOCCGC.

64. "Park Avenue Leads Day's Rental Lists," *New York Times*, June 29, 1943, 32.

65. 1940 U.S. census, Essex County, New Jersey, population schedule, Montclair, New Jersey, n.p., enumeration district (ED) 7-246, sheet 1B, household 21, Helen E. Stone; https://catalog.archives/gov.

66. Christopher Lehmann-Haupt, "Roger W. Straus Jr., Book Publisher from the Age of the Independents, Dies at 87," *New York Times*, May 27, 2004, B-10.

67. Lehman-Haupt, B-10.

68. Lehman-Haupt, B-10.

69. "210 East 77th Street, New York, NY 10075," Property Shark, accessed July 24, 2018, https://www.propertyshark.com/mason/Property/23927/210-E-77-St-New-York -NY-10075/#ny/nyc/sales_property_history.

70. Tom Miller, "The Pompeo Coppini Studio—210 West 14th Street," *Daytonian in Manhattan* (blog), March 28, 2020, http://daytoninmanhattan.blogspot.com/2020 /03/the-pompeo-coppini-studio-210-west-14th.html.

71. "Another Hotel for Girls," *New York Times,* September 17, 1918, 17.

72. "Apartment for New York Men," *New York Times,* January 31, 1915, 5.

73. Robert E. Thomasson, "YWCA Succeeding in Selling Properties," *New York Times*, September 8, 1974, 8-1.

74. FOC to Regina Cline O'Connor, n.d. (1949), FOCPEU.

75. FOC to Regina Cline O'Connor, n.d. (March 1949), FOCPEU.

76. "John Thompson, 84, a Professor and Poet," *New York Times*, July 6, 2002, A-14.

77. "Transatlantic Review," JSTOR, https://www.jstor.org/journal/tranrevi.

78. FOC to Regina Cline O'Connor, postmarked June 1, 1955, FOCPEU.

79. *The Correspondence of Flannery O'Connor and the Brainard* Cheneys, ed. C. Ralph Stephens (Jackson: University Press of Mississippi, 1986), 21, note 2.

80. "A History of the Provincetown Playhouse," Provincetown Playhouse, http://www.provincetownplayhouse.com/history.html

81. "About Us: Viking," Penguin Group USA, provided by Internet Archive, accessed July 19, 2019, http://us.penguingroup.com/static/html/aboutus/adult/viking .html site discontinued).

82. FOC to Viking Press, November 15, 1941, FOCPEU.

83. FOC to Regina Cline O'Connor, postmarked May 24, 1949, FOCPEU.

84. FOC to Regina Cline O'Connor, n.d. (1949), FOCPEU.

85. "Dr. John P. West," *New York Times*, December 2, 1978, 28.

86. Michael Grabelsky, "15 East 69th Street," Condopedia. http://www.condopedia .com/wiki/15_East_69th_Street.

87. Brad Gooch, *Flannery: A Life of Flannery* O'Connor (New York: Back Bay Books, 2009), 285.

88. 1950 U.S. census, New York County, New York, population schedule, Manhattan, n.p., enumeration district (ED) 31-1303, sheet 5, dwelling 54, Samuel Blackman; https://1950census.archives.gov.

89. "John M. Mck. Woodburn, '26." *Princeton Alumni Weekly,* December 5, 1952, 38.

90. "John M. Mck. Woodburn, '26," 38.

91. "John M. Mck. Woodburn, '26," 38.

92. Kenneth Slawenski, *J.D. Salinger: A Life* (New York: Random House, 2011), 197–99.

93. John Woodburn to FOC, February 3, 1948, FOCPEU.

94. Matt Falber, January 16, 2014, last modified Dec 06, 2017, answer to "Why is There No 4th Ave. in Manhattan?" The Blog, HuffPost, https://www.huffpost.com/entry /why-is-there-no-4th-ave-i_b_4611034#:~:text.

95. "The Woodstock Hotel," ProjectFIND, accessed April 16, 2023, https://www .projectfind.org/woodstock.

96. Ruth York to FOC, March 14, 1960, FOCPEU.

Bibliography

"26 Germans in Spy Ring Seized." *New York Times*, October 30, 1945.

"About the *Spalding County Times* (Griffin, Spalding County, Ga.) 1950–1952." *Chronicling America*, Library of Congress. https://chroniclingamerica.loc.gov/lccn/sn89053343.

Adickes, Sandra. "Terra Cotta Terrorized." *East Village Other*, March 15, 1966.

"All Health Foods Distributors Inc." *New York Age Defender*, June 12, 1954.

Anderson, Jack. "George W. Beiswanger, 91, Dies; Dance Critic and Esthetician." *New York Times,* October 11, 1993.

"Another Hotel for Girls." *New York Times,* September 17, 1918.

"Apartment for New York Men." *New York Times,* January 31, 1915.

"Archives: Books and Authors." *New York Times,* September 25, 1964. https://www.nytimes.com/1964/09/25/archives/books-and-authors.html.

Arnold, Tyler. "Report Finds 28 Credible Child Sex Abuse Claims of Georgia Priests in Last 70 Years." *Catholic News Agency*, March 29, 2023. https://www.catholicnewsagency.com/news/253972/report-finds-28-credible-child-sex-abuse-claims-of-georgia-priests-in-last-70-years.

Axelman, Arthur. "'Son of the Morning Star'—the Battle of Three Networks." *The Wrap,* November 10, 2011. https://www.thewrap.com/son-morning-star-battle-3-networks-32681.

Bewley, Ed. "Statewide Alert Out for Kidnap Suspect." *Herald-Tribune* (Sarasota), August 8, 1968.

Blumenkranz, Carla. "'Deeply and Mysteriously Implicated': Communist Sympathies, FBI Informants, and Robert Lowell at Yaddo." Poetry Foundation, December 18, 2006. https://www.poetryfoundation.org/articles/68753/deeply-and-mysteriously-implicated.

Blythe, Will. "Agee, Unfettered." *New York Times*, June 15, 2008. https://www
  .nytimes.com/2008/06/15/books/review/Blythe-t.html.
Bren, Paulina. *The Barbizon: The Hotel That Set Women Free.* New York:
  Simon & Schuster, 2021.
Brown, Ashley. "An Unwritten Drama: Sue Jenkins Brown and Flannery
  O'Connor." *Southern Review* 22 (Autumn 1986): 727–37.
Burton, Tony. "Novelist Elaine Gottlieb (1916–2004) Wrote a Short Story Based
  in 1940s Ajijic." *Lake Chapala Artists*, February 22, 2016. http://lakechapala
  artists.com/?p=3116.
"Carol Virginia Johnson (09/07/1928–06/10/2015)." *Victoria Times Columnist*,
  June 17–June 20, 2015. https://www.legacy.com/obituaries/timescolumnist.
Cash, Jean. *Flannery O'Connor: A Life.* Knoxville: University of Tennessee
  Press, 2002.
"Cast of Stock Players Do Well with Mystery." *Lake Placid News*, August 16,
  1940.
"Catharine R. Hughes Service." *New York Times*, August 4, 1987.
Chase, Chris. "At the Movies," *New York Times*, November 18, 1983.
"College Club Names Officers for Year." *Citizen and Chronicle* (Cranford, NJ),
  March 11, 1943.
Cook, Anna Maria Green. *History of Baldwin County, Georgia.* Anderson, SC:
  Keys-Hearn Print Co., 1925.
Cozzolino, Robert. "Dudley Huppler: A Chronology." In *Dudley Huppler:
  Drawings*, edited by Robert Cozzolino, 90–98. Madison: Elvehjem Museum
  of Art, University of Wisconsin–Madison, 2002. https://digital.library.wisc
  .edu/1711.dl/KZ7QLX3S54ZDT85.
"A Creative Commune in 1940s Brooklyn Heights." *Ephemeral New York*
  (blog), WordPress, July 28, 2011. https://ephemeralnewyork.wordpress.com
  /tag/george-davis-harpers-bazaar.
"Cyrilly Abel, Authors' Agent." *New York Times*, November 19, 1975.
Day, Dorothy. "Catholic Worker Movement." *Catholic Worker*, January 1976,
  republished in *Catholic Worker*, February 5, 2022. https://catholicworker.org
  /566-html.
"Denver Lindley, Editor, Dies; Translator of Mann, Maurois." *New York Times*,
  February 15, 1982.
Dowling, David O. *A Delicate Aggression: Savagery and Survival in the Iowa
  Writers' Workshop.* New Haven, CT: Yale University Press, 2019.
Drake, Robert. "The Writer as Observer, the Writer as Outsider." 1997.
  Republished in *For the Record: A Robert Drake Reader*, edited by Randy
  Hendricks and James A. Perkins, 287–99. Macon, GA: Mercer University
  Press, 2001.
"Dr. John P. West." *New York Times*, December 2, 1978.
Driggers, Stephen G., Robert J. Dunn, and Sarah Gordon. *The Manuscripts of
  Flannery O'Connor at Georgia College.* Athens: University of Georgia Press,
  1989.

"EcoTheater's Humanities Foundation Summer Guests." *Hinton News,* July 5, 1983.

"Edward Maisel." Paid Notice-Deaths, *New York Times,* March 30, 2008. https://legacy.com/us/obituaries/nytimes/name/edward-maisel-obituary?id =29192783.

Elie, Paul. *The Life You Save May Be Your Own: An American Pilgrimage.* New York: Farrar, Straus & Giroux, 2003.

"Elisa Loti Is Married to Dr. Mortimer Bader." *New York Times,* June 9, 1960.

"Esquire American Magazine." *Encyclopaedia Britanica,* July 20, 1998. https://www.britannica.com/topic/Esquire-American-magazine.

Evans, Curtis. "Hello, Miss Fenwick: Getting Reacquainted with a Crime Fiction Great." In *The Make-Believe Man/A Friend of Mary Rose* by Elizabeth Fenwick, 7–23. Eureka, CA: Stark House Press, 2022.

Eville, Bill. "For Phyllis Meras, Ink in the Veins Keeps the Spirit Young." *Vineyard Gazette,* May 13, 2021. https://vineyardgazette.com/news/2021 /05/13/phyllis-meras-ink-veins-keeps-spirit-young.

"Faculty Adds Thirteen New Members." *Colonnade,* September 30, 1939.

Farmer, David. *Flannery O'Connor: A Descriptive Bibliography.* New York: Garland Publishing, 1981.

"Father Arrested in Son's Seizure." *Herald-Tribune* (Sarasota), August 9, 1968.

Field, Edward. "Clifford Wright, Painting Yaddo Red." *Gay & Lesbian Review Worldwide* 11, no. 4 (July–August 2004). Gale Literature Resource Center. link.gale.com/apps/doc/A119024537/LitRC?u=lln_xavieru&sid=google Scholar&xid=03e3edaf.

Fitzgerald, Sally. "Flannery O'Connor: Patterns of Friendship, Patterns of Love." *Georgia Review* 52, no. 3 (Fall 1998): 407–25.

"Flannery O'Connor Buried." *New York Times,* August 5, 1964.

Florencourt, Louise, and Robert Donahoo. "Wondering and Wandering: An Interview with Louise Florencourt on Her Life and Her Family." *Flannery O'Connor Review* 20 (2022): 80–126.

Ford, Wayne. "High Court Upholds Life Terms for Athens Killer." *Athens Banner-Herald,* January 30, 2020. https://www.onlineathens.com/story /news/crime/2020/01/30/high-court-upholds-life-terms-for-athens-killer /1795772007/.

"Franz Horch Dies; A Literary Agent." *New York Times,* December 16, 1951.

"Frederick Rinehart, 78, Led Publishing Houses." *New York Times,* June 17, 1981.

Freeman, Fred [Fred Darsey]. "Letters from Flannery." Unpublished manuscript, 1973. SFPEU.

Fulton, Lyman. "Flannery O'Connor on the West Side: Dr. Lyman Fulton's Recollections of a Short Acquaintance, an Interview with Virginia Wray." By Virginia Wray. *English Language Notes* 39, no. 1 (2001): 71–78.

"Furnished Rooms–West Side." *New York Times,* April 18, 1950.

"Furnished Rooms–West Side." *New York Times,* November 6, 1951.

Futures for College *Women in New York*, vol. 1, October 1960–. New York: Alumnae Advisory Center, 1960.

Gates, Anita. "Alice Mayhew, Who Edited a Who's Who of Writers, Dies at 87." *New York Times*, February 4, 2020. https://www.nytimes.com/2020 /02/04/books/alice-mayhew-dead.html.

Gerald, Kelly. "The Habit of Art." Afterword in *Flannery O'Connor: The Cartoons*, edited by Kelly Gerald, 101–29. Seattle: Fantagraphics Books, 2012.

Gilman, Richard. "On Flannery O'Connor." *New York Review of Books*, August 21, 1969. https://www.nybooks.com/articles/1969/08/21/on -flannery-oconnor/.

Gooch, Brad. *Flannery: A Life of Flannery O'Connor*. New York: Back Bay Books, 2009.

Grabelsky, Michael. "15 East 69th Street." Condopedia. http://www.condopedia .com/wiki/15_East_69th_Street.

Graham Personals, Bluefield Virginia News, *Bluefield (WV) Daily Telegraph*, June 13, 1923.

Greene, James. "The Comic and the Sad." *Commonweal*, July 22, 1955, 404–05.

Gress, Kirsten. "Clifford Wright." ARS Longa.dk v/Kirsten Gress. http:// arslonga.dk/clifford_wright.htm.

Gussow, Mel. "James Laughlin, Publisher with Bold Taste, Dies at 83." *New York Times*, November 14, 1997.

Hamilton, Ian. *Robert Lowell: A Biography*. London: Faber & Faber, 1982.

Hapgood, Elizabeth Reynolds. "Foreword to the Second Edition." In *Stanislavski's Legacy: A Collection of Comments on a Variety of Aspects of an Actor's Art and Life* by Constantin Stanivslavski, edited and translated by Elizabeth Reynolds Hapgood, v–vi. New York: Routledge, 1968.

Hart, Henry. *James Dickey: The World as a Lie*. New York: Picador, 2001.

Hayes, Patrick J. "The Catholic Unity League." *Ecclesiastical Review* LXIX, no. 3 (September 1923): 297–99.

"Heirlooms Add Bit of Sentiment to Four Weddings." *Chicago Tribune*, November 15, 1936.

Hemley, Robin. *Nola: A Memoir of Faith, Art, and Madness*. St. Paul, MN: Graywolf Press, 1998.

Henry, Derrick. "George Haslam, 89, Teacher, Journalist, Art Subject." *Atlanta Journal-Constitution*, December 5, 2001.

"Henry V. Poor Buys Hoagland Residence on East Sixty-Sixth Street." *New York Times*, March 3, 1928.

"Henry W. Poor Fails: Loss Over a Million." *New York Times*, December 27, 1908.

Highsmith, Patricia. *Patricia Highsmith: Her Diaries and Notebooks*. Edited by Anna von Planta. New York: Liveright Publishing, 2021.

Hjortsberg, William. *Jubilee Hitchhiker: The Life and Times of Richard Brautigan*. Berkeley: Counterpoint; Reprint edition, 2013.

Hodgson, Godfrey. "Obituary: Patricia Highsmith." *The Independent,* February 6, 1995. https://www.independent.co.uk/news/people/obituary -patricia-highsmith-1571740.html.

"Home Town Is Proud of Dr. Margaret Sutton." Bluefield Virginia News, *Bluefield (WV) Daily Telegraph,* June 11, 1926.

"H. Stanley Hillyer, 67, Williams '08, Succumbs." *North Adams, Massachusetts Transcript,* January 3, 1955.

Hughes, Catharine. "Ionesco's 'Approaches to Truth,'" *Antioch Review* 21, no. 1 (Spring 1961): 105–12.

Jamison, Kay Redfield. *Robert Lowell: Setting the River on Fire.* New York: Alfred A. Knopf, 2017.

"John M. Mck. Woodburn, '26." *Princeton Alumni Weekly,* December 5, 1952.

"John Thompson, 84, a Professor and Poet." *New York Times,* July 6, 2002.

Jonza, Nancylee Novell. *The Underground Stream: The Life and Art of Caroline Gordon.* Athens: University of Georgia Press, 1995.

Kelley, Claire. "Remembering *Jubilee* Magazine." *Moby Lives* (blog), Melville House Publishing, February 13, 2013. https://www.mhpbooks.com/remem bering-jubilee-magazine/.

Kirk, Connie Ann. *Critical Companion to Flannery O'Connor.* New York: Facts on File, 2008.

Konsmo, Michael. "Robert Jiras." *Variety,* February 24, 2000. https://variety .com/2000/scene/people-news/robert-jiras-1117883538.

Krupnick, Mark. "Elizabeth Hardwick: U.S. Writer and Wife of Poet Robert Lowell, She Co-Founded the New York Review of Books." *The Guardian,* December 6, 2007. https://www.theguardian.com/news/2007/dec/06 /guardianobituaries.usa.

Langer, Emily. "Daniel Callahan, Preeminent and Probing Bioethicist, Dies at 88." *Washington Post,* July 23, 2019. https://www.washingtonpost.com/local /obituaries/daniel-callahan-preeminent-and-probing-bioethicist-dies-at-88 /2019/07/23/.

"Leaves for Georgia." Virginia Sidelights, Bluefield Virginia News, *Bluefield (WV) Daily Telegraph,* September 7, 1930.

Leeming, David. *James Baldwin: A Biography.* New York: Arcade Publishing, 1984.

Lehmann-Haupt, Christopher. "Robert Giroux, Editor, Publisher, and Nurturer of Literary Giants, Is Dead at 94." *New York Times,* September 6, 2008.

———. "Roger W. Straus Jr., Book Publisher from the Age of the Independents, Dies at 87." *New York Times,* May 27, 2004.

———. "Wilfrid Sheed, Writer of Gentle Wit, Dies at 80." *New York Times,* January 19, 2011. https://www.nytimes.com/2011/01/20/books/20sheed. html.

"Lenox Hill Home Sold to Operator." *New York Times,* December 3, 1931.

"Lettie Rogers, 39, Author, Teacher." *New York Times,* May 15, 1957.

"Levitt, Alfred H. (Alfred Hofmann), 1894–2000 Photographer, Painter."
Archives of American Art, Smithsonian Institution. https://www.aaa.si
.edu/collections/alfred-levitt-papers-9028.

"Local Artist Paints Picture at Coal Mine." Bluefield Virginia News, *Bluefield
(WV) Daily Telegraph,* August 19, 1937.

Lovegren, Sylvia. *Fashionable Food: Seven Decades of Food Fads.* New York:
Macmillan, 1995.

Lowell, Robert. *The Letters of Robert Lowell.* Edited by Saskia Hamilton. New
York: Farrar, Straus & Giroux, 2005.

Luo, Feijun, Curtis S. Florence, Miriam Quispe-Agnoli, Lijing Ouyang, and
Alexander E. Crosby. "Impact of Business Cycles on U.S. Suicide Rates,
1928–2007. *American Journal of Public Health* 101, no. 6 (2011): 1139–46.
https://doi.org/10.2105/AJPH.2010.300010.

Maass, Robert. "My Changeable Life: The Story of Marguerite Baralevsky
Langkjaer '24, from Czarist Palaces to Vassar, and Beyond." *Vassar
Quarterly* 50, no. 4 (June 1, 1984).

Macauley, Robie. "Who Should Mourn?" Letters to Editor, *New York Times,*
August 8, 1976.

Maher, John. "Obituary: Roslyn Targ, Longtime Agent, Dies at 92." *Publishers
Weekly,* November 3, 2017. https://www.publishersweekly.com/pw/by-topic
/industry-news/Obituary/article/75278-obituary-roslyn-targ-longtime-agent
-dies-at-92.html.

Mariani, Paul. *Lost Puritan.* New York: W. W. Norton, 1994.

Masterson, Paul. "Remembering Wisconsin's Forgotten Gay Artist, Dudley
Huppler." *Shepherd Express,* July 3, 2017. pherdexpress.com/lgbtq/my-lgbtq
-pov/remembering-wisconsin-s-forgotten-gay-artist-dudley-huppler.

Maurer, Mark. "The McGraw-Hill Building's Top Half to Receive Resi
Conversion." *The Real Deal,* June 27, 2018. https://therealdeal.com/2018
/06/27/the-mcgraw-hill-buildings-top-half-to-receive-resi-conversion.

"Mavis McIntosh Riordan, 83; Represented Noted Writers." *New York Times,*
August 6, 1986. https://www.nytimes.com/1986/08/06/obituaries/mavis
-mcintosh-riordan-83-represented-noted-writers.html.

Meras, Phyllis. "A Southerner and Her Stories." *Providence Sunday Journal,*
May 31, 1964.

———. "Talking to Writers." In *Pages: The World of Books, Writers, and
Writing,* edited by Matthew J. Bruccoli, 156–71. Detroit: Gale Research
Company, 1976.

Miller, Laura. "Death of the Red-Hot Center." *Salon,* August 11, 2000.
https://www.salon.com/2000/08/11/guide_intro/.

Miller, Tom. "The 1868 Grand Hotel—Broadway and 31st Street." *Daytonian in
Manhattan* (blog), July 3, 2010. http://daytoninmanhattan.blogspot.com
/2010/07/1868-grand-hotel-broadway-and-31st.html.

———. "The 1891 Margaret Louisa Home—No. 14 East 16th Street." *Daytonian
in Manhattan* (blog), March 8, 2011. http://daytoninmanhattan.blogspot
.com/2011/03/1891-margaret-louisa-home-no-14-east.html.

———. "The Pompeo Coppini Studio—210 West 14th Street." *Daytonian in Manhattan* (blog), March 28, 2020. http://daytoninmanhattan.blogspot .com/2020/03/the-pompeo-coppini-studio-210-west-14th.html.

Miner, Valerie. "A Writer Looks Back at His Sister, His Family, and Himself." *Chicago Tribune*, September 20, 1998. https://www.chicagotribune.com/news /ct-xpm-1998-09-20-9809200250-story.html.

"Miss Edith Ivey." *Macon Telegraph*, September 21, 1970.

"Miss Margaret Sutton Returns to New York." Bluefield Virginia News, *Bluefield (WV) Daily Telegraph*, July 27, 1939.

"Miss Oppenheimer Wed to a Physician." *New York Times*, March 31, 1955.

Monroe, Doug. "Asylum: Inside Central State Hospital, Once the World's Largest Mental Institution." *Atlanta*, February 18, 2015. https://www .atlantamagazine.com/great-reads/asylum-inside-central-state-hospital -worlds-largest-mental-institution.

"Mrs. Barbara P. Beiswanger." *Atlanta Constitution*, January 5, 1996.

"Mrs. Macleod Wed to John F. Day Jr." *New York Times*, May 16, 1955.

"Msgr. Daniel M. Dougherty Dies." *New York Times*, December 8, 1978.

"News of Advertising and Marketing." *New York Times*, November 22, 1956.

"Notes on Current Books." *Virginia Quarterly Review* 39, no. 1 (Winter 1963): *xv*.

"Novelist of Note: John Selby." Davies County Historical Society. March 2, 2004. http://daviesscountyhistoricalsociety.com/2004/03/02/novelist-of -note-john-selby.

"Obituary Note: Ellis Amburn." *Shelf Awareness*, August 21, 2018. https://www .shelf-awareness.com/issue.html?issue=3317#m41524.

O'Connor, Flannery. *Flannery O'Connor: The Collected Works*. Edited by Sally Fitzgerald. New York: Library of America, 1988.

O'Connor, Flannery. *The Habit of Being: Letters of Flannery O'Connor*. Edited by Sally Fitzgerald. New York: Farrar, Straus & Giroux, 1979.

O'Connor, Flannery. "Letters to Erik Langkjaer." *Asymptote*, April 2015. https://www.asymptotejournal.com/nonfiction/flannery-oconnor-letters-to -erik-langkjaer/.

O'Connor, Flannery, and Brainard Cheney. *The Correspondence of Flannery O'Connor and the Brainard Cheneys*. Edited by C. Ralph Stephens. Jackson: University Press of Mississippi, 1986.

O'Connor, Flannery, and Caroline Gordon. *The Letters of Flannery O'Connor and Caroline Gordon*. Edited by Christine Flanagan. Athens: University of Georgia Press, 2018.

O'Donnell, Angela Alaimo. *Flannery O'Connor: Fiction Fired by Faith*. Collegeville, MN: Liturgical Press, 2015.

Old, Corbin. "Miss Walker Is Married to Lt. Poor." *Richmond Times-Dispatch*, October 21, 1944.

Orgel, Irene. Biographical note. *American Scholar* 15, no. 2 (Spring 1946): 146.

———. *The Odd Tales of Irene Orgel*. New York: Eakins Press, 1967.

Pace, Eric. "Alfred Levitt, Prolific Painter and Photographer, Dies at 105." *New York Times*, May 29, 2000.

———. "Robie Macauley, 76, Editor, Educator and Fiction Writer." *New York Times*, November 23, 1995.

"Park Avenue Leads Day's Rental Lists." *New York Times*, June 29, 1943.

"Pauline Gilbert Is Married to Dr. Mortimer E. Bader." *New York Times*, August 1, 1982.

People. *Jet*. February 9, 1967.

"Personal Mention." *Union-Recorder* (Milledgeville, GA), August 31, 1909.

"Personal Mention." *Union-Recorder* (Milledgeville, GA), January 4, 1910.

"Personal Mention." *Union-Recorder* (Milledgeville, GA), October 19, 1909.

"Philip Rahv, Critic, Dead at 64; English Professor at Brandeis." *New York Times,* December 24, 1973.

Phillips, Harold. "Smart, Gay, and Every Inch a Pip." *Washington Times*, September 19, 1927.

"Popper, Hermine Rich Isaacs." Martin Luther King, Jr. Research and Education Institute. Stanford University. https://kinginstitute.stanford.edu /encyclopedia/popper-hermine-rich-isaacs.

"Priscilla Poor's Debut." *New York Times*, September 9, 1933.

Project JFK. "The New JFK Show: #237 Beverly Brunson the Great." YouTube video. May 22, 2019. 56:59, https://www.youtube.com/watch?v=f_Alq KsfN5w.

"Publisher: Thomas Y. Crowell & Co., New York, 1876–1979." The Lucile Project. http://sdrc.lib.uiowa.edu/lucile/publishers/crowell/cr_intro.htm.

Ramey, Phillip. *Irving Fine: An American Composer in His Time*. Hillsdale, NY: Pendragon Press, 2005.

"Record 'Phone Book Out; New Manhattan Directory Has 23,000 More Listings." *New York Times*, June 12, 1949.

Rivera, Larry. *The JFK Horsemen: Framing Lee, Altering the Altgens6, and Resolving Other Mysteries*. Crestview, FL: Moon Rock Books, 2018.

"Robert Hatch, 83, Critic and Editor." *New York Times,* June 3, 1994. https:// www.nytimes.com/1994/06/03/obituaries/robert-hatch-83-critic-and-editor .html.

"Rochelle Girson." *Gale Literature: Contemporary Authors*. Gale, 2002. Gale Literature Resource Center, document number GALEIH1000036945. link .gale.com/apps/doc/H1000036945/LitRC?

Rogers, W. G. Associated Press. Literary Guidepost, Associated Press. *Corsicana Daily Sun* (Texas), June 3, 1955.

Rothstein, Klaus. "Flannery O'Connor's Kiss of Death." *Asymptote*, October 2014. https://www.asymptotejournal.com/nonfiction/klaus -rothstein-flannery-oconnors-kiss-of-death/#:~:text.

Rourke, Mary. "Frederick Morgan, 81; Founder, Editor of Hudson Review Literary Magazine." *Los Angeles Times*, February 25, 2004. https://www .latimes.com/archives/la-xpm-2004-feb-25-me-morgan25-story.html.

"Ruby Hat Goes for 53k in Auction." ABC 13, Houston. November 8, 2009. https://abc13.com/archive.

"Ruth Poor Wears Veil Used by Four Others." *Daily News* (New York), June 25, 1936.

Samway, Patrick, SJ. *Flannery O'Connor and Robert Giroux: A Publishing Partnership.* Notre Dame, IN: University of Notre Dame Press, 2018.

Santoro, Lisa M. "How the Martha Washington Went from Women-Only Lodging to Hip Hotel." Curbed Classics, *Curbed New York*, September 21, 2016. https://ny.curbed.com/2016/9/21/13005332/nyc-hotels-martha -washington-history.

Schenkar, Joan. *The Talented Miss Highsmith: The Secret Life and Serious Art of Patricia Highsmith.* New York: Picador, 2009.

Scott, R. Neil, ed. *Flannery O'Connor: An Annotated Reference Guide to Criticism.* Milledgeville, GA: Timberlane Books, 2002.

"September 18, 1989: Playwright Maryat Lee Dies in Lewisburg." West Virginia Public Broadcasting, September 18, 2018. https://www.wvpublic .org/post/september-18-1989-playwright-maryat-lee-dies-lewisburg (site discontinued).

"Service Flag at the Baptist Church." *Union-Recorder* (Milledgeville, GA), April 24, 1918.

Sessions, William Alfred. "*Shenandoah* and the Advent of Flannery O'Connor." *Shenandoah* 60, nos. 1–2 (March 2010). https://www. thefreelibrary.com/Shenandoah+and+the+Advent+of+Flannery +O%27Connor.-a0233492505.

Sheed, Wilfrid. "Frank Sheed and Maisie Ward: Writers, Publishers, and Parents." The Good Word, *New York Times Book Review*, April 2, 1972, 24.

Shloss, Carol Loeb. "O'Connor's Real Estate: Farming Intellectual Property." In *Reconsidering Flannery O'Connor*, edited by Alison Arant and Jordon Cofer, 234–50. Jackson: University Press of Mississippi, 2020.

Shteir, Rachel. "Everybody Slept Here." *New York Times,* November 10, 1996.

"Signs Proclaiming 'Closing Out Sale' Send Owner to Jail." *New York Times,* March 2, 1966.

Sisario, Ben. "Stewart Richardson, 78, Editor with a Roster of Noted Writers." *New York Times*, July 8, 2004.

Slawenski, Kenneth. *J. D. Salinger: A Life.* New York: Random House, 2011.

Spain, Daphne. *How Women Saved the City.* Minneapolis: University of Minnesota Press, 2001.

Stelzman, Rainulf A. "Two Unpublished Letters by Flannery O'Connor." *Xavier Review* 5, nos. 1–2 (1985): 49–50.

Stern, Richard. "Flannery O'Connor: A Remembrance and Some Letters." In *The Books in Fred Hampton's Apartment*, 209–16. New York: E. P. Dutton, 1973.

———. "On Reprinting 'Golk.'" *Agni,* no. 26 (1988): 31–34.

Stevens, Tiffany, and Maura Friedman. "Still Silent: After 24 Years, a Family's Yellow House Sits Quietly." *Red and Black*, October 6, 2011. Last modified September 28, 2022. https://www.redandblack.com/magazine/35-years-later

-remembering-the-athens-murders-of-1987/article_cff0871c-3f6d-11ed-a736
-9f2c4f83d2e9.html.

"Students of Miss Treanor Performed a Musical in the College Chapel."
Union-Recorder (Milledgeville, GA), May 26, 1908.

"Suburban Theater to Give 'Kind Lady.'" *Standard Star* (New Rochelle, NY),
June 16, 1942.

Tanenhaus, Sam. "Hello to All That: The Irony behind the Demise of the
Partisan Review." Slate, April 16, 2003. https://slate.com/culture/2003/04
/the-demise-of-the-partisan-review.html.

"Theodore M. Purdy, 75; Book-Publishing Leader." *New York Times*, July 15,
1979.

"Theodore S. Amussen, Book Editor, Dies at 73." *New York Times*, December
26, 1988.

"Thirteen New Members Added to Faculty." *Colonnade*, October 4, 1930.

Thomasson, Robert E. "YWCA Succeeding in Selling Properties." *New York
Times*, September 8, 1974.

"To Tour Europe." Virginia Sidelights, Bluefield Virginia News, *Bluefield
(WV) Daily Telegraph,* June 26, 1932.

"Travelers Aid Society Benefit Committees for Garden Party on Friday."
Brooklyn Daily Eagle, June 3, 1934.

"Two More Debutantes Trip up to Altar." *Daily News* (New York), September
21, 1935.

"'U.S. Post Office' Is Sign Over Fire Station." Bluefield Virginia News, *Bluefield
(WV) Daily Telegraph*, April 7, 1938.

Van Gelder, Lawrence. "Catharine Carver, 76, an Editor of a Luminous List of
Writers." *New York Times*, November 16, 1997.

———. "Candida Donadio, 71, Agent Who Handled 'Catch-22,' Dies." *New
York Times,* January 25, 2001.

Vermeersch, Arthur. "Catholic Encyclopedia (1913)/Henri and Jules Desclée."
Catholic Encyclopedia, vol. 16: 1913. https://en.wikisource.org/wiki/Catholic
Encyclopedia(1913)/Henri_and_Jules_Desclee.

Virginia Sidelights, Bluefield Virginia News, *Bluefield (WV) Daily Telegraph,*
April 11, 1928.

Virginia Side Personals, Bluefield Virginia News, *Bluefield (WV) Daily
Telegraph*, August 16, 1931.

Virginia Side Personals, Bluefield Virginia News, *Bluefield (WV) Daily
Telegraph*, June 14, 1932.

Virginia Side Personals, Bluefield Virginia News, *Bluefield (WV) Daily
Telegraph* July 17, 1934.

"Vivienne Koch, 47, an Author, Critic." *New York Times,* November 30, 1961.

Ward, Estolv Ethan. "Organizing and Reporting on Labor in the East Bay,
California and the West, 1925–1987." Oral history conducted in 1987 by Lisa
Rubens, Regional Oral History Office, Bancroft Library. University of
California, Berkeley, 1989.

Weiss, Lois. "Literary Hotel to Return." *New York Post*, September 9, 2011. nypost.com/2011/09/09/literary-hotel-to-return.

"Where Boys and Girls Are Going to College." Bluefield Virginia News, *Bluefield (WV) Daily Telegraph*, September 21, 1924.

Whitt, Margaret. "Stopped by a Naked Woman: O'Connor's Departure from the *Kenyon Review*." *Flannery O'Connor Bulletin* 26–27 (1998–2000): 169–81.

"William G. Rogers Dies; Arts Editor for the A.P." *New York Times*, March 2, 1978.

Williams, Monte. "Instant Nostalgia as Two Havens for Young Women Close." *New York Times*, June 28, 2000.

Wilson, Andrew. *Beautiful Shadow: A Life of Patricia Highsmith*. London: Bloomsbury, 2003.

"The Winter Social Season Awakens." *New York Times,* November 5, 1916.

Winters, Shelley. *Shelley: Also Known as Shirley*. New York: William Morrow and Co., 1980.

Witt, Emily. "How Catch-18 Became Catch-14 and Finally Catch-22." *Observer,* July 20, 2011. http://observer.com/2011/07/how-catch-18-became-catch-14 -and-finally-catch-22/.

Wylder, Jean. "Flannery O'Connor: A Reminiscence and Some Letters." *North American Review* 255, no. 1 (Spring 1970): 58–65.

"Younger Social Set Entertained at Dance at the White House." *Washington Evening Star*, December 31, 1933.

Index

KATHERYN KROTZER LABORDE is a writer of prose and a Professor of English at Xavier University of Louisiana. In addition to various works of creative nonfiction that have appeared in journals and on websites, she is the author of *Do Not Open: The Discarded Refrigerators of Post-Katrina New Orleans* and *The Story behind the Painting: Frederick J. Brown's* The Assumption of Mary *at Xavier University.*

Printed in the USA
CPSIA information can be obtained
at www.ICGtesting.com
LVHW040238100824
787814LV00003B/231